Routledge Library Editions

ELEMENTS OF SOCIAL
ORGANIZATION

ANTHROPOLOGY AND ETHNOGRAPHY

Routledge Library Editions
Anthropology and Ethnography

RAYMOND FIRTH: COLLECTED WORKS
In 6 Volumes

ELEMENTS OF SOCIAL ORGANIZATION

RAYMOND FIRTH

Routledge
Taylor & Francis Group

LONDON AND NEW YORK

First published in 1971

Reprinted in 2004 by
Routledge
2 Park Square, Milton Park, Abingdon, Oxon, OX14 4RN, UK

711 Third Avenue, New York, NY 10017

Transferred to Digital Printing 2006

Routledge is an imprint of the Taylor & Francis Group

First issued in paperback 2013

British Library Cataloguing in Publication Data
A CIP catalogue record for this book is available from the British Library

Elements of Social Organization
ISBN 978-0-415-33016-9
ISBN 978-0-415-84844-2 (pbk)

Miniset: Raymond Firth: Collected Works

Series: Routledge Library Editions – Anthropology and Ethnography

A SYMBOLIC ACT OF FAITH

A corpse lies buried in the sand under the coconut matting. Pa Rangifuri, a man of Tikopia in the Solomon Islands, is preparing to pour a
libation to the spirit of the dead man, who is his father's brother. It is
believed that the spirit is sensible of this offering.

ELEMENTS OF SOCIAL ORGANIZATION

RAYMOND FIRTH

TAVISTOCK PUBLICATIONS

First published by C. A. Watts & Co. Ltd
in 1951, reprinted 1952
Second edition 1956
Third edition 1961, reprinted 1963, 1969

This edition published in 1971
by Tavistock Publications Limited
11 New Fetter Lane, London EC4

SBN 422 73920 0 (hardbound)
422 75320 3 (paperback)

CONTENTS

LIST OF PLATES

I am indebted to the authorities of the Musée de l'Homme, with the help of Mme. Denise Schaeffner, for Plate VII; to the Trustees of the British Museum, with the help of Mr. Adrian Digby, for Plates VIII (a) and X; to the Auckland War Memorial Museum, with the help of Dr. Gilbert Archey, Director, for Plate VIII (b and c); and to Mr. G. I. Jones for Plate IX (a). All other Plates are from my own collection. Plate V (*lower*) has been previously published by me in " Social Problems and Research in British West Africa," *Africa*, April, 1947.—R. F.

PREFACE 1971

THIS book was written as a re-crystallization of ideas first formulated in a series of lectures nearly twenty-five years ago. Many developments have since occurred in social anthropology, some mere fashions but most leading to more exact formulation of problems in the study and more precise investigation of them in the field.

New areas of interest have been explored. The recognition and construction of models has improved our analyses; hypotheses about the nature and relationships of social action have been refined. Not least as a factor in stimulating research and scholarly interchange of ideas has been the spread of social anthropology from its primary centre of development, Britain, through the general universe of scholars concerned with the sciences of man in the broadest sense.

The third edition of this book, ten years ago, took account of some of these developments. Since then, the study of systems of ideas, of myths, of symbols in different social and cultural conditions has taken an even more prominent place in the discipline. And though the 'anthropology of experience' has not yet become a major interest, some concern for the primacy of personal feeling in a research or teaching situation has become manifest. In some of its forms this could imply a kind of solipsism, which could render comparability of observation difficult. A trend of another order has been a growing concern for the relation of the anthropologist to the wider society, including that of the peoples he has studied, and his obligation to them has been emphasized.

I myself have been involved in some of these movements of ideas. Moreover, since the last edition of this book I have again made visits to Malaysia (in 1963) and to Tikopia (in 1966), where much of my earlier field research was carried out, and have recorded and to some extent participated in the changes taking place in those societies.

But while new theory and new field material could certainly improve the book, it is not so much a statement of what is known in and about social anthropology as essentially a set of my own reflections on some of the general aspects of the study. As such, in this series of standard works in Social Science Paperbacks, it has seemed to me that it can stand reprinting in its present form, and perhaps can be regarded as a contribution to the foundations on which the modern sciences of man have been erected.

RAYMOND FIRTH.

London, March, 1971.

INTRODUCTION TO THIRD EDITION

SINCE this book was first published, ten years ago, there has been a great development of interest in social anthropology. Public interest in the study has been stimulated partly by a desire to know more about the peoples of Asia and Africa who have recently attained political independence, and partly by a wider concern for any scientific discipline which can appear to throw more light on the refractory problems of modern social living. In more professional circles, colleagues in allied fields, e.g. sociology, psychology, political science, and even economics, have found it possible to integrate concepts from social anthropology, and some of the material provided by anthropological study, more closely with their own ideas and work. As a result, there is more understanding of what an anthropologist does, and more appreciation of the value of his comparative analyses of human behaviour, than ever before. At the same time, anthropologists have profited by this cross-fertilization of ideas. They have tended to give a less exotic, more precise and realistic air to their analyses. They have begun to give more attention to problems of recognizably general social import—migration, land tenure and utilization, social stratification, feudalism, local government, public health. They have increasingly left the primitive field and have examined with more confidence the institutions of rural, and even some urban, communities in the developed societies of the Orient and the West. They have given more depth to their work in various directions, notably in their increasing care for historical perspective.

Looking at the anthropological field in general terms, we can recognize marked developments in the study of problems of descent and kinship systems, of ritual, of witchcraft belief, and of symbolic behaviour. One great advance has been in the analysis of political institutions. A moderate interest in the allied subject of primitive law has long characterized social anthropology, but it is only recently that the study of the structures and operations of government and the workings of political forces have received much systematic attention from anthropologists. It is hardly an exaggeration to say that for many social anthropologists of the last decade, the main intellectual preoccupation has been problems of status and power. From Africa alone, the titles of such books as *Politics in a Changing Society*, *Bantu Bureaucracy*, *Tribes Without Rulers*, *East African Chiefs* are an index of the development of this line of inquiry, which has been put into a wider frame by work such as *Government and Politics in Tribal Societies* (see Appendix). Another field which has received increasing attention has been that of religion. Monographic studies on the Nupe, the Nuer, the Lugbara of Africa, the Coorgs of South India, the Javanese —to mention only a sample—have thrown much light on concepts of god and spirit, rites of sacrifice and communion, roles of priest, prophet, and shaman, over a wide societal range. Together with studies of African cosmologies, messianic movements in Melanesia, voodoo in Haiti, and more general works (see Appendix), they have helped to give a new depth to our understanding of problems of meaning in human behaviour.

The change has also been expressed in general theoretical terms. It is not now feasible to say that anthropologists are interested only in pattern and not in process. During the decade the more rigid structural studies characteristic of an earlier period have been supplemented by more flexible analyses directed to understanding social processes. Assumptions about the stability and integration of primitive societies have given way to a recognition of the force of contradiction in social principles and of conflict in roles. The effects of choice and decision-making by individuals in the context of social relationships have been seen to be of major significance in the interpretation of behaviour. Phenomena of social change have become an integral part of the material instead of being analysed in a special section, as the result of aberrant conditions.

There are plenty of passages in the early edition of this book which I would rewrite now if time and circumstance allowed, and I would wish to consider more deeply some of the philosophic implications. Much new material could be incorporated, either as fresh illustration or as enriching the argument. Though the original lectures on which the book was based did not include sections on status systems, politics and social control, the treatment could usefully be expanded to include them. Yet the book was written primarily to indicate a general point of view, and present a coherent theory in the comparative study of human institutions, and not to cover the entire field.

One cannot expect from an author a definitive judgement on the relevance of his work to developments in his science. But his own conception of its bearing may be an aid to its interpretation. On the one hand, I see this book as a continuation of the argument for the use of reason and systematic intellectual inquiry in the understanding of social affairs. No sensible man nowadays believes either that most human behaviour is motivated by reason, or that reason alone can solve most human problems. If he believes as I do in knowledge and in human personality as primary values in human life, he cannot defend his belief in them simply on the basis of reason. Plausible indeed in the complexity of human life, with its often inexplicable joys and sufferings, are the ideas of an extra-human source of values, an ultimate reality beyond human comprehension, a mystery in which full realization of the human personality can be found only by faith. There are no simple explanations in this field. But such limitations on the sphere of reason in human affairs are no justification for refusing to push reasoned argument as far as it will go in the interpretation of the diverse forms of belief and conduct of men in different types of society. From this point of view, the many variations of moral and religious belief and practice must be interpreted by the anthropologist as human constructs, often of a symbolic order, a part of the unending search of man to provide meaning to his life and ways of adjustment to the complex problems of social existence.

On the other hand, I have seen this book as part of the challenge to a rigid social determinism. Some views in social anthropology and sociology have regarded structure as the cardinal object of interest in social analysis, and would treat the behaviour of individuals as primarily determined by structural considerations—the outcome of their place in a system of roles, relationships, groups, social patterns. But while structural considerations are of great importance, normally occupying first place in the order of analysis, human behaviour is the resultant of many considerations, in which alternative modes of procedure are presented to individuals, and in which their personal choice, decision, and adjustment are therefore also of prime significance. Hence, subjoined to the concept of social structure must be another concept, whether entitled social organization or not, which is concerned with such processual activities. Over the last decade there has been a substantial shift in the direction of our general line of interest in social process. In this respect, as I see it, the book is a personal statement of a point of view which has come recently much more to the fore.

A few changes have been made in the text of this edition. Apart from the correction of occasional verbal errors, much reference material has been brought up to date or enlarged. (For convenience, these additions have been grouped at the end of the book in an Appendix, and the relevant footnotes or chapter endings in the text have been marked with an A. While I have not tried to recast the general argument in this text, I have expanded and supplemented my views in other publications, e.g. " Social Organization and Social Change," *Journal Royal Anthropological Institute*, vol. 84, 1954; " Some Principles of Social Organization," *Journal Royal Anthropological Institute*, vol. 85, 1955; " The Study of Values by Social Anthropologists," *Man*, 1953; " Problem and Assumption in an Anthropological Study of Religion," *Journal Royal Anthropological Institute*, vol. 90, 1960.

RAYMOND FIRTH.

London, May 1961

INTRODUCTION

THIS book consists in substance of the Josiah Mason Lectures, given in the University of Birmingham, at Edgbaston, in the Spring Term of 1947. Since I had the honour of being invited to deliver the first series of these lectures, it is appropriate to give here a brief explanation of their title and purpose.

In 1946 the Rationalist Press Association offered to found in the University of Birmingham a lectureship in commemoration of Sir Josiah Mason, a prominent Rationalist. The offer was accepted. The lectures, which are intended to be delivered annually, have as their main theme the illustration of the scientific approach to the problems of civilized society. Mason had had a long connection with Birmingham, and a very special connection with the University and with scientific disciplines there, which made it most fitting that his name should thus be perpetuated.

Son of a Kidderminster carpet-weaver, he was born in 1795, and died in 1881.[1] After experimenting in various lines of work, including his father's trade, he went to Birmingham at the age of twenty-one. There he succeeded in making a fortune in classical entrepreneur style, mainly by the manufacture of split key-rings and of steel pens, but aided by copper-smelting, nickel-refining, and other enterprises in the metal industry. Mason blended business acumen and benevolence in the Victorian manner. Professor Court has said, "He was a great getter of money and a great spender of it, not so much upon himself as upon others." He built almshouses and orphanages in the Midlands. He also built the Mason Science College in Birmingham, which was opened in 1880, and which served as the later foundation for Birmingham University. Self-educated, and a reader of history, science, and theology,

[1] For most of the detail in what follows I am indebted to Professor W. H. B. Court's brief memoir "Sir Josiah Mason: The Founder of a University," in *The Literary Guide*, London, 1947, Jan., pp. 3–4 ; Feb., p. 26.

though not of lighter literature, Mason clearly believed in the value of scientific knowledge, especially natural science, as a guide to experience, particularly industrial experience. Sectarian belief, apparently, he did not trust, and he took steps to ensure that no religious test was enforced for appointment or for student entry to the new college.

Like many others of his time, he built much better than he knew. His college, widened in scope and incorporated as a University, embodies a vision of a different kind from his, in which the humanities are intended to temper the austerities of pure and applied science. Yet his foundation gave a welcome impetus to higher learning, and a solid institution which others could expand and remould. It has become fashionable at present to re-discover the virtues of the Victorians, and, what is less defensible in such a different environment, to imitate many of their tastes. But a taste for sponsoring learning, even if it be associated with the commemoration of one's own name, is one of which every academic person must approve—provided that the purse does not have too many strings. It is unlikely that any very rarified passion for pure knowledge, for scholarship for its own sake, inspired Josiah Mason to found his new college. Nor, despite what we have now learnt or suspect about the hidden fires of some of his contemporaries, is it likely that his institution represented the realization of some secret ennobling dream, the fulfilment of some obscure longing which needed satisfaction in some consciously non-material objective. It was problems of technical and industrial training, not of sentiments and incentives, with which he was seemingly concerned. Yet, prosaic as may have been his academic interests, their pursuit demanded an effort of creative imagination which calls for respect. Mason gave more than money to his embryonic University—he gave it ideas and an organization. And he believed in the value of reason in general and scientific knowledge in particular as an aid to the solution of man's problems. It is for these things that he is to be commemorated.

The Josiah Mason Lectures are open to all members of the University. Seeing that this was the first series of lectures, and that the audience might include students and teachers from any faculty, I decided to discuss a subject of general scope. An obvious choice was an examination of the role of social anthropology in contributing to a better understanding of some of the problems of modern civilization. How far understanding may lead to improved control was a question to which the answer was implied rather than stated. In the set of lectures no more than an outline of my subject could be given. I divided it into two main sections: one dealing primarily with organization, the other with concepts and values. The one took up the theme of the relation between modern world situations and the primary observational field of social anthropologists, the small-scale, simpler, more " primitive " societies and cultures. The other discussed the attitudes of the social anthropologist towards concepts and values in four main fields or aspects of human social activity—economics, art, morals, and religion.

The lectures have now been revised to bring them more into keeping with written argument. Certain parts have been expanded for clarity or because I want to say more than was convenient at the time. I am grateful to my wife, and to those who took part in the discussions which followed the lectures, for suggestions and queries which have helped me in this expansion. I owe thanks also to Dr. David Schneider for helpful comment on the proofs.

To the Vice-Chancellor and various other members of the University of Birmingham I am greatly indebted for the courtesy of their invitation and for kindness and help. I have special acknowledgement to make to Professor P. Sargant Florence for his unflagging hospitality, which makes the stranger within the gates feel an honoured guest, and for his keen interest in the promotion of anthropology. Acknowledgement is also due to the Rationalist Press Association, whose consistent support of science led them to found the Josiah Mason Lectures, and who have suggested that these may find a wider audience.

RAYMOND FIRTH.

September, 1950.

CHAPTER I

THE MEANING OF SOCIAL ANTHROPOLOGY

SOCIAL anthropology aims at a reasoned comparative analysis of how people behave in social circumstances. But the study is a comparatively new one—less than a hundred years old. So its scope and methods are still not generally understood. Explanation is the more needed because the science is continually being re-defined. As with all scientific inquiry, the type of problems which seem most significant and the language in which their investigation is couched tend to alter with each generation of workers. Every study is sensitive to changing social conditions and the changing climate of social thought in general. As knowledge advances and technique improves, the framework of personal ideas in which each student of the subject tries to concentrate and express what he learns alters shape. Even scientific ideas are not immune to the influence of fashion. But social anthropology faces a special problem. Unlike most of the other sciences, its most-prized raw material is evaporating. The people themselves, of course, for the most part are not disappearing. But they have been altering their way of life radically, especially in those aspects which were the special province of the social anthropologist to study. Head-hunting, cannibalism, and human sacrifice have virtually disappeared; totemism, exogamy, polygamy, and the couvade have been much modified; even forms such as the joint family have undergone serious change. Faced by this loss or threatened loss of traditional subject-matter, social anthropologists have adapted themselves in various ways. Some have concentrated on the study of social impact and change. Some examine the special problems of race relations. Some pursue the vanishing primitive. Others look farther afield to the study of contemporary Western society. Others still try to define how society and psyche meet in the field of personality development. At the outset of this book, then, I give my own view of the main work of a social anthropologist: what he studies; what methods he uses; what results he gets; and how valid these results are likely to be.

One of the broadest ways of describing social anthropology is to say that it studies human social process comparatively. At this level of discussion we must neglect the metaphysical implications of the idea of process, save to say that the concept of change is basic to it. Social process means the operation of the social life, the manner in which the actions and very existence of each living being affect those of other individuals with which it has relations. For convenience of study, aggregates of individuals in their relational aspects are arbitrarily isolated as social units. Where these show a number of common features in distinction from other such units, they are conveniently termed societies. In considering social process, the magnitude of a society, the scale of the relations involved is significant; so also is the sequence of those relations in time.

Social process can be studied in the life of animals, and even of plants. The results are of interest to social anthropology. Studies of the learning process among social ants, for instance, or of the relations between apes in a colony can teach us something of the fundamentals of what life in a society must involve. Such empirical analyses of social behaviour help to throw light on the subtle relation between self-interest and the common need, between individual variation and the norm. They help us to distinguish between what is inherent in the very nature of association and what can be achieved only by planned action. Such results, achieved by patiently watching what animals and insects do, are very different from that translation of human behaviour into animal terms which is sometimes confused with them. Many a dog-lover uses his pet as a projection of his own personality. The brilliance of Capek's *Insect Play* lies not in its mimicry of insect life but in its dramatic and symbolic reminder of the eternal basic claims and limitations of the human self, and the problem of controlling them even by the exercise of reason and the whole range of other refined faculties of the human spirit. What the biological studies of social behaviour do above all for the study of man as a social animal is to emphasize the importance of systematic observation. What people do must be taken as the index to what they think and feel.

But if the anthropological study of human social process sometimes gets a lead from biology, it relies more directly on its companion social sciences. Anthropological generalizations about human society are collaborative, not definitive. Sociology and psychology share its general field. So does history. History, when it is interested in social process and not merely in personal events, supplies above all the documented time perspective on society. Sociology gives the massive structure of concepts and data derived mainly from observation of modern Western society—and the social sciences, after all, like modern industrial technology, are primarily a Western creation. Psychology analyses the social as seen in the individual, by classifying individual activity into types and setting them against the social environment. Where does social anthropology come in? In terms of such a thumbnail sketch, its conventional role is almost a regional complement to sociology. Historically it studies process in societies of people who are remote from us in their lives and unfamiliar to us in their customs. The Todas of India are polyandrous, the Menangkabau of Sumatra are matrilineal; the Aranda of Central Australia practise sub-incision, the Caribs of Central America practise the couvade; the Kwakiutl Indians of British Columbia compete in the potlatch, the Trobriand islanders of New Guinea exchange in the *kula*—such are some of the classic cases of anthropology. Reputable anthropologists have disdained to exploit the sensational. But respect for the science in learned as well as in popular circles rests in part on the ability of the anthropologist to discover and explain alien elements in human conduct.

An elaborate socially significant example of interpretation of the unfamiliar is in the analysis of Japanese institutions arising out of the last war. Japan is a society where concepts of personal obligation of a highly traditional, semi-feudal order exist side by side with technical and industrial standards of modern Western type. Her ritual and æsthetic values, exemplified in Buddhism and Shinto, brush painting, flower arrangement, and tea ceremony, are very different from those which the West has built up on a basis of Greek and Roman civilization and the Christian Churches. It is no accident, then, that among the more successful interpreters of Japanese attitudes were social anthropologists.[1]

At the same time the social anthropologist has never quite lost touch with modern Western society. In his studies of family and kinship, or of magic, religion and mythology, or of morality, he has kept the comparative point of view which makes him at least a lively spectator of what is going on around him. Historically, the influence of the great masters of synthesis in the science—Morgan, Tylor, Frazer, Westermarck, for instance—has contributed towards this from literary materials. This has been reinforced by anthropological field experience. Contact of the more primitive societies with the West has not only shown up the contrast; it has brought the West itself more fully under scrutiny. For the anthropologist, Western society is not a standard, it is only a species—or group of species.

But so far auto-analysis in anthropology has been the exception, not the rule. Most anthropologists have preferred to devote systematic study to another society than their own. What anthropological research has done increasingly is to enforce attention on to the general characteristics which underlie all societies. The contrast between Christianity and traditional ancestor-worship seen in so many tribal conditions, and often emerging in new prophetic and mystical cults, brings up problems of the basic nature of religion. Attack on and defence of the custom of bride-price—giving cattle or other goods at marriage in exchange for the wife—have emphasized consideration of economic factors as stabilizers of family relations. The ineffectiveness of European law to touch the real core of conformity and offence in a tribal society has stimulated examination of the general problems of allegiance and response to authority. By situations such as these the anthropologist has been driven beyond a simple

[1] See Ruth Benedict, *The Chrysanthemum and the Sword*, London, 1947. (A).

ethnographic or descriptive account of the customs of the people he studies to pose to himself general questions about the nature of society and of social process.

Anthropological field experience has another effect. Most social anthropologists have worked at one time or another among communities of small scale. This has led them to see how closely different aspects of social activity are related—institutionally and in the personal behaviour of individuals. A religious ceremony has its economic calculations about expenditure of time and resources; in an economic task the working party is held together by allegiances of a social and political order that transcend the material advantage gained. Research among small communities also helps the conceptual grasp of a society as a whole. By seeing the personal range, the investigator also finds it easier to see the range of relations possible and actual in all the social life, and to chart the major ones as an interlocking system. This is why social anthropologists are so conscious of the need for a basic theory of society. They recognize how important it is to have a general framework of theory, a conceptual apparatus for the study of social process. They see too the need for constantly re-examining the assumptions that lie behind the use of such concepts. If the theory of the anthropologist always tends to rise higher than its narrow base of fact warrants, this is his excuse. He studies social process in a few societies, and talks about Society. But more than any other social scientist, he is accustomed to observe how people really do behave in widely different social environments, and to look for the common factors and the variations in their conduct.

Look at the matter in another way. The social anthropologist has to isolate basic social situations from a wide variety of human circumstances. Philosophy, literature, and the social sciences all try, by their characteristic methods, to examine various kinds of human experience and draw conclusions from it. Literature proceeds to seek the general in the particular by bold selection and formal arrangement, by imagery and invention, by delicate allusion and suggestion. To lay bare the hidden springs of action, its privilege is to be the confidant of truth, to affirm, to be categorical, to fill from

B

the imagination all that cannot be learnt from inquiry. Philosophy is equally daring, but in another way. The philosopher takes not even truth for granted, but subjects the very basic categories of experience to his scrutiny—thought, action, personality, even existence and reality themselves. The social sciences are only the handmaids of truth. They take everything in human experience for granted—in the sense that since it is human, it cannot be without significance for the understanding of some facet of individual and social life. If literature proceeds by the way of imagination and philosophy by the way of scepticism, then the social sciences proceed by the way of acceptance and analysis. Social anthropology, in particular, is comparative. It looks for the widest possible range of experience against alien backgrounds. Yet if experience is to be meaningful, it must be susceptible of regularity. To extract regularities from unfamiliar, obscure bodies of experience, and express them as more general principles or tendencies of familiar, intelligible kind is one way of defining, rather abstractly, the aim of social anthropology.

Take a simple example of how an event quite remote from our own experience can be treated in terms of principles of social significance. At first sight, we take people's names for granted, as tightly attached to them, almost a facet of their personality. This is not so everywhere. And even in our own type of society a woman changes her surname on marriage. In Tikopia, a small and distant island of the Solomons, both men and women invariably take new names at marriage. They leave their simple bachelor names to be used only by their most intimate kin, and adopt for general social inter-course names compounded of a house-site name and a title of respect. A married man is called *Pa*, meaning literally "Father," but equivalent to our *Mr.* Thus there is social recognition that he has acquired a domicile of his own and a new status preparatory to the founding of a family. Since the house-site concerned has been very likely occupied by his for-bears, the new name itself will have probably been borne by one or more of them in time past. Years ago, in Tikopia, a Polynesian was talking to me about personal names. I knew him as Pa Rangifuri. But he told me that he used to be called by a different name, and that he changed it because he wanted children.   Pa Rangifuri on marrying had first taken the name of Pa Rangieva, given to him in commemoration of an ancestral kinsman.   After some time, seeing that no children had been born to him, Pa Rangieva recollected that the former bearer of the name had had no children likewise.   This, he thought, was a bad omen.   He declared that his name must be changed.   So his father then gave him the name of Pa Motuapi, after the house in which he himself was living.   A younger brother then took on the name of Pa Rangieva.   He too dropped it in turn as time passed and he had no offspring. Finally, the father was elected as chief of the clan and took the corresponding title, dropping his name of Pa Rangifuri.   Pa Motuapi, who by this time had had children, adopted this name, by which I knew him.

These proceedings may seem to us quite irrational.   It is true that here is a case of defective knowledge, of mistaken association.   We know that a mere name cannot affect procreation.   Yet the events fit into some fundamental social patterns: of the social identity, status, and role of the individual; of that concern for the future and interest in the past which may be called preoccupation with social sequence; as well as of the tendency to attribute causal connection where there is only strong emotional interest.

One might think that personal names, being so intimately associated with individuals, would be regarded in every society as a purely private matter, mere labels to be changed at whim. The contrary is the case.   In some societies individuals are certainly allowed great freedom to choose new names.   Yet every society has some rules about personal names, and they fit into the group structure accordingly.   A personal name is an indicator of the place of the individual in society.   But the patterns which they follow vary from one society to another. Muslims and Christians think it natural that one should be able to tell from a personal name whether the holder is male or female.   In many societies this is not thought important, and one cannot tell the sex from the name.   We may think it unimportant to use personal names as historical records.   In many non-literate societies it is customary to give children names which refer to and keep in memory events of importance to the parents or the society. Many societies emphasize social relationships and differences of social status by name-avoidances: one must not mention the names of relatives by marriage, or the names of dead kin. To European society this respect-taboo seems strange. But we have a respect-taboo of our own—we do not normally expect children to call their parents by their Christian names. A personal name is a very convenient mechanism for preserving continuity in identification of people in their social contacts. But while the Christian West has the pattern of surname or family name, making it easy to follow lineal descent, the Muslim East is content with the patronymic, linking child with father alone.

Again, change of name is a symbolic act, signifying change of social personality. In Muslim society it is not felt necessary to mark the new status of marriage by name-change. In Western society it is normal for a woman to change her surname then, but it is not thought necessary for a man to do so; the emphasis is on patrilineal descent. But this is not the sole determinant. The Tikopia go farther; though their society is oriented at least as strictly as ours towards the male line in descent and succession, both man and woman assume a new name on marriage. In such a small community less importance is attached to preserving a male descent-name than to marking the establishment of a new social unit. What is given social recognition in the naming system is the " settling-down " of the young couple in a house of their own; and in their titles, the prospect of their founding a family. In regard to the begetting of a family, there is looking both forward and back. Hence the inference that if there are no children the name must be wrong has a social force. In some societies the emphasis is more on the retrospective aspect. The name of an ancestor or elder kinsman is taken, to reflect the social significance of the links with the past, to grip past generations into the life of the present. In some cases, as in parts of Bantu Africa, to give a person an ancestor's name means that he is believed to reincarnate that ancestor's spirit. In other cases, as in Tikopia, it means only that there is recognition of his continuing spiritual interest in his descendants, and of the perpetuation of his memory and their use of his cultivations, his tools, his house. But in some societies, again, the emphasis is prospective. A child does not take its name from its parents; on the contrary, in the institution of teknonymy they are known as "Father and Mother of So-and-so." The personal name can then be more than a label for an individual, an aid to recognition of him. It is an index of social position. It can take on the character of a social instrument, enforcing attention on new social responsibilities.

In the light of this, the Tikopia case cited is much more than misplaced association. It is an example of one type of preoccupation with social sequence. It illustrates a structural relation between system of personal names, system of residence, procreation of children, family constitution, and religious belief in ancestral guardianship.

The problems with which the social anthropologist is concerned, when framed in a very general way, are of some such order as this: What are the main patterns of human behaviour in any society? How far does conformity to these patterned relationships draw people together in groups? How do the groups interact to allow of the operation of what can be called a society? What are the controls for group action and for individual action of an interpersonal kind? How far do rational considerations enter in the field of controls? How far does loyalty to a group operate in the face of self-interest? What are the sets of values which give meaning to the behaviour of people in social circumstances? By what symbols do they express these values? How do the patterns of behaviour stand up to changed circumstances? What kind of authority and guidance does tradition supply? How quickly can values and symbols change? What kinds of strain are most severe on human relationships? These questions represent only a few of the important problems. But in that form the problems are hardly capable of any direct or useful answer. They must be broken down into much more specific questions, involving the search for types and variants of social relationship, and the correlation of these with other elements of social behaviour. Social process can be discussed in gross, but must be studied in detail. This means the analysis of material from particular societies, particular situations, even particular persons.

There is one complicating element here. I mentioned at the beginning that the conventional material of the social anthropologist was fast disappearing, as Western technology, economic evaluations, and institutions have hit the more primitive peoples. This has in reality widened, not narrowed, the range of data open to the anthropologist. But it has set him two difficulties to tackle, of closely related kind. One is that of isolation of a relevant field of inquiry. To select any set of people as a physical unit, or any set of relations as a social unit, for consideration as a " society " is always an arbitrary proceeding. The problem has been least apparent in the case of a remote, almost self-sufficient Pacific island community. It is most evident in the case of an African tribe having its members living intermingled with those of other tribes and in symbiotic relationship with them. It becomes increasingly difficult as Westernization—or " modernization " as some prefer to call it—links people more closely into a common system of values and institutions, with increased movement of population as well as ideas. Definition of a group for study then becomes more clearly arbitrary. The second difficulty is that of finding sufficient regularity in the behaviour of members of the group to allow of adequate generalization. The range of variation in individual conduct in modern conditions may be so much greater than in traditional conditions that it may be hard to establish a norm. Where traditional restraints have broken down and every man does what seems fit to him, there may not be much meaning in a concept of the " custom " of the society. Yet, though conformity to a recognized rule may no longer exist, some statistical frequency is commonly observable in the people's actions. In such conditions the anthropologist's generalization needs a broader base of observation than before.

Detailed analysis of some aspects of these situations will be given in Chapter III. But here a reference to the issues of Westernization is necessary to show the kind of material it presents to the anthropologist. The process has been going on for centuries. But since the beginning of the Industrial Revolution the amazing advance of modern technology is devouring natural resources at an unprecedented rate, and digesting them to serve an ever-expanding variety of human purposes. The accent is changing from development of resources to conservation. Exploitation of Nature is coming to be regarded as no less dangerous and immoral than exploitation of man. Even the soil's fertility itself is in jeopardy. To secure the proper technical utilization of such resources old forms of organization are being revitalized, and new forms of organization are being created or foreshadowed, vaster in scale and more infused with conscious purpose than before. All such technological and economic activity involves human changes of magnitude. In many cases it is deliberately introduced to provoke such human changes, to advance human welfare. Yet the development of the concept of the human being as a value in himself has meant that, as far as possible, changes are envisaged in their total effects, and that no change is justified if it involves the permanent degradation of any man.

Yet here enter the social difficulties, and here too the anthropological problems begin to emerge. For the process of change is never smoothly accomplished. Take the question of incentive. There may be general agreement that economic development may be desirable; it may even be conceded by many that it is within the grasp of those who reach out for it. Yet the workers may be slow to respond—whether Russian peasants, African ground-nut farmers, or English miners. The relation between their present standards of consumption, their incomes, and their future prospects may be such in their eyes as to offer too little inducement to improve production materially or, even more so, to alter radically their technical methods. Rarely, however, is the problem simply one of technological conservatism and economic calculation. Into the consumption standards enter a range of factors of a kind most difficult to reduce to measurable values, of any quantitative type. Preferences for the social aspects of the customary working patterns, for the distribution of daily and seasonal leisure time in such a way as to give full scope for existing recreations, for the kind of social relations which would be disturbed by break-up of existing social units—this is but an indication of the factors which may operate. The role of the social anthropologist consists in part in the analysis of these factors—especially where the groups concerned have been traditionally outside the orbit of the Western industrial system.

Even apart from such planned economic changes, the worldwide spread of communications and the intensive development of market relations have created a group sensitivity among the individual non-Western communities. Isolation may be a bar to progress, but the loss of it brings unforeseen difficulties. Throughout the world at the present time there is what may be described as a " crisis of the peasantry." This is occurring not simply because of the peasant's low standards of productivity and of living—as is often alleged—but also because of the strains thrown on his social mechanisms by his and other people's efforts to raise those standards.

Efforts to mitigate the strains, or to provide new mechanisms to bear the burden, are well to the forefront of policy in responsible government circles. A variety of measures is adopted. Projects of fundamental education supply literary and technical training, stimulate organizations for self-help and self-expression for the community, and try to develop local leadership. Administrative measures aim at a closer association of the people with the machinery of government through the establishment of native local authorities and the incorporation of larger numbers of local people in the public service. These and analogous aims are expressed in terms which imply the need to secure the rights and interests of the common man. Stress is laid on securing the co-operation of the people—building from the bottom up; on development of community, not merely sectional or individual capacities; on the need for a democratic foundation as the ultimate basis. At the same time there is stress on the need to develop initiative and a sense of responsibility in those who should ultimately take control of their own destiny. Some think that all this can be done without destroying the tribal or other indigenous forms of society, others think that only radically new forms can do the job. Here the pessimist sometimes expresses the view that voluntary organization in the long run will not be able to secure the efficiency required, and that some form of compulsory authoritarian discipline will be needed.   Others again argue that what is needed first of all is a political re-basing of the society.   In the Colonial territories the principles of tutelage, trusteeship, or partnership, announced as the policy guide of the metropolitan Power, have been challenged as only a moral cloak hiding the nakedness of economic exploitation or strategic retention.   It is beginning to be generally acknowledged that it is no more compatible with human dignity that one man should be the political vassal of another—at least in name—than that he should be his economic and legal chattel.   Whether the concept of self-government favoured by some metropolitan Powers meets the full requirements of freedom is a moot point.   And the moral obligation of economic development is beginning to be stressed in a new form as an offset against the cry for local self-determination, now that the resources of some Colonial Powers are shrinking and their need for strategical security is expanding.   But if the nineteenth century has seen the passing of serfdom and slavery, the twentieth century may well see the passing of the Colonial system.   Most radical of all, the Communist policy claims to treat local nationalist movements not in themselves but as stages in a more fundamental emancipation, which will solve by a final synthesis all the economic, social, and political problems.

Social anthropology does not take sides on such questions. Criticism or defence, either of the activities involved or of the value systems which lie behind them, is out of place.   But the science is affected by them.   They enter as factors in the total situation with which the anthropologist is concerned.   If, in pursuance of a new administrative policy, an ordinary village African is made a member of a Native Authority—a kind or rural district council—his social behaviour is affected.   He gets certain new privileges, certain committee rights; he also has new obligations.   He has to help control his neighbour's sanitation and access to water ; he shares some control over local taxation; he has to put community interests before those of his family.   He becomes a different social personality, and his new relations are part of a modified social structure.   The economic behaviour of the ordinary Malay peasant who relies on his rubber-trees to bring him in some extra cash may be affected by the outcome of negotiations about the production of synthetic rubber, with British dollar needs and American strategic considerations both operating powerfully. The anthropologist does not study the operation of these external factors as such; but he does study the peasant society and economy in which their effects are manifest. Here is one sphere where the wider interest of the anthropological problems becomes apparent. For the working of the African Native Authority depends ultimately on the social relations of the men who compose it. Lacking any thorough-going authoritarian powers of enforcement, they can be effective in administration only by the extent to which they have the acquiescence, loyalty, respect, and allegiance of the people they represent. How far the bases of co-operation lie in the recognition of traditional forms of authority and leadership under a new guise; of the validity of the social and economic bonds of family and lineage or other kin ties; of respect for newly acquired education or wealth, are questions which the anthropologist helps to analyse. Or consider the economics of the Malay peasant. One of the problems of great concern to the administration is the heavy burden of indebtedness he bears. The level of his debt is to some extent bound up with the prices of the products which he sells to the external market, especially the price of his rubber. But his debts are not automatic. They are incurred to meet what he regards as important social liabilities—not merely the feeding and clothing of his wife and children, which he can usually manage, though sometimes at a pinch, from his normal output—but disbursements at the marriage of his son, at religious festivals, for charity, or even to help a kinsman out of financial embarrassment. Examination of indebtedness needs a social as well as an economic analysis. In this way the work of the social anthropologist can have a bearing on concrete as well as on abstract problems.

This indicates, too, that the province of social anthropology is much wider than the simple, small-scale " primitive " or " preliterate " peasant cultures outside the Western world. Our studies still deal largely with these. But the boundaries are neither technological nor geographical. In China, anthropologists have been analysing the structure of the peasantry and gentry in rural areas, problems of labour efficiency and management in new factories set up during the war, and the relations between personal development and family life. In India they have been investigating conditions among Hindu caste groups in towns as well as among the agricultural masses. In Japan, Mexico, the Caribbean Islands, French Canada, they have carried out studies of community organization and values. In the United States anthropologists have collaborated with the Bureau of Indian Affairs to investigate the problems of the Indians of the South-West. American anthropologists have turned also to studies of personality and character-formation in civilized as well as primitive communities: others have studied the conditions of negro communities in the Black Belt of the South; still others have produced urban studies in which analyses of class structure and status have played a prominent part. English anthropologists have done most of their work abroad, but some study has been made of kinship organization and other problems in English working-class society.

The nearer the anthropologist approaches to the study of contemporary civilization, the more he must be aware of the contribution of other social sciences to the problems. He must also define his own limits of inquiry more carefully. It is sometimes thought that he holds a special clue to the understanding of human behaviour. If so, it can only be through applying scientific method more rigorously, or studying some aspects of the subject which other disciplines neglect.

When the first public announcement of the Josiah Mason lectureship was made, one of the speakers on the occasion expressed the hope that the lectureship would not be confined to the study of Melanesians or Polynesians. He wished it to include a scientific study of British institutions—even more so of Irish institutions, which seemed to need a special type of inquiry to explain! Such a joking remark prompts a few reflections. Eire's present situation, marked by rural difficulties, by direction in public as well as private affairs by a powerful Church, by strong cultural as well as political nationalism, and by an ambivalent attitude towards Great Britain, has a complex history. On the social and economic side, for instance, events of a century ago have left their mark. In the ideology of the present situation, records of the potato famine, the system of absentee landlords, the exaction of rack rents cannot be ignored. To understand something of the emotional attitude which so often emerges without apparent cause when relations with England are discussed, consider some of these earlier records. A century ago, in their shortsightedness and intransigence, there were English landlords who were attempting to deal by force with rent evasions created by the poverty and ignorance of their Irish tenants. Hired "process-servers" pursued wretched tenants for non-payment of rent. "Grippers" chased them to arrest and imprisonment. "Keepers" watched lest they steal their own crops by night and cheat the landlord's distraint. "Drivers" took off their poultry and cattle to the pound. Acts of even greater violence were the response. The landlord's men were terrorized and beaten up by young men, disguised in skirts, with blackened faces, calling themselves "Molly Maguires." Agents who carried out evictions and greedy tenants who dared to replace those who were evicted were faced by threats, assault, and even murder by men of the "Ribbon Code," whose expressed aim was to redress all alleged wrongs connected with the management of land.[1] Such events were local and temporary in their duration. But they indicate that the tradition of real or fancied wrongs might well outlast the economic conditions which made for immediate difficulty.

It is clear even from this one type of material that the examination of such economic conditions, especially on the historical plane, is no job for an anthropologist alone. To explain the genesis of modern Irish society needs demographer, economist, historian, sociologist, political scientist—perhaps even psychologist as well. Is there a role for the social anthropologist? It is part of the task of anthropology to study the everyday contemporary life of the people, particularly in its more intimate domestic and associational aspects. Something of this has in fact been done, precisely in Eire.

[1] See descriptions, e.g., by W. Steuart Trench, *Realities of Irish Life*, London, 1869, *passim*.

About a decade ago two American social scientists explicitly applied anthropological methods to the collection and interpretation of material on Irish rural life.   They analysed the Irish peasant family and rural community structure, showing the social network by which the greater part of the Irish population is bound together.   They pointed out the strength of family and kinship ties, and their importance in rural cooperation, even though now operating on a decreasing scale. They showed how the sons in the peasant family remain dependent on and subordinate to the father until a comparatively late age, so that sociological adulthood comes much later than physiological adulthood.   They showed also how such persistent and recalcitrant demographic factors as continuous emigration for about a century, declining population, delayed marriage, and rise of bachelorhood rate still resisted efforts at amelioration, and profoundly influenced the condition of the Irish peasantry.[1]   In this first-hand community study these anthropologists made a contribution of a novel type in Irish studies.

These examples indicate not only the potentialities of anthropological research, but also the closeness of its relation to research in other disciplines, including psychology and sociology.   What are the features which distinguish social anthropology?

They lie firstly in the intensive detailed character of the systematic observation of the behaviour of people in group relations.   The anthropologist above all sees at first hand what people actually do.   For this concentrated observation of small-unit behaviour, usually made with the aid of vernacular language, I have suggested the term micro-sociology.[2]   This is on analogy with micro-chemistry, micro-biology, or micro-geography, each of which deals with very small samples of its material, or with items of very small magnitude.   The anthropologist deliberately selects either his small community or a small sample of a large community, because of the greater

[1] Conrad M. Arensburg and Solon T. Kimball, *Family and Community in Ireland*, Cambridge, Mass., 1940; cf. also J. M. Mogey, "The Community in Northern Ireland," *Man*, 1948, 98.

[2] Raymond Firth, "The Future of Social Anthropology," *Man*, 1944, 8.

accuracy of first-hand observation.   He can get not simply a
general pattern, but also the degree of variation from it, and
perhaps the reasons.   Moreover, he can check what he is told
by seeing what people actually do.   But if the distinguishing
feature of the anthropologist is micro-sociological technique,
his theory is macro-sociological.   He uses the microcosm to
illumine the macrocosm, the particular to illustrate the general.
His small sample or his small unit of 1,000 or so people is made
the basis for generalizations which cover the whole community, or even reach out with hypotheses—about family,
marriage, magic, or morals—to put a question mark against
the whole of human culture.   The principles upon which this
small sample is taken to be representative are very important.
They involve really the assumption of homogeneity in the
material, of uniformities in what people do.   But one of the
weaknesses of social anthropology still is that they are so
rarely stated and examined.

The second characteristic feature of the social anthropologist's inquiry is that it is holistic in implication.   Any particular
item selected for examination is always considered with some
regard to its place in the total phenomena in the life of the
human group concerned.   What Malinowski expressed as the
functional point of view is always basic to our study and interpretation of social material.   What has been put forward on
the highest metaphysical level by Whitehead and others, as the
essence of the " organic philosophy," may perhaps be borrowed as an analogy on a lower level by the social scientist.
If the underlying activity of nature is a system of interlocking
concrescent processes, each developing and realizing its appropriate value, then human activity partakes of the same general
character; it is part of the dynamic process of the world.

The third characteristic is the emphasis the social anthropologist gives to comparison.   Comparison is inherent in all
scientific work, at the simplest levels of observation and inference.   But the essence of the comparative method in social
anthropology is that comparison is made between items of
behaviour in different major social units, with the object of
establishing types and seeing variants from them.   The selection of items of behaviour and the identification of the major

social units rest on abstraction.   Hence the question that is
sometimes posed—Should we compare social actions of individuals, institutions, or whole societies?—can be answered only
according to the degree of abstraction that is judged to be
necessary for the problem in hand.   But if the relational idea
emphasizes totality, the comparative one emphasizes isolability.
Form is important, the defining element which gives the isolate
its special character.   If it be argued that form is nothing but
a specific order of relations, then it can be said that what the
anthropologist compares are differences of relational order.   If
he is comparing forms of marriage, for instance, he is noting
differences in the order of relations between men and women
in specific legal circumstances.   Perception of *order* is then
fundamental to our inquiry.   And from this angle the intensity which has been mentioned as the first characteristic of
anthropological study is a continued testing, by empirical
reference, of the grounds for the attribution of order to the
material.

The intensive character of anthropological observation gives
reality to the data : the science deals with the behaviour of
real people.   The relational character gives the aim of looking
at social life as a process, of finding meaning in effects and not
simply in appearances.   The comparative character gives
generalizations which apply to human beings in many different
kinds of social circumstances.   Social anthropology aims therefore at being truly a science of Man, and not
simply a science of ourselves.

In examining the validity of the methods used by the social
anthropologist, there are three problems which must be considered : the problem of observation; the problem of assignment of meaning; and the problem of expression.   I shall
consider these in turn.

How does the social anthropologist set about reaching his
primary objective—correct observation?   The two main senses
he uses for the collection of his data—sight and hearing—are
vitally important for accurate field-work.   An historian may be
deaf, a jurist may be blind, a philosopher may be both, but it is
essential to an anthropologist to hear what people are saying, to
see what they are doing.   It is human social behaviour, verbal

and non-verbal, which is the raw material for study. In stressing this, the anthropologist does not necessarily share the general assumptions of behaviourist psychology. But whether it be speech or any other type of bodily act that is under observation, the anthropologist assumes that these phenomena have a reality of their own, that their existence does not depend simply on his perception of them. He is aware of the possibility of " observer-effect," of his noted presence acting as a conditioning element to the behaviour of others. But he assumes that his senses can give him a correct rendering of events with a degree of accuracy which depends largely on his proximity. Problems of intuitional comprehension, empathy, existential thinking, he leaves on one side. What is, however, worthy of his attention is the extent to which his sensory perceptions can cover the relevant field of observation, and the extent to which the memory-factor enters into his reproduction of what he observes. Testing of the adequacy of these elements has not yet gone far in anthropology, though to some extent practical tests are applied by the field worker himself through repetition of his observations, and through necessary guessing in advance as to what is going to happen in the everyday life of the people.

In social behaviour, people have physical relationships to objects and to other people. Take an early and apparently simple stage in the development of man as a social being—young children in social play. They give things, they take things, they walk towards others or away from them, they touch them or refrain from touching; continually they talk—to one another, to themselves as an accompaniment to action, to objects, with variations in inflexion, emphasis, and speed. These physical relationships shown in sequences and associations of such behaviour are given meaning by the intellectual and emotional appreciation of the watching parents, who are looking all the time for the clues. So also with the anthropologist in his field experience. He ascribes ends to social acts. He infers from them social relationships—that is, their ends are regarded as transcending the sphere of influence of single individuals, to affect others in the community. Now physical behaviour is a flow, a continuum. We talk of an act as being

repeated, but " repetition " is only a convenient expression for
close similarity; it is not identity.   Even in the simplest social
acts, such as the repeated proffering of a toy by one child to
another, time has passed between the acts, slight muscular
changes have occurred, there has been some displacement of
the body.   Even a cinema film record would show a slight
variation.   Yet we regard the social relation as the same when
analogous physical acts take place on later occasions.   We see
sufficient elements of likeness to allow us to attribute identity,
to abstract and generalize into a type of social relation.   Such
inference by abstraction and generalization is carried throughout the whole range of social situations observed, or envisaged
through description by others.   The physical acts of giving,
for instance, enter, together with other actions, as basal behaviour into such diverse social relations as buying and selling,
gift-exchange, transfer of goods at marriage or funeral, compensation for injury, paying respect to a person of superior
rank, offering to gods or ancestors.   The ways and contexts
of giving and the amounts given are seen to have a certain
regularity for the community under observation.   They vary
only within certain limits, which can be more or less precisely
defined.   According to the precision of definition of these
limits, such actions, and such social relations, are predictable,
in terms of probability of occurrence.   If event a occurs, then
events b and c are likely to occur, and their magnitudes are
likely to be of a given order.   In Tikopia in 1929, if a man of
a given rank and kinship group died, it was possible for me to
predict in advance who would occupy the position of chief
mourners, for how long in each case, and what would be the
number, size, and content of the various packages of food and
other goods involved in transfers between persons and groups.[1]
Yet there are always certain possibilities of variation.   Abstraction from the conditions of original observation has involved approximation, allowing the possible entry of new
factors into the situation under examination.   And in this the
effects of human choice and decision have always to be
considered.

[1] I have given a brief account of these proceedings in *Primitive Polynesian
Economy*, London 1940, pp. 324-31.   (A).

C

Social anthropologists are usually said to study a society, a community, a culture. But this is not what they *observe*. The material for their observation is human activity. They do not even *observe* social relationships; they infer them from physical acts. The anthropologist as observer is a moving point in a flow of activity. At any one time he has only a limited field of social observation—the people whose acts he can see or hear, or about whose acts he can get description by others who have observed. Rarely does he observe a small group such as a simple family in *total* activity over any considerable length of time—say, a complete day. And still more rarely, if ever, does he observe *all* the members of one of the larger groups, such as a lineage or age-set, in action all together. Yet his published analyses are full of general statements about what families, lineages, age-sets do, and even about the attitudes and interests of whole societies. We are told that the Tanala are vastly more interested in their cattle than in their rice cultivation, though the latter is of much greater economic importance to them; that the chronic state of the Iatmül culture is one in which the norms are weakly defined; that only a killer's opinions had weight in the conversation of the head-hunting Kalingas of Luzon. We normally accept such statements. In them the anthropologist ascribes regularities, he imputes ends. What is his justification for doing so? It is primarily the degree of uniformity of his experience as he moves through his field of social observation. He applies a rough index of conformability to new items of behaviour as he isolates them from the flow. Relating them to ends previously considered, and to behaviour previously observed, he attempts to estimate how far they conform. Significant variation leads him to further investigation and collection of more instances, until he has established the reason for the variation—or until he has separated another isolate and related it to a fresh set of ends and circumstances. In this process of isolation and selection, in identification of common ends or recognition of disparate ends, the estimate of what is significant or non-significant in variation is very important. Let us now turn then to a brief consideration of the problems of meaning.

In his study of behaviour the anthropologist works by

contextualization. He assumes that if he grasps the context adequately, he can apprehend the meaning of the behaviour. The context of associated circumstances allows him to see the end of the activity and the value attached—that is, the quality of the relationship inferred. To give a simple example: if the anthropologist is travelling on the Plateau of Northern Nigeria, as I was a few years ago, he may meet men from the Bi Rom and other pagan tribes living there. They will probably shake their clenched fists in the air as he approaches. According to his fears or his politics, he may interpret this as a symbol of anger or of solidarity among fellow-workers. In time, he will find it is merely the normal greeting. How are the conditions of contextualization arrived at and the correct value given? If one has no guide to interpret, simply by a process of hypothesis and trial and error. The anthropologist notes the associated activities and conditions: the grin which frequently accompanies the fist-shaking, the lack of threatening gesture with spear or axe when these are carried, the regular speech sound—*sho*—accompanying the raising of the fist, the absence of any apparent reasons for aggressive display. He checks his tentative classification of this as a greeting symbol by watching when pagan people meet one another. He may also pluck up courage and experiment. He may test his inference in reverse by clenching his own fist and shaking it at the next inoffensive old man he sees in the path. If nothing but cordiality and a similar response ensue, he is satisfied for the time being. There are still other possibilities—that the sign is a greeting only between men, or between equals, or between travellers; that its use is perfunctory, as a meeting rather than as a greeting sign proper. The problem of meaning is not exhausted, but it may be regarded as sufficiently illumined for the sign to be used by the anthropologist as a stepping-stone in his further analysis of the behaviour of the people.

This simple example emphasizes, too, that for the anthropologist, almost more than for any other field scientist, research means a process of learning and practising new modes of personal behaviour. His is not the dispassionate eye behind the microscope or the hand holding the test-tube. He is observing amidst his fellow human organisms. He is adopting for much of the time their patterns of living, greeting, eating, and perhaps even of participation in ceremonial life. Many of his inferences are thus tested by the best measuring-rod—the results of his own action upon them. If his scientific inferences are wrong, he gets into practical difficulties.

Another aspect of the problem of meaning is that of relevance. While the meaning of an item of behaviour can be established by contextualization, there is still the question of what items are to be selected for consideration. It is impossible to grasp the complete flow of events. The observer must select according to his particular interest. He wants to perceive order or regularity in a certain field, or, in other terms, to test a hypothesis about a certain order of relations. The problem is one of relative significance, of choosing for examination those items which if omitted would distort the order sought, and discarding those which have no effect upon the order, or only a minimal effect. Here again this is a matter of trial and error. This may be illustrated by an example.

As one day I was sitting cross-legged on the mat floor of a palm-leaf-thatched house of a chief in Tikopia, my eye was caught by a vermilion paint-mark on a gravestone of the chief's father. Then I saw other paint-marks on some of the timbers that supported the roof. What did they mean? Were they relevant to my problems? I was studying mainly at that time the organization of turmeric manufacture in its relation to the religious beliefs and ritual of the people. The marks did not look promising. I idly wondered how a splash of this turmeric pigment could get so far from the scene of action when everyone had been so careful, and none of the paint had been flying about. Then I thought further. They looked like smears made by someone who had been casually wiping paint-stained fingers on the wood—to clean them, or for sport. I could not get up to look closely, because the chief's house was a temple as well as a dwelling. Where the grave-mats of his ancestors lay, beneath the marks, was a sacred part of the floor. Since the work of manufacture was over, and all had turned out well, the marks, which were fresh, were probably of no account. But it was just as well to make sure, even though all the rites were apparently over.   Perhaps these marks were not so casual, after all?   It is the business of the field-anthropologist to tie up all the ends of his inquiry if he can, to account for every article, every piece of behaviour that appears in a situation.   This balancing of his field-work account books, to see that he leaves no unexplained item, is necessary to ensure that he is observing the correct relation of services, attitudes, values, structural elements.

Inquiry revealed that the marks were not at all haphazard. I was first told that they were to signal the end of the turmeric-making—as marks of the importance of the chief's house where the work had been carried on.   They were to call the attention of anyone who should come into the house—" a sign of the turmeric-making, to call attention to the pigment that has been hung up."   I pointed out that the marks were small and the cylinders of turmeric pigment which had been prepared were large enough to call attention to themselves.   But this was ignored by the chief and his people, who insisted that the marks were an announcement of the turmeric-making.   I finally concluded that it must be a kind of formal token, a glorification in privilege, not a factual notification.   Later the deeper significance appeared.   They were intended as a notification not to men, but to spirits !   As religious symbols they were tokens of thanksgiving—of acknowledgement to gods and ancestors that the turmeric had been successfully produced. As specific symbols, each was dedicated to a particular spirit, known by a personal name and a genealogical position.   Their interpretation rested upon a further piece of symbolism—the theory of the visible, material representation of the invisible and immaterial.   In this building, rough and smoke-stained, each gravestone represented an ancestor, each wall-stud and rafter on the sacred side of the house was dedicated to, and even regarded as embodying, a spirit.   The procedure of turmeric-making was brooded over by a whole order of spirit beings— from one point of view a vast human fantasy construct.   Yet this conceptual world had got to be actualized, made concrete, for it to be effectively usable.   Its symbolic presentation was both homely and varied.   The finger-mark of pigment was regarded in this metaphorical language as a " decoration " for the god or ancestor represented by the timber so marked, just as similar marking is used to decorate men for a ceremony. This symbolic mark was also intended to tell the spirits of the completion of the turmeric manufacture—one does not mind telling the gods what they already know.   As a mark of thanksgiving the symbol stands for an emotional attitude.   Yet an intellectual element of calculation also enters in.   If no thanksgiving was offered that year, there might be no adequate yield of turmeric the next.   Moreover, the marks were not isolated examples; they were part of a series, spaced out in time and place, and themselves acted as indices to mark off the approach to further ceremonial events.

Here, then, that which at first sight seemed as if it might be irrelevant to the problem turned out to be part of the structural scheme of actions which made up the institution. Should, however, it have turned out not to be symbolic of relations between the alleged spirit world and the human world, it might still have been relevant to another problem. If, for instance, the marks had been merely casual, or for recreation, they would have served as an indication of the degree of licence allowed to behaviour in a sacred building.

Scientific observation of phenomena and attribution of meaning to them can only be done in reference to a set of theoretical concepts, which also serve for the expression of the results of the inquiry. The anthropologist is perpetually grappling with new ways of expressing or subsuming reality by verbal propositions. He realizes that these propositions, and the concepts they use, do not represent the reality of his observation directly. Terms such as *society* ; *community* ; *structure* ; *function* ; *organization* ; represent only certain characteristics or facets of it. They imply qualities which the observer thinks he can recognize and to which he gives names in order that the discussion may go on. One of his obligations is to see to it that the reality to which these names correspond is the context of his observations, and not simply the context of discussion itself. He must not carry on his argument entirely in the air. The task before him is to try to secure the greatest degree of abstraction with the greatest degree of correspondence with reality. The extent to which this is possible varies with the degree of uniformity of the material under study. That is why it is important to look back continually at individual behaviour to see the extent of variation it shows from the abstracted norm. The notion of a system is basic to our study of society. But this notion can be imposed on our perception of social relations as well as aid us in such perception.

In the description and analysis of the group life of human beings the most general terms used are society, culture, and community. Each is commonly used to express the idea of a totality. As abstractions they can give only a selected few of the qualities of the subject-matter they are meant to represent. Naturally, then, the definition of them has tended to mark contrasted rather than shared qualities. The types of contrast made familiar by German sociologists have drawn a distinction between the more purposeful associations serving individual ends and those arising from less-well-defined principles of aggregation. This has value as an analytical device, to classify social relationships. But at the broadest level, to cover almost the complete range of association, this mutual exclusiveness is misplaced. The terms represent different facets or components in basic human situations. If, for instance, society is taken to be an organized set of individuals with a given way of life, culture is that way of life. If society is taken to be an aggregate of social relations, then culture is the content of those relations. Society emphasizes the human component, the aggregate of people and the relations between them. Culture emphasizes the component of accumulated resources, immaterial as well as material, which the people inherit, employ, transmute, add to, and transmit. Having substance, if in part only ideational, this component acts as a regulator to action. From the behavioural aspect, culture is all learned behaviour which has been socially acquired. It includes the residual effects of social action. It is necessarily also an incentive to action. The term community emphasizes the space–time component, the aspect of living together. It involves a recognition, derived from experience and observation, that there must be minimum conditions of agreement on common aims, and inevitably some common ways of behaving, thinking, and feeling. Society, culture, community, then involve one another—though when they are conceived as major isolates for concrete study their boundaries do not necessarily coincide.

These boundaries are in any case arbitrary. The human associational process is such that men are continually overcoming barriers to social intercourse—even those they themselves have erected. Sexual and economic relationships, involving also the use of language, create such links that unless there is stark physical isolation, no society can be given a definite limit. The Australian aborigines and the white men who have pre-empted their land are often conceived as being nearly at opposite ends of the scale of human achievement. Yet the cattle-station owner, the prospector, the dingo-trapper, the missionary, have brought the blackfellow within the European economic orbit, and miscegenation has reinforced the social tie which exists even where it is least acknowledged. Fields of social relations, not clear-cut societies, must be the more empirical notion of social aggregates.

In studying a field of social relations, whether we are using the notions of society, of culture, or of community, we can distinguish their structure, their function, and their organization. These are separable but related aspects. All are necessary for the full consideration of social process. Briefly, by the structural aspect of social relations we mean the principles on which their form depends; by the functional aspect we mean the way in which they serve given ends; by the organizational aspect we mean the directional activity which maintains their form and serves their ends. Each of the critical words here is heavy with implications for our study. So we had better examine each concept in turn.

To the layman the term social structure may sound simple enough. In fact anthropologists and other social scientists—for example, Herbert Spencer—used it for many years without feeling the need to define it. They simply took it as meaning generally the form or morphology of society, and took for granted that everyone would know broadly what the idea meant. They were concerned with substantial propositions rather than formal propositions. When, forty years ago, a pair of economic historians set out to examine the results of the eighteenth-century enclosure of the common fields, they said, " Our business is with the changes that the enclosures caused in the social structure of England. . . ."[1] They assumed that every reader would accept this to mean changes in the form of English society, especially rural society. Their analysis accordingly dealt with such themes as changes in the system of social classes in the village, the conversion of the peasant to a labourer, modifications in his rights to assistance, in his relations to the courts, the magistrates, the parish authorities. When later two other social analysts made what they termed " A Survey of the Social Structure of England and Wales,"[2] using a great deal of statistical material, they also did not give any specific definition of what they meant by social structure. It was merely stated that the aim of the book was to treat contemporary social data from the morphological point of view; to construct a picture of social conditions as a whole; to present a coherent picture of some of the more important aspects of social life in this country so far as they can be illustrated by statistics. It was assumed that what was wanted was classification and assessment of magnitude of social units of the more important types, and demonstration of the relations between them. The analysis began with population units, and went on to examine units of marital association, housing, urbanization, distribution of industrial facilities, of occupations, of national income, of social services; special attention was also given to such important matters as the breadth of the educational ladder.

As against this rather broad use of the term social structure, many social anthropologists and some sociologists have in recent years spent much time in trying to get a more precise idea of its meaning. Their differences of view suggest that any science must have a budget of terms of general application, not too closely defined, and that " structure " may be one of these. On the other hand, they have drawn attention to

---

[1] J. L. Hammond and Barbara Hammond, *The Village Labourer* (first published in 1911), Guild edn., 1948, vol. I, p. 19.

[2] A. M. Carr-Saunders and D. Caradog Jones, *A Survey of the Social Structure of England and Wales as Illustrated by Statistics*, Oxford, 1927. This book bears also the sub-title of *The Structure of English Society*. (A).

significant elements in the social process, and in the process of social study itself.

The idea of the structure of society, if it is to be in conformity with the general concept of structure, must fulfil certain conditions.[1] It must be concerned with the ordered relations of parts to a whole, with the arrangement in which the elements of the social life are linked together. These relations must be regarded as built up one upon another—they are series of varying orders of complexity. They must be of more than purely momentary significance—some factor of constancy or continuity must be involved in them. Current anthropological usage of the notion of social structure conforms to this. But there is room for difference of opinion as to what kinds of social relations shall be of main account in describing a social structure, and how much continuity they ought to have before they are included. Some anthropologists have argued that a social structure is the network of all person-to-person relations in a society. But such a definition is too wide. It makes no distinction between the ephemeral and the more enduring elements in social activity, and makes it almost impossible to distinguish the idea of the structure of a society from that of the totality of the society itself. At the opposite extreme is the idea of social structure as comprising only relations between major groups in the society—those with a high degree of persistence. This includes groups such as clans, which persist for many generations, but excludes those such as the simple family, which dissolves from one generation to another. This definition is too narrow. A different idea of social structure stresses not so much the actual relations between persons or groups as the expected relations, or even the ideal relations. According to these views, what really gives a society its form, and allows its members to carry on their activities, is their expectations, or even their idealized beliefs, of what will be done, or ought to be done, by other members. There is no doubt that for any society to work effectively, and to have what may be called a coherent structure, its members must have some idea of what to expect. Without

[1] See, for example, Bertrand Russell, *Human Knowledge*, London, 1948, pp. 267 ff.

some pattern of expectations and a scheme of ideas about what they think other people ought to do, they would not be able to order their lives. But to see a social structure in sets of ideals and expectations alone is too aloof. The pattern of realizations, the general characteristics of concrete social relations, must also form a part of the structural concept. Moreover, to think of social structure as being comprised only of the ideal patterns of behaviour suggests the covert view that these ideal patterns are the ones of primary importance in the social life, and that actual behaviour of individuals is simply a reflection of standards which are socially set. It is equally important, I think, to stress the way in which the social standards, the ideal patterns, the sets of expectations, tend to be changed, recognizably or imperceptibly, by the acts of individuals in response to other influences, including technological developments.

If we bear in mind that the only way in which we can learn of a person's ideals and expectations is from some aspect of his behaviour—either from what he says or from what he does— the distinction between the norms of action and the norms of expectation to some extent disappears. The concept of social structure is an analytical tool, designed to serve us in understanding how men behave in their social life. The essence of this concept is those social relations which seem to be of critical importance for the behaviour of members of the society, so that if such relations were not in operation, the society could not be said to exist in that form. When the economic historian describes the social structure of eighteenth-century rural England he is concerned, for instance, with relations of different classes of people to the common land and to one another. These were fundamental to the society of the time. As the common-field system changed to one of private enclosure, consequential changes affected the various classes. The small farmer and the cottager, for example, emigrated to an industrial town or became day labourers. The relations of the new type of labourer with his employer and with the local authorities, now that he was deprived of land and many other rights to minor income, were very different from before. The social structure of the country had radically altered—though the ideals of many people were still much as before, and even some of their earlier expectations lingered on.

In the types of society ordinarily studied by anthropologists, the social structure may include critical or basic relationships arising similarly from a class system based on relations with the soil. Other aspects of the social structure arise through membership of other kinds of persistent groups, such as clans, castes, age-sets, or secret societies. Other basic relations again are due to position in a kinship system, status in regard to a political superior, or distribution of ritual knowledge. In many African or Oceanic societies an important structural element is the special relation between a mother's brother and a sister's child. The senior has obligations to protect the junior, to make him or her gifts, to help in sickness or misfortune. So important is the relationship that where a person has no true mother's brother he is provided socially with a " stand-in." This will be a son of the dead mother's brother, or some more distant kinsman who will act as representative of the mother's brother, take on the kinship term, and behave appropriately. Such a relation, then, is one of the cardinal elements of the social structure. If, through external influence on the society, the role of the mother's brother becomes less marked, and the duties cease to be performed, then the structure of the society has altered. Different social structures are contrasted in terms of the differences in such critical or basic relations. For example, among some Malays, in the matrilineal communities of Negri Sembilan, the mother's brother has the role just described. But among other Malays elsewhere in the Malay peninsula this relative has no special importance. On the other hand, in accordance with Muslim law, all Malays attach great importance to what is termed a *wali*. This is the guardian of a young woman for certain legal purposes, including marriage. The *wali* represents her in the marriage contract, and must give his consent to the union. Usually it is the girl's father who is the guardian. But if he be dead, then the grandfather, brother, or other nearest kinsman of the girl, according to rules laid down in the Muslim books of the law, takes his place. In some circumstances the duties and powers of guardians go so far as to allow a guardian in the ascending male line the titular right to dispose of a maiden's hand without her consent.   The *wali* relation is therefore a major element in the structure of a Muslim society.   In comparing different Malay and Muslim social structures as such, then, the difference between the role of the mother's brother and that of the *wali* is a useful structural feature.

This discussion of the notion of social structure has taken us some way towards understanding the kind of questions with which anthropologists are concerned in trying to grasp the bases of human social relations.   It also helps to clarify two other concepts, social function and social organization, which are as important as that of social structure.

Every social action can be thought of as having one or more social functions.   Social function can be defined as the relation between a social action and the system of which the action is a part, or, alternatively, as the result of the social action in terms of the means-ends scheme of all those affected by it.[1] By Malinowski the idea of function was extended into a major scheme of analysis of social and cultural material. The basic emphasis in this scheme has influenced modern social anthropology considerably.   It stresses the relation of any social or cultural item to other social or cultural items.   No social action, no element of culture, can be adequately studied or defined in isolation.   Their meaning is given by their function, the part they play in an interacting system.   In studying the grosser units, the more abstract sets of behaviour patterns known as institutions—such as a marriage system, a family type, a type of ceremonial exchange, a system of magic —the scheme distinguishes various associated components. The charter is the set of traditionally established values and principles which the people concerned regard as the basis of the institution—it may even be embodied in a mythical tale. The norms are the rules which govern the conduct of the people; and these must be distinguished from their activities,

[1] See A. R. Radcliffe-Brown, " On the Concept of Function in Social Science," *American Anthropologist*, 1935, vol. 37, pp. 394-402; B. Malinow-ski, *A Scientific Theory of Culture*, Chapel Hill, 1944, p. 53.   Illuminating treatment of the general theme is given by Talcott Parsons, *Essays in Sociological Theory Pure and Applied*, Glencoe, Illinois, 1949, *passim*.   (A).

which may diverge from the norms according as their own individual interests pull them. The institution is carried on by means of a material apparatus, the nature of which is to be understood only by consideration of the uses to which it is put, and by a personnel, arranged in the appropriate social groups. Finally, there is the function or set of functions to which the institution as a whole corresponds. By function in this sense Malinowski meant the satisfaction of needs, including those developed by man as a member of a specific society as well as the more directly biologically based needs.

This imputation of needs to human social behaviour raises some difficult questions. Needs can be fairly easily recognized in the sense of those proximate ends giving immediate direction to an activity and normally envisaged by the participants themselves. The proximate ends of a feast, for instance, clearly include the aim of consuming food, and this in itself involves certain social and economic consequences. But it is less easy to identify and separate ultimate ends—those which give basic significance to the activity as part of the total pattern of the social life. The ultimate end of a feast is not the satisfaction of hunger, which could be done much more simply. Is it a form of sociability, the pleasure in assembly and excitation through company? Or is it in the exchange system of which a single feast is only one item? Or is it in the status-display and personal enhancement for which the feast gives opportunity? Or is it a form of mystic compulsion, by which periodic assembly is necessary to the integration of the social body? The more abstract the conception of needs, the greater is what may be called the personal refraction of the student—the conditioning of the social image by his own views of purpose in social life. At a certain point in the analysis, indeed, it becomes difficult to do more than infer the human needs from the behaviour that is being studied—men act socially in such and such ways, therefore we judge from this consistent behaviour that some social need is met. For reasons such as these, many modern social anthropologists, while drawing much from Malinowski, have found it preferable to approach the classification of types of social action through study of the structural aspects of behaviour. Elements which can be isolated by reference to their form, their continuity of relation, are more easily classed.

But any attempt at describing the structure of a society must embody some assumptions about what is most relevant in social relations. These assumptions, implicitly or openly, must use some concepts of a functional kind, by reference to the results or effects of social action. This also includes some attention to the aims or directional quality of the actions. Take the exogamy associated with a lineage structure. The exogamous rule requiring that a lineage member shall not marry anyone who is a member of the same lineage is said to be one of the defining characteristics of that structural unit: it helps to mark off lineage members as a body. But for this statement to be true it is assumed necessarily that prohibition of marriage has some effect upon actual marital attitudes; that this effect is considerable; and that there are also positive effects on non-marital behaviour. The translation of " forbidden to marry " into " reinforcement of lineage ties " may be justified, but only after consideration of effects. From this point of view one may use a term of A. N. Whitehead's, and say that the function of a social action or relation is the " concern " which the action or relation has for all other elements in the social system in which it appears. Even minimally, their orientations are affected by its presence. As it tends to exhibit variation, so also do they tend to vary within the total sphere of social activity.

The study of social structure needs, then, to be carried farther, to examine how the forms of basic social relations are capable of variation. It is necessary to study social adaptation as well as social continuity. A structural analysis alone cannot interpret social change. A social taxonomy could become as arid as classification of species in some branches of biology. Analysis of the organizational aspect of social action is the necessary complement to analysis of the structural aspect. It helps to give a more dynamic treatment.

Social organization has usually been taken as a synonym for social structure. In my view it is time to distinguish between them. The more one thinks of the structure of a society in abstract terms, as of group relations or of ideal patterns, the more necessary it is to think separately of social organization in terms of concrete activity.   Generally, the idea of organization is that of people getting things done by planned action. This is a social process, the arrangement of action in sequences in conformity with selected social ends.   These ends must have some elements of common significance for the set of persons concerned in the action.   The significance need not be identical, or even similar, for all the persons; it may be opposed as between some of them.   The processes of social organization may consist in part in the resolution of such opposition by action which allows one or other element to come to final expression.   Social organization implies some degree of unification, a putting together of diverse elements into common relation.   To do this, advantage may be taken of existing structural principles, or variant procedures may be adopted. This involves the exercise of choice, the making of decisions. As such, this rests on personal evaluations, which are the translation of general ends or values of group range into terms which are significant for the individual.   In the sense that all organization involves allocation of resources, it implies within the scheme of value judgements a concept of efficiency.   This infers a notion of the relative contributions which means of different amount and quality can make to given ends.   The sphere of allocation of resources is one in which economic studies are pre-eminent.   (See Chapter IV.)   But of necessity economics has been restricted primarily to the field of exchange relations, especially those which are measurable in monetary terms.   In the social field beyond this the processes resulting from the possibilities of choice and the exercise of decision are also of major importance.

As an example of social organization in a peasant society let us consider once more the institution of the *wali*.   Among the people of Acheh in Sumatra,[1] according to the Shafi'ite law which they follow generally, it is only an agnate in the ascending male line—a father or a father's father—who has the right to give a maiden in marriage without her consent.   If she is a minor she is incapable of giving any valid opinion.   So where

[1] See C. Snouck Hurgronje, *The Achehnese*, Leyden and London, 1906, vol. I, pp. 330–46.

such a guardian is lacking, if the girl is under age, strictly speaking she cannot be married.   But the Achehnese have a strong prejudice against allowing a maiden to stay unmarried until she has come of age; they say it spoils her beauty.   Now, since there may be many girls who have lost both father and grandfather, Achehnese custom and Shafi'ite rule are in opposition.   But the dilemma is easily resolved.   A way out is found by using the Muslim right of appeal to the tenets of another school of law—in this case that of Hanafi.   This school allows any *wali* to give his under-age ward in marriage without her consent.   It throws the net of guardianship wider too, and allows a maternal kinsman to be selected as *wali* if the kinsfolk on the father's side have died out.   On the other hand, this school lets a woman have discretion later. When she comes of age, if she has been married in this way she is entitled to demand a separation from her husband if she wishes.   The essence of all this is that the structure of the *wali* relation—a very important one for the constitution of Muslim marriage and family in Acheh, as in every Muslim society— offers a number of courses of action.   The relatives of a girl who is under age and who has lost father or grandfather have to decide how they will organize her marriage.   Will they follow the Shafi'ite or the Hanafi'ite procedure in the appointment of her guardian?   If the latter, will they try to marry her off or not?   Into such decisions many elements may enter, including the rank of the girl and financial considerations. The *wali* relation, then, is not of itself a permanent, simply definable morphological element in Acheh society;   it is maintained and given its ultimate form by organizational decisions which resolve amorphous situations.

This example draws attention to further elements in social organization.   It implies the recognition of a time factor in the ordering of social relations.   There is the conception of time as necessitating a sequence or serial order in the allocation of units towards the required end.   Appointment of a guardian is not automatic;   kinsfolk must meet, discuss, agree, consult the religious authorities, and in general arrange an elaborate sequence of actions, at some sacrifice of their energies.   Sequence development and the limitations on alternative routes

D

of action thereby are an important aspect of organization. There is also the conception of time as setting limits to activity through processes of human metabolism. In the example just given, the development of the Achehnese maiden ensures that after a certain point of time she will be entitled to take her own decision as to marriage, and so alter the form of the organization. The concept of social organization also allows attention to magnitudes. As in this example, amounts of wealth, rank of persons, numbers of kin, and other quantities are involved as bases for social action of different kinds.

Organization demands also elements of representation and responsibility. In many spheres, in order that the purposes of a group may be served, there must be *representation* of its interests by individual members. Decisions which purport to be group decisions must in fact be individual decisions. There must be some mechanism then, overt or implied, whereby a group concedes to individuals the right to take decisions on behalf of the totality. In this concession lies difficulty—of reconciling possibly conflicting interests of sub-groups, because the individual who is selected as representative must, in ordinary circumstances, be necessarily a member of one sub-group. There is a danger, then, that instead of attempting to secure the wider interests of the totality, he will act so as to secure in the first place the interests of the particular group element to which he belongs. By *responsibility* is meant ability to envisage a situation in terms of the interests of the widest group concerned, to take decisions which shall be conformable to those interests, and willingness to be held accountable for the results of those decisions. In this respect conflict at every level of group unity is possible. A person belongs to a simple family, to a larger kin group, to a local unit, and these may be only some of many components of a large social unit which he is representing. For him to assume effective responsibility, and for other members of all these constituent groups to concede to him agreed representation of their interests, there must be an effort of projection by all parties concerned—a concept of incorporation of immediate in less directly perceptible interests. The more limited this projection, the more restricted the social organization.

This is seen, for instance, in the history of commercial administration in the East. The function of serving as an "employment agency" for one's kinsmen has been traditionally regarded as one of the prime duties of a man who has attained to a position of power. This has become increasingly a handicap to efficiency in Oriental countries such as China, where industrialization and modern commercial life have reached large proportions. For industry in China it is said that the problem of efficient personnel has been as important as the problem of mechanization. The question of the relation of nepotism to effective service has been basic. For large business concerns there seems to have been fairly general agreement that nepotism has meant better jobs but worse work. For the small shopkeeper the employment of kinsfolk has been justified by the argument that, though often less efficient, they are bound to the family, are more trustworthy, and do not steal.[1] The type of attitude which leads men to further small group interests by appointing kinsfolk to jobs irrespective of their efficiency tends to cater for other kinds of satisfaction in the traditional form of the society. In effect, it is a diffused mechanism of providing social support with public resources, but without bringing the persons concerned before the bar of a public judgement. It would seem that in Communist China perception of all these implications of the family system has been seen. The result has been reorganization and an emphasis on extra-familial groupings, which stress wider types of responsibility and canalize economic efficiency.

The concept of social organization is important also for the understanding of social change. There are structural elements running through the whole of social behaviour, and they provide what has been metaphorically termed the social anatomy, the form of a society. But what is this form? It consists really in the persistence or repetition of behaviour; it is the element of continuity in social life. The social anthropologist is faced by a constant problem, an apparent dilemma—to account for this continuity, and at the same time to account for

[1] See Olga Lang, *Chinese Family and Society*, New Haven and London, 1946, pp. 181 ff.

social change. Continuity is expressed in the social structure, the sets of relations which make for firmness of expectation, for validation of past experience in terms of similar experience in the future. Members of a society look for a reliable guide to action, and the structure of the society gives this—through its family and kinship system, class relations, occupational distribution, and so on. At the same time there must be room for variance and for the explanation of variance.

This is found in the social organization, the systematic ordering of social relations by acts of choice and decision. Here is room for variation from what has happened in apparently similar circumstances in the past. Time enters here. The situation before the exercise of choice is different from that afterwards. An open issue, with elements as potentials in several directions, has now become a resolved matter, with the potentials given a specific orientation. Time enters also as a factor in the development of the implications of decision and consequent action. Structural forms set a precedent and provide a limitation to the range of alternatives possible—the arc within which seemingly free choice is exercisable is often very small. But it is the possibility of alternative that makes for variability. A person chooses, consciously or unconsciously, which course he will follow. And his decision will affect the future structural alignment. In the aspect of social structure is to be found the continuity principle of society; in the aspect of organization is to be found the variation or change principle—by allowing evaluation of situations and entry of individual choice.

After this abstract consideration of a framework of ideas for our analysis, we can now see how some of the operations work out in practice in a type of community normally studied by anthropologists.

CHAPTER II

STRUCTURE AND ORGANIZATION
IN A SMALL COMMUNITY

IT is convenient to study social process in a concrete way
in a particular community. A human community is a
body of people sharing in common activities and bound by
multiple relationships in such a way that the aims of any individual can be achieved only by participation in action with
others.[1] One important sense of the term stresses the spatial
aspect—the people forming the community are normally in
collective occupation of some territory. This gives their relations a directness and intimacy which are part of their special
quality. Such community life has its structure and its organization, as already defined. Carrying the analysis further, we
may distinguish four constituents essential to social existence in
a community. These are: social alignment; social controls;
social media; and social standards.

All community life involves methods of grouping and
grading people for the effective carrying out of the various
types of activity demanded by the common existence. This
social alignment, including "social structure" in the narrow
sense of the term, comprises not only corporate groups of
more permanent type, based on sex, age, and kinship, but also
associations of persons for such common aims as work or
recreation. The division of the people of the community by
occupation, their grading by rank and in any ritual hierarchy,
are included, as also their arrangement by social role and social

[1] One definition of community lays emphasis on common *interests* or
aims. These may be assumed to be always present to some degree. But
they are a matter of inference rather than of observation, and are best
omitted from a preliminary statement. Moreover, the interests of different
members of the community may be common at only a very superficial
level, beneath which they may diverge, or be fundamentally opposed.

41

status.   Social alignment is in essence the ordering of the personnel component of the community.   Community life involves also systems of beliefs and procedures by which activity can be guided and controlled.   These *social controls* include the general system of technical and empirical knowledge by the aid of which people manipulate much of their environment, and also the systems with a marked non-empirical component, often of high emotional quality, regulating magical and religious behaviour in particular.   They include also the specific formulated sets of rules of etiquette, morality, law, and ritual, and the charters of mythology, as Malinowski has termed them, which serve to validate social behaviour.   Social controls are the regulative factors in community life.   This life requires a material basis for activity, and a basis for communication.   Material goods, on the one hand, and language, on the other, form the *social media*.   Material objects affect community life in a number of ways.   They facilitate activity —like tools and transport; they crystallize and incorporate expenditure of effort; they serve as a reservoir of effort against future needs; they are the object of property relations, of holding and transfer; they are the object of emotional attitudes. By their durability, they give manifold links with the past, and so are perpetual conditioning factors to activity.   Language provides a vehicle for the expression of thought and emotion. As a means of communication it conveys the meaning of action, serves as a substitute for action, and induces action in others.   Moreover, as with material objects, it acts through memory as a preservative of action and of ideas about action. Language and material goods, then, provide the apparatus whereby social relations are carried on in the community.   All community life involves also a system of standards, giving rating in the choice of activities and judgement on the effectiveness of performance.   These *social standards* represent systems of values, in their expression as activity.   Value is a term to which many meanings have been given.   But for our purposes we may take it to mean the preference quality assigned to an object in virtue of a relationship between means and ends, in social action.   The notion of value involves judgement on a preference scale, a grading.   It implies primarily positive qualities, ideas of desirability or worth. Every value has an emotional charge as well as an ideational component. But values do not serve only to express feelings; they stimulate and guide conduct. Moreover, they are not in entire independence of one another. They are in an inter-connected system, albeit of varying integration for individuals and social groups. Classification of values is difficult. But for our purposes here it is convenient to consider these social standards of preference as applied in regard to six major types of quality: technological; economic; moral; ritual; æsthetic; associational. Let us take a simple example—their possible application in a situation where food is concerned. The technological standard is applied to its preparation—for instance, how efficiently it is cooked. The economic standard is applied to its value for exchange purposes. The moral standard can be applied in regard to the propriety of having food of such quality, or indeed of having food at all, when other more needy people are going hungry. The ritual standard can be applied in respect of whether the food is licit or forbidden by a particular religion—as beef to a Hindu, pork to a Muslim, meat to a Roman Catholic on Fridays. The æsthetic standard is applied to the way the food is presented—its patterns of colour, its shape, its taste. Finally, the associational standard is applied to the way in which it affects social relations; partaking of food together may have a value for social co-operation.

Community studies, with varying emphasis on aspects of social alignment, controls, media, and standards, are of a vast range. Regional novelists, students of folk art, geographers, historians, rural and urban sociologists have all contributed. The names of Maine, Le Play, Park and Burgess, Seebohm Rowntree, Thrasher, Zorbaugh, Kolb, Brunner, Sims, Sanderson, give only an indication of some of the lines of approach from the more specifically social side. We must be content to take up two points which are directly relevant to our analysis.

The first concerns the importance of what most sociologists speak of as "primary groups." These are small-scale units—families, work groups, neighbourhood groups, play groups—

the members of which are in close personal contact in daily
life. Such groups are primary in the sense of being the
smallest types of co-operative unit in society, the bricks from
which the community fabric is built. To some extent they
may also be regarded as primary in the ontogenetic sense,
in that they include those groups in which the growing
personality of each child develops as a member of the
community.

Such primary groups are socially vital. They offer many
types of personal satisfaction—in opportunities of feeling
secure amid group support of exercising power over others,
of showing skill and petty inventiveness in adapting things to
immediate group needs, in getting gratifications of a moral
kind, through the display of love and self-sacrifice. They are
essential also for co-operation, in economic and other fields.
Upon the simplest primary groups are built others of a more
complex and formal character, though no very clear-cut line
can be drawn. Even when an element of organization has
been applied to them, such groups still preserve much of their
spontaneous, personal character. Games clubs, literary and
dramatic institutes, local branches of trade unions, ordinary
working teams, have social functions apart from their pro-
fessed aims. Their members are united by more than a single
nexus; they get to know more than the purely functional
characteristics of one another. This strengthens their common
action.

An instance of the strength of groups built upon the primary
tie of neighbourhood is given by the local air-raid defence
organization in Britain during the war. For technical reasons,
to secure man-power and rapid mobilization, the comparatively isolated, almost anonymous individual in the city flat or
tenement was caught up with a group of his neighbours into
a street fire-party. This was also sound sociology. Within
the given area of operations this type of organization which
drew on the local community promoted efficient co-operation
by breaking down class and other affiliations and by giving
increased personal contacts in small groups. Fire and bomb
struck the neighbourhood, and evoked a neighbourhood
response. This type of organization may have been equally

valuable at the time outside the immediate technical sphere. The shared experiences at work—tragic, comic, and merely mundane; the recreation in common, often developed when off duty by dart-matches and vegetable-growing;—all this tended to preserve and steer personal values and maintain morale amid the strain of war.

Such primary and allied small groups are essential for social processes in a wide field. In a democratic society consent of the individual is ultimately necessary for the implementation of programmes. His consent does not emerge simply from him as an isolated rationalizing entity; it is not formed in him simply by what he reads in the newspapers or hears on the radio. It crystallizes from exchange of views with his fellows in his family or in other small groups. The opposition expressed to planning of social affairs often seems to be based in part on a real or imagined threat to the existence and enterprise of those small groups, the members of which all know one another and work through that knowledge. What is feared? The threat of anonymity is feared. It is felt, even obscurely, that personal contact in the making of decisions is a strong, vital, and necessary thing in the life of society. It is felt, too, that these small social units blend various kinds of obligations and incentives in such a way that they realize their particular aims through a wide range of satisfactions.

One problem in the welfare of modern society is to identify the most significant functions of the primary groups and support them where possible. An illustration here is the discussion as to the role to be played by parents in the education of a child. An allied problem is to elucidate the most relevant other small social units and maintain or develop them to serve as a focus and outlet for the activities of their members. At the same time they must be allowed to modify their sectional behaviour as necessary to fit themselves smoothly into the wider organizations of community life. Here come some fundamental differences in point of view. On the one hand, there is the support given to the family in its fullest functions, including political and religious education, by most Western systems, including the Christian Church. On the other hand, in a field entered by Communism, as in China, the influence of the family is denigrated, since it opposes small group interests to those of the whole new society.

The second point to be considered now is the importance often attached to the small community as such. The growing scale of organization in the modern world, and the need to utilize large units for many types of effective social action, has tended to reduce the sphere of influence of the small community—as, for example, the country village. Yet it is often argued that there is utility in the life of the small community, not merely as a survival of traditional forms, but as a means of personal development and social integration. This point of view lies to some extent behind experiments in economics and education, and the provision of amenities for the small rural community now being carried out in many parts of England. More specifically, it animates the arguments of men like A. E. Morgan in the United States.[1] An engineer by profession and an educationist by emergence, he became impressed by the conviction that the small community is an essential element in the good life, and indeed in the very survival of our Western civilization. Arguing that modern men are bluffed by the prestige of bigness, by the so-called efficiencies of mass production and centralization, Morgan holds that the small intimate group within the scope of a man's acquaintance remains the primary pattern for society and the hope of its salvation. Modern society demands much more than the small-group pattern alone can give. This Morgan recognizes, as would be expected from his engineering experience. He concedes the need for large-scale organization and control, and for the application of mass power to meet the vast and varied needs of contemporary society. Yet his thesis is that these should not dominate the individual personality, which requires a vital co-operative small community type of organization as the source from which to draw what he would term good leadership and the right values. Such arguments are often obscure and shot through with unstated value judgements. In

---

[1] Cf. F. G. Thomas, *The Changing Village, An Essay on Rural Reconstruction*, London, 1939; A. E. Morgan, *The Small Community, Foundation of Democratic Life, What it is and How to Achieve It*, New York and London, 1942. (A).

particular they often fail to give full weight to the difficulty of providing an adequate economic base to the small community, and they ignore the elements of friction and instability in its implied class structure. But the emphasis on the social importance of groups which provide face-to-face contacts does link up with the more objective findings of social psychologists and sociologists.

What emerges from many of the scientific community studies in the West is the comparatively undifferentiated character of the small community, its strong social solidarity, and the close integration of its social, economic, and other activities. Such a community is not uniform. There are, what James West in his study of the community of Plainsville with its population of 275, called discrimination systems, as well as significant differences of role and status. But demographic factors are important in the organization of community affairs. Mere size tends to govern the quality as well as the quantity of social relations. Highly developed specialization of roles, and many economies of scale in production and distribution of goods are not possible. Personal relations are multiplied thereby. Choice is influenced by the plurality of relations between persons. Different types of primary group tend to coincide or overlap in large measure. Members of the same family are likely to find themselves in the same church and school, at work side by side, in the same recreational groups, perhaps marrying spouses who are already their kinsfolk and related to one another. Such coincidence tends to mitigate the clash between the values of home and school, work-team and church, which so often occurs in a highly differentiated larger community.

The African, Oceanic, and other small communities studied by anthropologists show this close interweaving of all aspects of social activity. They are socially compact. Economic, ritual, and recreational affairs, for instance, are often difficult to disentangle within a complex institutional sequence of events, such as an initiation ceremony, a harvest festival, or even a funeral. Community cohesion, though varying according to such structural factors as the system of kinship grouping, rank, and religious ties, is normally strong. But the scope for social differentiation is usually very much greater than in the small community of the West. The total range is not necessarily wider, since many kinds of economic and political specialization are equally barred. But the great variety of structural arrangements, in kinship grouping, age-grading, sex, and seniority emphases, and the formalization of many relationships which in the West are left informal, allows of much subtle difference in the social position of members of the community. Even quite a small Melanesian community may have a complex clan structure. This will separate out the roles of men in a working group, forbid some to eat one kind of food and others another, partition them off in a complicated give-and-take of marriage arrangements, and dictate the land each shall till. This in turn may be crossed by other structural elements, resting on a rank–wealth alignment, and linked with elaborate privileges to use specific sections of a club-house. Reference has been made in Chapter I (p. 32) to the importance of the mother's brother relationship in Oceanic communities. The formalization of this and other kin relations, such as that of father's sister or of cross–cousin, adds further to the process of social differentiation. One can define the social position of a Melanesian in his community, as it were, by superimposition of a series of charts of clan structure, marriage rules, food taboos, rank–wealth grades, club-house divisions, kinship roles. By comparison with the position of a member of a Western community, that of the Melanesian shows a sharper social differentiation. Analogous structural elements exist in the West, but they are on the whole less formalized and more open to alteration by the individual concerned.

Now let us introduce more precision into the notion of the small community as studied by anthropologists. Most anthropologists select for their work both a unit of general survey and a unit of personal observation. The former is commonly a tribal or other cultural group, and may be of almost any size, even tens of thousands of people. Its boundaries delimit the area to which the conclusions of the scientist are expected to apply. This unit of general survey is traversed on occasion to examine the uniformity and variation of practice to be found in it. But the weight of the analysis rests on the unit of personal observation. This latter, chosen with an eye to its representative character, is usually not much more than 1,000 people, and is often considerably less. This unit is submitted to systematic study over a considerable period of time, in order to elucidate detailed social relations between as many persons as possible. In it one or more sub-units may emerge for intensive analysis, these usually comprising the households with which the investigator has most intimate daily contact. In some cases the unit of general survey and the unit of personal observation tend to coincide. This was so in my own research in Tikopia. On this small island of a few square miles and about 1,300 people, almost all their major doings could be observed at first hand, in their general assemblies and in their family affairs. Contrast with this the studies by Fortes and his colleagues of the structure of the Ashanti of Ghana, by Evans-Pritchard among the Nuer of the Sudan, or by Schapera among the Tswana of Bechuanaland, or my own work and that of my wife among the coastal Malays of Kelantan. There it was not possible to study closely more than a small fraction of the total community. Methodologically, the width of the gap between unit of general survey and unit of personal observation is important, since if the investigator is to apply his generalizations over the wider community he must be sure that the unit he selects for close study is sufficiently representative.[1] Apart from this, the difference may be reflected in structural and organizational relations.

The small community which is the unit of personal observation is of two types: the integral community and the sectional community. The integral small community, such as that of Tikopia, is structurally self-contained. The system of clans and other kinship units, the pagan religious system, the political

[1] In his study of Ashanti domestic organization, Fortes states that the two rural areas selected, with populations of about 900 and of just over 4,000, seemed to include most of the variations observable outside large towns and industrial centres. Schapera argues that in conditions such as the Tswana present the field-worker must either use some method of sampling or admit that the data he collects may be biased (M. Fortes, p. 61, and I. Schapera, p. 106, in *Social Structure: Studies Presented to A. R. Radcliffe-Brown*, Oxford, 1949).

system of chiefs, and their supporters, are primarily independent of external social arrangements. The sectional small community, on the other hand, is structurally a part of a wider entity. Clan membership or a religious system, or a superior political authority, are shared with other communities of the same kind. With the lessening of the degree of personal contact in the totality of community affairs, different patterns of organization are necessary. Where personal meeting is not possible to the same extent, more unknowns enter into choice, local autonomy is restricted, the techniques of conveying decisions in themselves require extra organizational roles. This has a more than purely political significance: it may radically affect the economic organization, for example, as by stimulating the growth of a class of middlemen.

But the isolation of any community nowadays is only relative, and even remote Tikopia is not completely self-contained. It has certain limited relations, at long intervals of time, with a neighbouring island, seventy miles away across the open ocean, and with an even smaller population. There are some kinship ties between them, and a recognition that these folk have a similar social system. But this does not make of Tikopia a sectional community. Its people do not depend on their neighbours for fulfilment of their wants. Their social systems are interlinked only peripherally by bonds which affect only a few individuals. Of more importance to the structural integrity of the Tikopia community are its contacts with the Western world. As a part of the British Solomon Islands Protectorate, it has a somewhat tenuous recognition of an external government. As a community within the sphere of influence of the Melanesian Mission, it has been subjected to some proselytizing influences, with the result that half of the community had become nominally Christian by the time I was there. But in their religion, as in their politics, the Tikopia were still following out highly localized patterns, with the minimum of outside interference or interest. This is a marginal case of a phenomenon very common with the small community—the lack of coincidence between effective areas of organization. The Tikopia Christian, entirely dependent for most of his social life on his fellows, needs for the ultimate supply of his religious doctrine and ideals the stimulus of an external body : his social and his religious systems are not completely coincident. So also the Malay fisherman of Kelantan depends for his subsistence in part on an economic market for dried fish in Singapore, run by Chinese ; and for his religious satisfactions he relies in part on a Muslim system which has its fountain-head in Mecca. Where there is a marked distinction between effective areas of organization, it may be very difficult for a member of the small community to cope with, and indeed to comprehend, the effects of a disturbance in the wider area. This will be referred to again in Chapter III.

To examine the processes of social organization in a small community I propose to take examples from Tikopia.

In many respects this community is the antithesis of any known in Western civilization. Geographically, it is extremely isolated, lying more than 100 miles to the southeast of the Solomon Islands chain, a solitary ancient volcanic crater far out in the Pacific Ocean, visited from the outside world on the average perhaps once a year. Technologically its culture is very undeveloped. The people use some steel tools, obtained by gift or barter from European vessels that call, but these are scarce and precious, and comprise almost solely axes, adzes, knives, and fish-hooks. Their houses and their canoes are built without nails, lashings of braided coconut fibre being used instead. What calico cloth they have is worn mainly at festivals, or used as religious offerings to their gods, and the people still wear their traditional barkcloth, made from the fibrous inner bark of the paper-mulberry tree. Their outrigger canoes are small, heavy craft, carrying at a maximum six or seven men, and are invaluable for fishing, but very risky for the ocean voyages in which they sometimes indulge. Their introduced steel tools must have materially lightened the labour of wood-working and clearing of brushwood in agriculture, and increased considerably their catches of fish. But otherwise they are practically self-sufficient. Save for these tools and a few luxuries like sugar, which they get rarely, they produce all they consume. They have practically nothing for export, it being as much as they can do to scrape

together a few mats, fans, and coconuts for barter when /a
ship comes. In 1929, they neither used money nor understood
the relative values of the European coins they had seen.[1]

Such a small-scale community with poor resources means
that it is relatively undifferentiated in some ways, especially by
Western standards. The small population means a lack of
extensive markets for goods and a lack of avenues for diversi-
fied employment. The people have elaborate systems of
exchange among themselves, but these fulfil social rather than
directly economic ends. Whole-time specialists in production
and a developed class of middlemen are absent. Individual
producers are unable to accumulate large capital stocks from
profit margins and to undertake large enterprises of a new
type. There is no rentier or capitalist class. Social and
economic relations tend to merge, as in mediæval Europe.
Moreover, a kinship, and not a cash nexus, governs relations
between producers, or between producers and consumers. In
this respect Maine's classic phrase applies—relations tend to be
determined by status rather than by contract.

Here there is nothing like the condition of noble harmony
sometimes still postulated as the birthright of natural man,
and projected romantically into the life of such relatively
primitive communities. In Tikopia there is no great wealth
or grinding poverty. The people know that their resources
are small, and their margins are such that a drought or a hurricane may bring famine. Ordinarily, however, the canons of
hospitality are such that no one need go hungry while any
household has food which he can be invited to share. The
Tikopia are very conscious of their cultural unity and distinct-
ness. They have a strong regard for their own institutions,
and a belief in the rightness of their common values. The
members of the community are bound together by a variety of
interwoven ties. These ties are given expression on their

[1] Some analysis of Tikopia society has been published in various books
and articles. See, e.g., *We, The Tikopia: A Sociological Study of Kinship in
Primitive Polynesia*, London, 1936; *A Primitive Polynesian Economy*, London,
1939; *Work of the Gods in Tikopia* (London School of Economics Monographs on Social Anthropology), 2 vols., London, 1940; " Totemism in
Polynesia," *Oceania*, I, Sydney, 1931. (A).

general festival occasions, when what they describe as "the whole land" assembles for a dance or the celebration of a chief's feast. But there are marked features of structural differentiation, and in line with these are jealousies and feuds, part superficial and ceremonial and part compounded of underlying ill feeling.

The structural basis for this social differentiation is complex, though not unusual even in such a small community. It consists, first, of the division of the community into two main geographical districts, each with its own name and its own place in tradition and myth. Between these districts there is rivalry—in flying-fish netting, in dancing, in dart-hurling, and in the many affairs of daily life. It is expressed not only in comparison of achievement, but also in boasting and slander. The coming of Christianity, which by 1929 had been adopted by one district but not the other, has both expressed and intensified the feud. Secondly, the social structure is based upon the clan and kinship divisions. There are four of the major units, the clans, with important social and ritual functions. To some extent the district feud is both expressed and perpetuated in clan jealousies. But though the members of the clans are to some extent concentrated locally in the various villages, this is so to only a limited degree, and the interdigitation of their residence helps to mitigate the intensity of local feuds. Each clan is composed of a number of large kinship units, of the type known generally as lineages.[1] These are known to the Tikopia as "houses," a term which emphasizes their ultimate growth from a simple family base. The Tikopia lineages are patrilineal, membership being traced through the father along the male line to an original male ancestor.[2] The

---

[1] In a previous publication I have referred to these as *ramages*, a term which stresses their segmenting or ramifying character rather than the line of descent. A distinguishing feature of the Polynesian variety of lineage is its non-exogamous quality, as against the exogamy of the ordinary African lineage.

[2] The tie of some lineages to the primary "house" which gives its name to the clan is through a woman, but this does not invalidate the patrilineal principle. Nor does the non-exogamous character of the lineage; though intra-"house" marriage is possible, and a person is related to his lineage co-members through his mother as well as his father, it is the tie through the father alone that is significant for membership of this unit.

E

lineage alignment is an important element in the Tikopia social structure. Though it does not regulate marriage, as do many other lineage systems, it is the basis for land-holding and use, it provides significant units for many kinds of exchange of goods and services at marriage, funerals, initiation ceremonies; and within the clan structure it has a basic part to play in the religious system. The senior man in each lineage acts as its major representative in public affairs. In particular he fills a specific post as a ritual elder responsible for maintaining proper relations between his group and the ancestors and gods from which it is believed to be descended. This function, performed both in private and public rites, is regarded as a privilege as well as a duty.

A third basic element is the structure of authority expressed primarily in the position of the chiefs. Each of the four clans has its leader, called by a title meaning " chief." This man is *de facto* head also of the primary lineage giving its name to the clan. The status of the chief is supported not so much by his seniority in descent—he is elected, possibly from among several suitable candidates—as by the power credited to him in the religious sphere. He, it is believed, is the possessor of secret knowledge which gives him influence with the feared clan gods, and he is the main intermediary between them and men. The four chiefs are ranked in a hierarchy which is expressed in the sequence in which they perform ritual on public occasions, in their seating when they are together, in the order in which food and other gifts are laid before them. At the same time, they and their immediate lineage members form a recognized class of " chiefly houses," distinguished from the " houses " of commoners by various privileges, observable especially on occasions of personal friction and clash. They are separated from the common people by myths of ancestral origin, by different avenues to power and influence, and to some extent by a marriage bar, though this is theoretical rather than actual. In times past the chiefs even preached limitation of families to the common people as a religious pronouncement with the expressed object of conserving food supplies. The four leaders, despite personal jealousies and the structural antagonisms arising from their clan headship, preserve a great show of deference and good manners to one another in public. Each has great influence with his clan members, and in cases of need exerts an autocratic authority from which there is no direct appeal.[1] His authority is recognized in certain circumstances by members of the other clans as well. Banded together as "the wave of chiefs" their public weight is irresistible. Here, as elsewhere, it is the ultimate religious sanction on which their authority relies. Temporal power is believed to reside in the possession of spiritual weapons.

A fourth element in the structure of the Tikopia community is the distribution of wealth. It will be realized from the prior description that this means essentially the distribution of land. But this is a mutable rather than a fixed structural element. Differential family growth, in altering the man-land ratio, affects the control of wealth by kin groups and by individuals from one generation to another. Hence in Tikopia inequality in rank is paralleled by, but not coincident with, inequality in wealth. A chief has titular control over all the lands of his clan members, and does derive a small income from ceremonial gifts from them, such as first-fruits. But the heads of some of the lineages among the commoners are more wealthy in land resources than some of the chiefs.

Here, then, in this small community of not many more than 1,300 people are the structural materials for elaborate personal differentiation: local divisions, descent divisions, rank divisions, wealth divisions. There are many other differentiæ also, bound up with the structure of the kinship system. The relation of father to son is one which is classed by the Tikopia as being in a "heavy" category, being marked by formal respect from the junior to senior, with taboos on bad language and on interference with head or body, and conventional wailing when the elder has received injury. This type of behaviour is extended to cover classificatory as well as true kin. Analogous formalized relations, with varying emphasis on restraint or on freedom, on protection, assistance, and support, exist

---

[1] Its effects are mitigated by conventional mechanisms. See my "Authority and Public Opinion in Tikopia," in *Social Structure: Studies Presented to A. R. Radcliffe-Brown*, ed. by M. Fortes, Oxford, 1949, pp. 168–88. (A).

between a person and his father's sister, his mother's brother, his cross-cousins, and his relatives by marriage. These relations are so balanced that they form a consistent, interconnected system, by which every member of the Tikopia community finds his social obligations and privileges defined. Moreover, they cut across other structural elements. Thus they mitigate social tensions and serve in very powerful fashion as factors of social integration. Kinship ties, carried into effect on formal and informal occasions, help to bridge the class gap between chiefly and commoner families, re-group and bring together people from different districts, clans, and lineages, and even help to soften the asperities of inequalities in wealth.

The social structure does not, then, merely impose limits on freedom of action; it offers positive advantages to the individual who conforms to its principles. I use the word *conform* advisedly. Certain elements in the social structure are firmly fixed; it does not lie within the province of the individual to alter his position in regard to them. His membership of a lineage and clan, and of the commoner or chiefly class, is unalterable. It is true that, like all elements of the social structure, this exists only through common recognition of the appropriate social standards. If Tikopia were another type of community it might be possible for a person to leave his lineage and clan, and be adopted into another, or by his industry, thrift, and economic ability to raise himself from the commoner class into that of the chiefs. But if such radical displacement were possible, the society would not be the same. On the other hand, in Tikopia it is perfectly possible for a person to leave his present home and move to the other side of the island, to another district. After a period of settling in, he and his descendants are accepted as district members. Such a permissible change of allegiance means that this district alignment is one of the flexible elements in the social structure, where alternative action is possible. What is not possible is for a man to take no action at all. He must conform to the structural principles of local grouping, but, unlike the position in his lineage alignment, he can exercise choice as to which group he will take for his alignment. In terms of group recruitment or assignment one can speak of automatic fixed assignment to a lineage, and automatic but optional assignment to a district.

In kinship, as distinct from lineage relations, the assignment is automatic if the genealogical position of the individual be considered alone. For the bulk of his kin ties, his rights and obligations are settled by his birth. But not entirely. He can refuse to conform to what are recognized as being the obligations proper to a certain kinship status—as a father, as a brother-in-law, as a son. More than this, since the kinship system extends to kin beyond the immediate family circle, and includes them in the family terms in " classificatory " style, the individual at a certain point can even decide whether or not he will adopt a given kinship status. He does not simply decide not to behave as a brother-in-law ought to; he refuses to *be* a brother-in-law. How can this happen? Very simply, in the Tikopia kinship structure. If a man marries a woman of his own lineage, then her brothers become his brothers-in-law, in the ordinary way. Normally, his brothers would take on the same status to hers, and the whole group of men would share this relationship. But if the woman is of her husband's lineage, then her brothers will be closely related already to the man's brothers. His brothers may be unwilling to sacrifice this tie and undertake new obligations and status. They may say to him, " You make your brothers-in-law alone." They refuse therefore to conform to the structural implications of an act which is one of the most important creators of social ties. There are, then, situations in the social order in which choice of social alignment is allowed. Such a choice, and its consequences, are part of the social organization.

An example will bring out this organizational aspect. Structural relations on the occasion of a Tikopia marriage demand that a gift of food and valuables should be made from the kinsfolk of the groom to those of the bride, and should be divided among these latter. On one occasion, I noted, a kinsman of the bride—one of her mother's patrilineal relatives—did not have any goods allotted to him as a present. The reason given was that he came as a cook instead to the house of the groom's kin. Why he should thus forego his right to a

share of the marriage goods is an illustration of the relation of
organizational to structural principles.   (See Figure below.)

Men and women in Tikopia have different roles in the work
of preparation of food at a marriage feast.   But among the
men there is a structural division, each section being marked

Structure of Social Relations

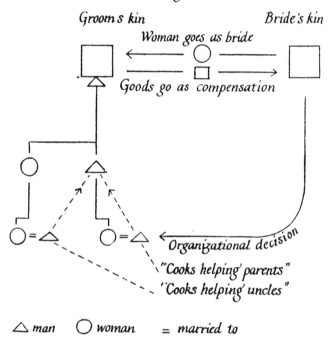

Relations of kin groups and cooks at a marriage feast.

by a name.   There are the "cooks who help the parents,"
who come because their wives are daughters of the men of
the main lineage concerned.   There are also "cooks who help
the uncles," who come because their wives are daughters of
women who have married out of the lineage a generation
earlier.   They are daughters' daughters of the men of the
main lineage, or, as the Tikopia prefer to regard it, they are
"sacred children" to their mothers' brothers there.   This
structural attribution is pursued a long way: "It goes as far

as the mother's brother relation is recognized "—far beyond the immediate blood tie into the classificatory sphere. Now, the emphasis on this structural principle is important for the organization of affairs.

Cooking in Tikopia is one of the main regular jobs. On occasions of ceremony, demanding elaborate food and involving large numbers of people, it amounts to the proportions of a major task. It is a hot and unpleasant task in that tropical climate. Economic co-operation, then, is not left to chance, to good will, or even to the attractions of a free market for such labour by the direct incentive of payment. It is made to rest on what purports to be an absolute, undeniable basis—the kinship tie of male affinal relationship. Other helpers are there round the oven—blood kin, neighbours, friends. But to rely simply on such a general labour field might result in shirking and failure, or in having to pay a higher price for the work than it was worth. What happens is both a utilization of the structural principle and a strengthening of it. The marriage tie is made the basis of service as a cook. But the cook gets a reward, when the work is done, by giving him a part of the food, and on ceremonial occasions a present of bark-cloth or other goods as well. This distribution of goods reinforces the social and economic ties between the groups concerned in a marriage. More than this, it also serves as an occasion for paying attention to the next generation—for letting the mother's brothers in the officiating group help their " sacred children," the offspring of the women who have married from their group. For on such occasions maternal uncles often make specific presents to their nephews and nieces—the children of the cooks.

Cooking for a large feast demands not only labour, it demands also control over labour in terms of the passage of time. In a Tikopia oven, heat is supplied by stones raised to a high temperature in a fire in a hole in the ground. The food is put in, and the oven covered with leaf-pads. Proper timing is important to get good results. So as not to waste fuel and energy, the raw food should have been scraped and peeled by the time the firewood has burnt down and the stones are red hot. While the food is cooking, coconut meat must be scraped and squeezed to press out the cream to pound up with the cooked vegetables to make puddings. Scrapers, bowls, pounders, leaf-wrappings and platters, and the various kinds of vegetables have all to be assembled at the right time, and their use co-ordinated among the twenty or thirty people gathered together to cook. And the cooking of the food has to fit in with other phases of the ceremonial. Hence among the cooks there must be some idea of the relations which should exist between the passage of time and the progress of the work. There must be ideas about the proper integration of technical processes, apparatus, and effort to secure the result. There must also be some attribution of responsibility for results. This is provided for in terms of the structural principle. "The ordinary people come along and sit down," the Tikopia say, "but the cook walks about; he goes and looks at all things. The man who is giving the feast does not speak to the crowd; he speaks only to the cook; he speaks to the cook to look after things. He doesn't scold the crowd (if things go wrong); he scolds the cook." And among the cooks themselves the prime responsibility is not left to chance. The senior cook is the man who is married to the senior woman of the kin group of the man who is the host at the feast. He takes the brunt of running the cooking; he also gets the best present when the affair is over.

But the efficacy of the structural principle is not rigid. Response to it may vary. Here personal decision comes into play. For instance, in such a community a man is often related by kinship to both sides in a marriage ceremonial. Sometimes he elects to play a role on both. But more often he chooses to assist one party. Such was the case in the example mentioned above. The man chose to rank himself as a cook for the bridegroom, not a kinsman of the bride. His reason here seemed to be essentially that it was better to respond to the obligation to go and work rather than to sit and receive presents without effort. His decision resolves an incompatibility of two structural principles. One principle is that on public occasions when his lineage is involved as a main party a man's duty is to go and align himself with it. The other principle is that marriage ties oblige a man on public occasions to contribute to the cooking arrangements of his wife's kin. He may get some material return from both. There is in Tikopia no further structural principle which can be called upon to resolve this dilemma of incompatibility. Relative nearness of kinship is a help. But the choice is essentially a personal one; the decision and responsibility for it are personal. These are part of the organizational machinery by which the society's affairs proceed.

Our aim is the understanding of social process. For this it is essential to understand the principles of the social structure. But that by itself is not enough. It is necessary to see how in any given case social activity is the resultant of a complex set of elements, including direct response to structural principles, interpretation of them, choice between them, by regard to personal interests and experience, temperamental dispositions, and the pressures exercised by other individuals striving to accomplish their own ends. Social process involves progress in time, and alteration in social position of individuals. Social events are not a simple reflection or exemplification of elements of the social structure. They affect situations in such a way that action becomes irreversible, new sets of choices are needed, and by the carrying into effect of new decisions the structure of the society itself is laid open to modification.

A further, more complex, illustration from Tikopia community life will demonstrate this dynamic aspect of social organization.

The event, in which I was at one point a participant as well as an observer, was of a dramatic, though not unique, kind. The initial stimulus was a tragedy. The eldest son of the chief of the village where I was living was a man of middle age, by name Pa Rangifuri,[1] who was a friend of mine, and a kindly, honest, simple man. Shortly before I arrived in Tikopia he had the misfortune to lose his elder son at sea. The boy, called Noakena, was a self-willed, headstrong lad, resentful of discipline, and imbued with the idea of his position as the virtual heir ultimately to the title of his grandfather, the chief. It was generally thought in the village that the lad had

[1] See p. 6 and Frontispiece. He became Ariki Tafua in 1936 and died in 1951, being succeeded by his younger son.

taken a canoe and gone off to sea to seek his fate because his father had scolded him, and he had refused to accept the criticism. His father gave an additional reason. One of the popular recreations of the Tikopia is the dart match, a formal competition between two groups of men, each side striving to produce the longest throw of a dart on a long open space rather like a cricket-pitch. One side is called the Bachelors, the other the Benedicts, though these terms have no literal meaning, and the sides really reproduce the traditional rivalry of districts and clans already referred to. Noakena had gone to a dart match as a novice on the day of the evening he went off to sea. In virtue of his social position, he might have expected some recognition, since novices in Tikopia often get special treatment at dance festivals and other public occasions. One of the other chiefs present did indeed call out to his side to let the dart of his nephew win. But the players disregarded this, and the boy had no success. He came back to his father in a rage, cursing, "May their fathers eat filth, the Benedicts; they didn't let my dart win. Why, the dart pitch there, does it belong to them? . . ." and more to the same effect. He had this much on his side, that the game has a ritual as well as a recreational significance, and his clan gods were believed to have a prime responsibility for the dart pitch. His father told me he thought this affair probably spurred the boy on to be fractious, so that when scolded he flung out of the house, took his canoe, and went off. He was never heard of again. The painful associations of the dart game were such that the father did not go to it any more when the period of mourning was over.

The custom in Tikopia when anyone has been lost at sea is for the relatives to wait for a year or so until some vessel from abroad has arrived. If it brings no news, it is almost certain that the lost one has been drowned. They then carry out burial rites as if for a corpse, but with mats and bark-cloth only, in an empty grave. This is called " spreading the grave-clothes, to make the lost one dry." The symbolism is that the grave-clothes provide dry garments for the spirit of the dead, whose body has gone to its last resting-place in the ocean with wet garments clinging round it. The time had now come, according to the talk in the village, to think of

" spreading the grave-clothes " for Noakena. This was very much in the mind of Pa Rangifuri, as subsequent events showed.

A funeral rite is a social rite *par excellence*. Its ostensible object is the dead person, but it benefits not the dead, but the living. As E. M. Forster has said, " The dead who seem to take away so much, really take with them nothing that is ours." As anthropologists have so often stressed, it is those who are left behind—the kinsfolk, the neighbours, and other members of the community—for whom the ritual is really performed. This is eminently clear when the ritual takes place for a person who has been lost at sea. One view of funeral ritual emphasizes the need, for hygienic purposes, of some standard means of disposing of the corpse of the dead. But here is no corpse, only a void. Why, then, go to the trouble of simulating burial rites and expending time and energy, as well as valuable property? Any theory of social process must be able to put forward hypotheses to account for such behaviour.

The first element in such hypothesis is the resolution of uncertainties in the behaviour of the immediate kin. For the father and mother of the dead boy, in particular, his loss has left a gap. The keenness of the edge of their grief may have become blunted, but their acceptance of his death is still emotionally difficult. Their attitudes and patterns of behaviour still waver between making allowance for him and his interests, and recognizing that he must be excluded. In time they will knit up the torn ends of their sentiments, and resolve their actions accordingly. But the funeral ritual gives a social backing to their attempts at adjustment, provides them with a cathartic mechanism for a public display of grief, and sets a period to their mourning. In essence, the community says to the relatives: " Your boy is dead; he is now buried. Wail for him in one final outburst, before us all. We expect it of you, and we demand it of you. Then tomorrow you will return to a normal social existence." The ritual is then a symbol of finality.

The second element is the fulfilment of social sequence. Radcliffe-Brown has argued that one of the basic functions of ritual is that it serves to maintain and reinforce the system of sentiments on which the existence of a society depends. In this sense the burial of the grave-clothes of a person lost at sea helps to sustain the appropriate attitudes of the members of the society to one another : by stressing the dead, they emphasize the value of the services of the living. Moreover, there is a value, moral as well as æsthetic, in completion of pattern. Every major stage which a person reaches in his social life is marked by some formalization, some ceremonial. So one who has been heralded as a member of a society cannot be allowed to pass out of it entirely without valediction. A proper progress through life means a funeral. Whether the body is present or not, the ritual must be performed. The death of every person must be followed by a reaffirmation of the social character of human existence.

The third element is the social importance of the economic aspect. This is not incidental. · On the one hand, there is the general principle of social life, that sentiment receives credence only when it is backed up by concrete expression. On the other hand, the mobilization of goods and the passage of them from one person to another have social effects. Every funeral means expenditure—in Tikopia bark-cloth, food, wooden bowls, ornaments, fish-hooks, and other valuables are accumulated and transferred according to traditional rules. In our Western society much of the funeral expenditure is commercialized—it goes to the undertaker and other people who provide the services accompanying the disposal of the dead. In a small-scale community of simple technical type, such as Tikopia, all the goods are disbursed among members of the society primarily in virtue of their kinship ties and obligations. Some kin are responsible for digging the grave and burying the body; others for wailing at appropriate times; still others for cooking the food to sustain the mourners. Each of such services obtains recompense. The whole occasion is marked by a complex interchange of goods and services. Some of the more immediate kinsfolk are the heaviest providers of goods, others are, on balance, heavy gainers. But these transactions do not stand alone. Another funeral in another family reverses them. Hence there is every incentive for all parties interested in paying debts or getting them paid to have the appropriate funeral rites whenever anyone dies. This is the more so since the magnitude of the transactions is in itself a source of pride and prestige. With all but the immediate kin of the dead person the secondary elaborations may well outweigh the importance of the primary social fact. Concrete economic pressure may then add to the incentive for the full ritual procedure of the normal life-cycle of a person to be carried out in detail, even when the body of the dead is absent.

These three elements are relevant to the performance of funeral ritual in any type of society. But in this immediate context they help to explain why the proposal to hold a mock-burial rite for the boy drowned at sea had social backing in this Tikopia community.

At the same time, there was also talk in the village about a ritual dance festival which was going to be celebrated by the old chief, father of Pa Rangifuri and grandfather of the drowned boy. The feast was to be one of the series which every chief should give as his seniority advances. As such it would be a celebration of the clan gods,[1] a grand entertainment to his fellow chiefs and the public. It became increasingly clear that it would not be possible to carry out both the funeral rite and the dance festival in close succession because of the very large quantities of food and bark-cloth which each would need. The resources of the group, though considerable, could not stand the strain. So an important question of public interest was—which would take place first? Pa Rangifuri, naturally, wanted the rite for his son performed first. His structural obligations imposed this upon him. He had been in mourning, with food taboos and abstention from public affairs, for about a year, and wanted to be free. And, finally, he had been very fond of his son, and his sentiments were deeply engaged on the side of doing what was proper by him. Moreover, he argued, very reasonably, that he preferred to

---

[1] The chief was a Christian. But his faith in the old gods was not seriously shaken, and the songs composed for the occasion began in traditional style, with invocation of all the pagan deities! Politeness was observed, however, by including in the list a song to his new God!

wail for his son first, and then stand up and dance in the festival later, rather than to get his mourning lifted and dance, and then have it reimposed. How could he dance with tears still unshed?—he said.

But Pa Rangifuri had five brothers. In Tikopia relations between brothers are expected to be equable. They are sharers in the family property, of which the most important item—land—is held jointly, though they may divide it on the death of their father. Hence they are all interested in any event, such as a feast, which will draw on family resources and involve all of them in contributions of labour as well as of private goods such as bark-cloth. But while in general affairs they are on an equal footing, it is the eldest who has normally most influence. He is distinguished by a special term, indicating his seniority, and he tends to be the administrator of the joint property after his father's death if the brothers keep together. With a chief's family these distinctions are sharpened because of the problem of succession. In theory, succession to chieftainship is open. In practice, if the chief has grown sons, the system is one of primogeniture. Hence beneath the superficial good relations between brothers and their general structural equality there are possibilities of jealousy and intrigue developing. In this case the brothers of Pa Rangifuri were suspected of wanting to hold the dance festival first. To them this would be the more exciting affair, with probably more opportunity for personal assertion, in dancing, in organizing roles. It was thought that they wanted to skim the cream of the food supplies available, as it were, rather than have to put up with a mediocre quantity after the funeral rites. It was thought that since they lived closer to the old chief, they were secretly trying to influence him to follow their wishes. The attitude of the chief himself was not publicly known—nor indeed apparently to his sons. But if the public estimates were correct, a decision would evidently have to be made soon.

A dramatic incident brought matters to a head. As I was writing in my house one morning, people called me out. They said that Pa Rangifuri had gone striding to his house in great anger—they did not know why. I went to his dwelling, and found him there, very angry and in a state of great excitement. We pressed noses in the usual Tikopia greeting, but he hardly paid me any further attention, though he was usually solicitous. A few of his close kinsfolk were beside him. All of them were clearly very much disturbed. One of them lay with his nose pressed to Pa Rangifuri's thigh. This was a conventional token of sympathy, expressing also a rather flattering respect. Pa Rangifuri was uttering broken, almost incoherent, statements in a high voice. Tears were streaming down his cheeks. His body was quivering. He kept bursting out with wild remarks. "I am going to leave the island and commit suicide. I only wanted to cut bark-cloth for my child. They said that *their* axe should cut first, but was it for a dirge? No! it was for the dance!"—and the like. More people came into the house, including a couple of older men. Gradually, as they asked him what was the matter and spoke soothingly to him, he calmed down, and made some explanation. We then began to understand what had happened. He and his wife had intended to go and cut paper-mulberry trees in one of the family orchards in order to prepare some bark-cloth against their son's funeral rites. They had gone to the chief to tell him in the ordinary way—in effect, to get his permission. The old man had been very curt, and had snapped at them without giving any very clear idea of whether he approved. He was so short that Pa Rangifuri thought that his brothers must have been successful in persuading the old man to give priority to the dance festival and postpone the funeral. So, he explained, he felt anger rise up in his body. He wanted to show fight to his father. He wanted to drag out of the house the brother whom he suspected of being the ringleader in influencing the chief against him. But in Tikopia the person of one's father is sacred. And when one's father is a chief one must be especially careful not to show violence before him. So instead he got up, threw himself out of the door, and stalked back to his house. This was the gist of his account. But his gesture of flinging away in a rage, though it avoided an open breach, was impolite enough to offend the chief seriously, and to cause the whole village to be deeply concerned.

What could the people of the village do? Would they take sides? Would they cower away and let the principals settle the matter between them? Tikopia conventions do not operate in that way; patterns of *rapprochement* are laid down.

Some of the people were with the chief, soothing his outraged dignity. Others were with Pa Rangifuri. The people in his house were very tactful. They agreed with him about the correctness of his wanting to cut bark-cloth. They said it was right to want to hold the funeral rites before the dance festival. But when he spoke about going off to sea, or of cutting himself off from his brothers, they respectfully dissented. They told him not to speak like that. They took the pathetic line. They appealed to his affection for them, who would be left behind if he went off to sea. They would be without protection—not entirely an empty form of words, since the eldest son of a chief has traditionally an important role in looking after the welfare of commoners. This type of talk is customary when a man of rank has taken offence—or indeed when any person is seriously disturbed. People sit near him with sad, serious faces, listen to him, agree with his self-justification, but dissuade him from any talk of violent action. They do not adopt any ethical attitudes. They do not say that suicide is wrong, or talk of it as silly; they do not say that the man is exaggerating the whole affair.

After Pa Rangifuri was calm, people suggested *rapprochement*. They asked him to go and see his father—in effect, to make his apology. At the same time they suggested that I, as his bond-friend, should conduct him there. This is also the custom, that some neutral party of rank should play the part of mediator and escort. If I had not been present, then one of the elders, or the son of another chief, would have been drawn into service. After a time Pa Rangifuri agreed. I took him by the wrist, he rose, and we went to the chief's house. (When I heard him narrate this part of the incident later, he said that I gripped him by the wrist and dragged him to his feet, otherwise he would not have gone! Such is the function of the escort: to save the *amour propre* of the principal.) When we entered the chief's house I sat down without a word, to see what would happen. The old chief sat with set stern face, and head averted from his son. Pa Rangifuri took on a very humble air. He crawled over the floor-mats in abasement, touched his father's knee with his nose in respect, and began to wail a dirge. This was his formal apology. The old man sat like a statue, not moving a muscle except to suck at his pipe. Then, after a few mintues, he turned and said to his son, " Why are you crying? Keep still!" He lifted up Pa Rangifuri's head and pressed noses with him in token of forgiveness. But Pa Rangifuri continued his wailing in spite of repeated commands to stop, thus demonstrating his contrition. At last he stopped, blew his nose, wiped his eyes, and sat up.

Then he consented to chew betel offered him by his father. His mother and other people in the house began to reproach him for his hasty action. " Why did you not wait to listen to further talk? Your father was only waiting for you to ask him to come with you and cut trees for bark-cloth." Then the chief himself began to speak—not reproachfully, and in a gentler, more reasoning tone than I had ever heard him use with his sons before. He explained that he was only waiting for Pa Rangifuri to come and give him the word. But one of his nephews had made him angry. This man had stolen a march on him by cutting the first tree in one of his orchards —where the chief had intended to fell the first tree himself with his own axe to make bark-cloth as an offering to his principal god. That was why he had spoken sharply—he had not been angry with Pa Rangifuri, nor had intended to block his plans. The old man concluded by asking his son if he would go and fell trees for bark-cloth in the orchard that very day. After some hesitation, Pa Rangifuri, who had not tried to justify himself at all, agreed. He was then lent his father's new axe, which had not been used before, and which it would be a privilege for him to handle. So the matter was settled.

The funeral was then tacitly agreed upon. The next day I had more talk with Pa Rangifuri, who soon brought up the topic of his dead son. He said rather bitterly, " He abandoned me and went off to sea." He told me that his father had

F

now set aside valued neck ornaments, that his brothers and some other kin had given beads and cloth, and that all these things were to be buried in the grave the following night, during the ceremony. He was now satisfied that the correct course would be followed. His personal outburst had precipitated a decision which meant the fulfilment of structural obligations. (Plate II.)

Why should his outburst have occurred at that particular time? There is nothing laid down in the structure of Tikopia kinship rules enjoining protest of this type if the fulfilment of kin conventions is delayed. On the other hand, though Tikopia are easily moved to the open expression of emotion, and see no shame in what to a Westerner would be a lack of restraint in their public behaviour, to give an explanation simply in terms of Tikopia temperament, or the personality of the father himself, is inadequate. Some trigger action is needed to explode the emotional charge which is there in a situation of the type described. This trigger action was supplied by Pa Rangifuri himself, unwittingly, through a dream.

In my talk with him he proceeded to describe to me a dream he had had during the night before he had quarrelled with his father. He said that the spirit of his son had come to him—it was the first time since the boy had been lost, months before. He said that in his dream he had been in one of the family orchards. His son had climbed a coconut palm and was twisting off a coconut. He called to him, "Noakena, Noakena." The boy answered, "What?" "What are you doing?" "Plucking coconuts for the store-place." "Hand me a coconut" ("and I reached out my hand," Pa Rangifuri said to me.) "Leave it till I throw it down," the lad replied. "Oh! Hand it to me," said the father. "Leave it till I throw it down." The boy then came down the palm, went some distance away, and climbed another tree. The father called out to him again by name, several times, but there was no reply. "Again I called, 'Noakena, curse you! Why don't you answer me?' And then I heard him grunt at me, '*Ngu ! Ngu ! Ngu !*' in a high tone, and then he was gone away. I then returned to my house—but I was already sleeping in my house; it was only my dream that was going on."

Pa Rangifuri then described how two women appeared to him in the dream. One of them was his sister, who had died in Anuta, the neighbouring island, but who in the dream had assumed the form of a girl living in a near-by house. Each woman had a basket under her arm. He called to each woman in turn, but neither would answer. One turned her face away. Here Pa Rangifuri's wife, who was listening to the story, interjected, " A pair of female deities " (who bear the baskets of disease). " They are evil. Look at So-and-so, who saw them; a death occurred soon after in his house." " Be quiet," said Pa Rangifuri, " while I tell my dream." He continued, "Then I came to my house and slept—but I was already asleep all the time. Then Noakena came to me, crawling through the doorway like this." (He illustrated the action—the Tikopia doorways are very low, and make it necessary for one to come in on hands and knees.) " He came to my side, and I looked on his face and body. He crawled to where I lay, and leant over and said to me, ' Have you said that I shall be made dry? ' Then I stirred. I stretched out my arms to embrace him, and called out, ' Oh! alas! my baby! ' And then my hand hit this box " (standing by his bed mat). " I awoke, I sat up and grasped the bark-cloth——here it is " (displaying it at the head of his mat). " I unfolded it and laid it out " (as an offering to the dead boy's spirit) " saying, ' Thy making-dry is there.' And then I sat down and wept for him. . . . Next day I said to my wife, ' Let us go and cut some bark-cloth for the two of us '— meaning to make preparation for the funeral."

I wrote down the salient features of this dream episode on the spot, as Pa Rangifuri was talking, and added further notes immediately afterwards. And although concerned in the first place with the scientific record and interpretation, I could not help being moved by the story. The man was full of sincerity, and obviously had been deeply affected. His face showed his emotion, and his voice was husky and broken, and near to tears. His cry as he opened his arms to demonstrate how he tried to hug his son to him and struck only the wooden box was poignant in its recollection of the incident. It can be understood, then, that when Pa Rangifuri went to see his father the morning after his dream he was in a highly emotional state, ready to react violently to any opposition to his impulsion to proceed with the funeral rites. He said of his acts then, " My belly was like as if a fire had entered into it."

This case raises a number of psychological issues. The dream was obviously an expression of the dreamer's paternal sentiments. It expressed also his sense of conflict and frustration, not only at apparently being thwarted and opposed by his brothers, but also at being deserted by his son. It reflects both aggression and remorse in regard to the boy. The dream symbolism, which is elaborate, can only be touched on. The coconuts and the tree are probably sex symbols. But overtly, they have significant ritual associations. They are a symbol for the head of the principal god of the clan. The wordless *ngu ngu* uttered by the boy in the dream is conventionally the typical sound of a certain type of sea spirit in the Tikopia religious system. The dream as a whole dramatized the belief that the boy is now a spirit. From the point of view of social organization an important feature of the dream is the way in which it serves as a galvanizer or propellant to the dreamer, inducing him to take action to redress his unbalanced emotional state. The psychology is not our concern here, but its social effects are significant for our analysis.

The analysis has shown how unreal is the concept of group solidarity if applied without qualification in the examination of social process. The family, the lineage, for many public affairs do act as a unit. But in others the members supply separate forces of influence which may operate in opposition as well as in harmony. Fortes remarks of the Tallensi that in all social activities in which brothers take part as the sons of their father they are merged, as it were.[1] Our example has indicated how far from the truth this would be if applied to the Tikopia. Fraternal clash of interests, breach of etiquette between father and son are uncommon enough in public

---

[1] M. Fortes, *The Dynamics of Clanship Among the Tallensi*, London, 1945, p. 199.

expression to be dramatic when they occur, but they are recognized among the frictions of Tikopia social life.

Social organization, the handling of personal relations, includes mechanisms for dealing with such frictions. Some societies have legal mechanisms available in the last resort. But in the small community we have taken for analysis it is difficult to classify or separate out specifically legal procedures, if only because one commonly cited criterion of law—the politically organized force of the society—is lacking in a unified form. But what concerns us here is not a nominal classification of procedures for dealing with conflict, but the means of operation and their efficacy. In a small community, with a high degree of interpersonal contact between all its members, comparatively informal procedures can be very effective. In a community of larger scale, where it may be difficult to find individuals with personal knowledge of both parties to a dispute, more formal procedures of settlement must be adopted. The case we have cited shows a prominent member of the community, under emotional strain, breaking rules of etiquette towards his father and his chief, and indulging in extravagant language, including threats of suicide. Other members of his community, though disturbed, are not at a loss. Their actions follow a defined pattern—which could be seen if space allowed the description of other cases of social conflict. Let us consider the outstanding elements, expressed in the behaviour of various individuals, jointly or severally.

The people give social support to the distressed man. They do not leave him alone; they rally round him. They call upon the structural principles of the society by mobilizing those to whom, by closeness of kinship or seniority of status, he is most likely to listen. To begin with, they are quiescent, showing only by small signs that they are beside him, and sympathetic; they behave to him in ways which emphasize his position as the centre of the scene, and his status. They treat the whole matter as one of great concern. They proceed to gather its full import, by questioning, and they stimulate the person to express himself freely, to talk himself out. They agree with his self-justification. What they reason with are his proposed actions. They neither scoff nor contradict; they accept his standpoint to some degree, but appeal to his affection for them, and to his vanity, not to press his proposals to the full.   In effect, they purport to attack his rational arguments by the arguments of sentiment; in reality, they subdue his emotions by reason.   If necessary they call in a neutral party to lend weight to their case, and in particular to enable the person concerned to redress the situation without losing self-esteem.   In this way a person who is socially displaced is helped to restore himself.   He is allowed to expend his emotion, gather indirectly the opinion of his fellows, and regain his position by appearance of concession rather than compulsion.   Catharsis and sentimental appeal are used as levers of reorganization of relations.

These levers vary in effectiveness, one of the important factors involved being the amount of time available.   The Tikopia, like most Polynesian peoples, are prone to suicide attempts.   "The tendency to depart from situations of personal shame," as it has been called, is marked among them. This refusal to face the full implications of a social situation may take one of several forms.   Hanging with a cord is a suicide method adopted by men and women.   But the commonest method used by a man is to take a small canoe and put off to sea, perhaps with paddle and mat sail and a few coconuts, perhaps without provisions.   A woman, who ordinarily never enters a canoe, simply swims out to sea until she is drowned or the sharks get her.   When the suicide attempt is known, rescue parties go out, and not uncommonly are successful in recovering the person, whose desire for self-sacrifice has possibly abated with the nearness of death.   In fact a suicide attempt can be a means of exerting social compulsion on the community, of throwing the onus of responsibility upon others, of securing rehabilitation as through a purge, by offering all that one has, even life itself, to fortune. Morselli, Steinmetz, and above all Durkheim, have examined the sociological aspects of suicide, and shown how, despite its private, intimate nature, the practice is not to be regarded as a purely personal decision.   It reflects to a considerable degree other social factors.   Said Morselli, " The psychical life of the individual is but the reflex of the nature and characteristics of the social aggregate in the midst of which it thinks, wills and acts." But there is some difference of opinion as to what this relationship is. Durkheim went so far as to argue that the rate of suicide of a community is an index of its social cohesion. On this view, the greater the incidence of suicide, the weaker the social integration. An alternative view is given by Nadel, who argues for a correlation between social rigidity or inclusiveness and the incidence of suicide. The less the latitude given to misfits, the fewer legitimate alternatives of living offered, the more is the predisposition to suicide. The Tikopia evidence shows that a distinction of significance is that between suicide attempted and suicide accomplished, and that the incidence of suicide accomplished has to be interpreted in relation *inter alia* to factors of social organization. Tikopia is a society which can be said to have a high degree of social cohesion, through its interlocking mechanisms of social co-operation and very distinct community consciousness. Yet its suicide attempt rate is high. On the other hand, it is not a society which can be called rigid in not offering outlets for abnormal behaviour. Institutionalized roles, such as that of spirit medium, and institutional persuasion procedures, such as that just described, may give people ample opportunity to re-dress their social balance. The actual suicides that occur are a function of time and opportunity as well as of disposition. Suicide in Tikopia is not condemned, but neither is it encour-aged by public opinion—as in Japan. Mobilization to prevent it is quick once the attempt is discovered. The social organ-ization then acts as a distinct restraining influence on suicide, both by providing cathartic mechanisms to turn aside an attempt and rescue mechanisms to render an attempt unsuccessful.

Now let us endeavour to identify more closely some of the major elements or principles involved in social organization, as seen in concrete activity. The first element is that of *co-ordination*. For the continuance of the processes of social life, items hitherto unconnected must be brought into relation, in reference to a common end. From the point of view of our social analysis, these items are really activities or behaviour-configurations of persons, though they are exercised in regard to media such as material goods or language. Even at the simple economic and technical level of a small community such as that described in this chapter, such co-ordination of the use of resources, including the time and energy of human beings, is a serious process, involving at various points much deliberation.

The need for such co-ordination arises from the basic lack of correspondence between elements in an existing situation and what is deemed to be required. It involves a projective effort. In the economic sphere, for instance, the amount of available resources is inadequate, or they are present in a form inadequate to satisfy the requirements. In the social sphere the disposition of the human elements is such that some different arrangement is thought to be desirable. But in any act of human effort the element of uncertainty must have allowance. In an economic affair such as a feast, for physical reasons of illness, or for social reasons of pique or apathy, the requisite amount of labour may not be forthcoming. In a social affair such as a marriage one or other party to the ceremony may fall out, or impediments may be raised by kinsfolk on various grounds. In the most mundane affairs the element of uncertainty has to be resolved as far as possible by judgement of probabilities. Where judgement will not carry, resort is often had to faith. But in the last resort these probabilities, or the faith which replaces them, relate to the behaviour of men. Even events in Nature can be seen in this light. Should a hurricane strike the food-crops of a community, for instance, it is not simply the natural phenomenon that must be taken into account in the subsequent organization; it is also the probable reactions of men to the news, and to the resulting famine. As Frank H. Knight has shown, the basic fact of organized activity is the tendency to transform the uncertainties of human opinion and action into measurable probabilities by making an estimate or approximate evaluation of the capacity of men. In a highly differentiated economy it is for the ability to make estimates which are on the whole ratified by subsequent events that profit accrues to the entrepreneur. In a small community of the more primitive type the rewards are more diffuse; they are expressed in social status and social esteem. But there must be substantial ratification, or the structure of the society could not survive, and there would be constant flux in the social position of members of it. The high status of the magician, spirit-medium, or diviner in many small communities is due to his general percipience in estimating how his fellows will probably behave— in conditions when he diagnoses wrongly as well as correctly. We may list *foresight*, then, as the second element of major significance in social organization.

The third element is *responsibility*, to which some reference has already been made. This has two aspects—*assumption* of responsibility by an individual, on whom falls the onus of ultimate decision; and *assignment* of responsibility by others who are agreed that he shall take this onus on himself. In a highly differentiated Western society this process of assignment is often of a very elaborate character, formal and institutionalized. In a small community of the more primitive type the assignment is more often tacit, springing as an implication from the social structure. In many such societies, having chiefs as an element of the social system, one of their primary functions is to assume responsibility for many of the most important decisions in the life of the community. The decision may at times emerge almost spontaneously, without any very conscious formulation, from the consensus of opinion of those by whom a chief is surrounded. But he bears the onus of it, and he reaps the praise that signalizes the successful outcome of the activity. At other times, as in the case cited in this chapter, the chief must make a decision which is by no means apparent from the circumstances, and without which the social life would be confused, with conflicting parties. Decision in such cases demands not only some degree of knowledge of human reactions, based on experience, but also firmness of opinion and attitude. Any act of social organization has the seeds of conflict. Not only are there possibilities of clash in regard to the best methods of accomplishing the agreed common aim. Disagreement over the choice of aims may promote a rift in the social group or may spring from pre-existing divergence of interests. This may be personal, depending, say, on differences of individual sentiment, or it may be structural, depending on difference of status. Whether the disagreement is overt or covert, some resolution at the overt level is usually sought, and found. Where such resolution comes by the decision of a chief, it is significant that it is rarely a bare decision. There is usually some concession made to either party.

This raises the fourth notable element in social organization, what may be termed the *basic compensation* that underlies the contribution of each factor to the situation. Malinowski emphasized the importance of such a principle under the name of *reciprocity*. This term, however, implies primarily the concept of an exchange relationship, whereas something wider is needed to convey the essential return. This basic compensation accrues not only for what can be recognized as a specific service, such as a certain piece of work, or an act which clearly facilitates the organization of the activity; it may correspond to the mere presence of a person, or to his acquiescence. It commonly does not accrue in material goods, though in the small primitive community material goods are often given in compensation for services or acts which would not call for such in our Western society. It is essentially the social price for participation in the activity. It may be paid in prestige, in politeness, in a seat at the gathering, in listening to what a man says instead of ignoring it.

These four principles—co-ordination, responsibility, foresight, basic compensation—cannot easily be given quantitative expression. But in the examination of concrete cases of social organization it may be possible to give some idea of their magnitudes, and thus to offer a basis of inter-social comparison.

Degree of co-ordination can be expressed to some extent in scale and time span of the relations of the persons involved. Responsibility can be expressed as a function of the number of persons, range of statuses, and type of social groups represented. Foresight cannot be expressed as valid judgement, but can be considered in terms of preparations made in advance to meet estimated needs—mobilization of goods over time, for instance, to prepare against a marriage ceremony. Basic compensation can be expressed simply only in material terms, but some measure of it can be obtained in cases where refusal to co-operate can be matched against co-operation.

At the present stage of social anthropology such type of measurement is only beginning.

Where the scale of co-ordination is considerable and the area of responsibility is wide, one event in the social organization may have marked effects on the social structure. This is so, for instance, in the field of law. In a small community of the type we have been discussing, a single decision by a chief may change radically the practice of the community in some major respect. So in Tikopia, the decision of one of the chiefs to become a Christian brought with it a long train of consequences which affected the traditional religious ceremonies, the relations between chiefs, attendance at dance festivals, and a number of major economic exchanges. Similarly, the decisions of Tswana chiefs in their courts of law have done much to modify marriage custom and property relations in the tribes. In all such cases foresight that from loyalty and other reasons the people would accept the change has been justified in the event. It may be assumed also that some elements of basic compensation were available to the people in their conformity.

Organizational analysis can be carried out further, as at the level of the organization of personality in terms of a theory of motivation. But effective linkage of the various types of analysis has still to be made.

The next chapter is concerned with some aspects of social change. In this field it should be clear, too, that we are not dealing with automatic processes but with the results of specific social organization, in terms of the principles discussed here.

CHAPTER III

SOCIAL CHANGE IN PEASANT COMMUNITIES

Over the last half-century social anthropologists have taken a more dynamic view of their problems. Fifty years ago the communities they studied were often almost isolated from the civilized world. The people in them might still be using stone axes, wearing bark-cloth, ignorant of reading and writing and the use of coinage, and be practising an economy which, if not entirely self-subsistent, did not depend on production for a Western market. The anthropologists' study of the " savage " could include material on head-hunting in the Solomon Islands, killing of twins in Africa, or strangling of widows in Fiji, without it being thought that he was a sensation-monger delving into the memories of an almost forgotten past. But the antithesis between the apparently unprogressive primitive and the self-consciously developing civilized man was so strong that the anthropologist tended to assume too easily that he was dealing with static conditions. Even where he made such an assumption merely as a device to make his analysis simpler, he tended to express his results as if they had a timeless quality. They created the impression that they were meant to convey the permanent essence of a people's life. Some textbooks still carry on this fiction of stasis. They speak, for instance, of the totemism of the central Australians or the shamanism of the Siberians as if these had remained unaltered since they were described at the turn of the century. Discussion in this " ethnographic present " can be justified when it is simply a comparison of abstract types that is wanted. But the use of this tense has often meant a disregard of dating and sequences, a lack of that sense of history which a social anthropologist should have if he is to do justice to his records and be of proper help to his successors.   With such a process of literary embalming, it is sometimes even impossible to find, as in some accounts of Oceanic culture, whether or not a custom has died out.   Even where some radical change in the social institutions of a people could not be passed over, as with the disappearance of head-hunting in the Solomons, the anthropologist was apt to take a retrospective, even nostalgic, point of view.   He was more concerned with what had been lost than with the positive implications of the change.   The removal of incentives to the building of large canoes formerly needed for the head-taking raids drew more attention than the new possibilities for social intercourse in peaceful conditions or the effects of the development of coastal as against hinterland settlements as the fear of war receded.

Two obvious reasons led to a changed approach : alterations in the nature of the material, and alterations in the climate of opinion in which the social sciences as a whole operate. When people hitherto primitive take to using steel axes, wear cotton clothing, write letters and read newspapers, grow cocoa, rubber, or ground-nuts for sale, and spend the proceeds on a bicycle or a gramophone, they must think and act very differently from before.   The anthropologist has had to study the new social relations.   Terms such as " culture-contact " and " acculturation " were introduced to express the way in which new patterns of behaviour or types of relationship were acquired and incorporated into a primitive system. The emphasis here was on the primitive system as primarily passive, a recipient of new elements.   The second factor in modifying the traditional viewpoint of the social anthropologist has been the general change of opinion regarding social stability and social process.   As the twentieth century has revealed a much less assured social order than seemed to characterize the nineteenth century, and a world in which change can be regarded as normal rather than exceptional, the anthropologist's analysis has tended to take on a more dynamic character.   He conceives of primitive people not simply as accepting civilization when it is introduced to them, but as reacting in positive fashion to each new element as it is presented to them.   Moreover, he conceives them as autogenetic in their culture—initiating new ideas and new ways of behaving, if only on a small scale. Ideas of the equilibrium of a primitive social system being its most characteristic state are no longer so common. The dynamic picture demands recognition of the possibility that the operation of a social system, however simple, involves continual tendencies to change. Basic relations in the system are not of a balanced order; they are often unbalanced, requiring continual re-adjustment in order that the system may work at all. This operates at all levels of activity in the social system. The principle of basic compensation—one of the root principles of social organization—operates precisely because individuals are attempting, wherever they can, to remedy or utilize the asymmetry of the structural arrangements in the society as a whole. Anthropologists as yet have not succeeded in working out a satisfactory dynamic theory of society from their own data. Most of them are not prepared to accept a Marxist or other ready-made frame of concepts. But without being very abstract, they have provided a general idea of what has happened to primitive societies of different kinds under the impact of Western influences.

In such descriptive analysis the anthropologist approaches the work of the historian. He becomes a recorder and inter-preter of social changes. His data are given a time co-ordinate, and can be compared in sequence, and not only in typology, with those of other social scientists. But the work of the anthropologist in this respect differs significantly from that of most historians. More conscious of the theoretical issues of social process, the anthropologist is more concerned that the minutiæ of events recorded should be seen to be relevant to some problem in social relationships. He relies far more as a rule on his own personal observations than on documents. This gives him the great advantage of being able to give first-hand evaluation to events. He can collect the type of information which he thinks is most appropriate to his inquiry. What would an historian not give for the privilege of a personal scrutiny of men and affairs in his period, to be able to talk to his characters about their motives and to fill the gaps in his documents? But the anthropologist usually has to pay for this privilege. He has bartered time-span for being able to rub shoulders with reality. He usually sees his community for only a year or two at a time. Rarely does he return later to measure interim changes. He lacks the long series of documents which give the historian a sequence of contemporary or near-contemporary pictures of events. So, to give depth to his analysis, the anthropologist has to make many assumptions. He relies upon ideas about social homogeneity or the continuity of social process, or about the historical meaning of traditions. Sometimes he translates differences in contemporary social conditions in related communities into differences in stage of development. He turns space into time. He can fairly assume something about the continuity of the society he studies—he knows it will not vanish like a fairy castle when he leaves. But what he assumes about the past and what he estimates about the future will depend very much on his theories about the nature of society in general. So an added care is needed when he makes his personal observations, which must give so important a base for his projections on the time-scale.

A theoretical framework for the analysis of social change must be concerned largely with what happens to social structures. But to be truly dynamic it must allow for individual action. As a member of a society, each separate individual is striving to attain his ends, interacting with other members in the process. All of them are largely governed in their behaviour by the set of established basic relationships of the social structure. This embodies sets of expectations as to what people will do in virtue of their social roles, and ideals as to what they ought to do. So the conduct of the individual has a complex scheme of motivations. His own interests, recognition of interests of other members of the society, and recognition of the structural values by which he has been guided so far in his career, all affect his patterns of behaving. Some change necessarily occurs at every step in the action process. No act can be precisely a repetition of that which has gone before, although both may have been carried out as responses to similar stimuli, in the same general scheme of motivations. The pattern, then, is the main theme, not an identical procedure. But at any step in the action process new motivations may present themselves to the individual. These may arise from his perception of advantages to be derived from the social system, hitherto unperceived by him. Or they may arise from the entry of new factors into the social environment, offering new opportunities or enforcing new ways of protection. Into the social process of an agricultural community, for example, drought, flood, tempest, accidents to animals or gear, discovery of a new crop strain, present the members with problems which they can solve only by modifying their activity. Even the demographic process of waxing and waning of population necessitates a different handling of resources. All this demands a new adjustment by the individual in his daily activity. But he has also to maintain some orientation to the values which have hitherto held a powerful place in his motivational scheme. He must also have regard to the ways in which other members of the society are likely to react to the new factors in the social situation, and to his own response to them. The outcome is likely to be some organizational change. There will be a re-planning of time, of the order in which fields will be ploughed or harvested, of the ways in which different members of the household will co-operate to carry out the daily tasks. Preferences will be other than before. Choices will fall differently between the new range of alternatives. Activity will take new directions, and form new combinations.

But a distinction can be drawn between organizational change in general and that massive form of it which is structural change. In the one case the pattern of procedure does not alter radically. The organizational change does not alter the basic relations between the members of the society so much as to be termed a modification of the social structure. Structural change may not imply a high degree of coincidence between the new motivations of any large number of members of the society. But it does imply large-scale shift in the pattern of their activities. This may mean a new common orientation. It may involve only a greater dispersion of their goals. But the observer can recognize that a former basic relation has lost its magnitude, its force, its frequency. He may be able to see a new relation directly substituted for it, or several new relations may have arisen. The potato and the pig, for instance, when introduced among the Maori of New Zealand, radically altered the economic structure. They reduced the amount of labour put in on other crops, and on fowling; they altered the production balance as between men and women; they gave commoners a chance of earning relatively higher incomes and elevating themselves in the social scale; they even helped to change the scheme of ritual by reducing the amount of economic magic demanded. To-gether with other factors, such as the musket, they were the basis of some important structural changes in Maori society.

It can be argued that structural change cannot be brought about by individual activity. This is true in the sense that no individual alone can change the form of society. The great man does not make history : human relations in the narrow personal sense do not really alter the fate of nations. But, on the other hand, the social structure cannot change *per se*. It is intelligible only as an aggregate of human relations and attitudes. When, then, the form of these relations and attitudes alters, it is as individuals that people respond to stimuli. When the patterns change, it is individuals in the last resort who change them.[1] When they act in response to forces stronger than themselves, these forces are composed of the acts, opinions, and attitudes—or imputed acts, opinions, and attitudes—of other individuals.

Structural change is a product of social interaction, in which pressures are felt, advantages perceived, responsibilities recognized. This involves governance of conduct by sets of values which have common elements for significant sections of the society. For a new pattern of behaviour to be adopted, the values governing the old pattern must have some degree of plasticity. Ends must be capable of being met by al-ternative means to those hitherto in use. Structural change implies that there was some imperfection in the previous means–ends schedule of a substantial number of members of

---

[1] For the conventional aesthetic view see, e.g., Emile Mâle, "It is not the Multitude that creates, but individuals" (*Religious Art from the Twelfth to the Eighteenth Century*, London, 1949, p. 29).

G

the society, and that adjustment is possible. Two effects can occur. One is a process of what may be called social convection. When some members of a society change their behaviour from what has been recognized as an established pattern, the reactions are likely to involve other members too. By imitation, by resentment, by the need to repair the breach in their accustomed ways, they tend to modify their own conduct likewise. The other effect may be called a process of social conduction. A change in established patterns tends to bring unforeseen results in its train. The functional inter-relation of activities is very delicate. So people who have adopted an innovation may find themselves facing a situation to which they must conform, though very much against what they would have chosen in the beginning could they have known. These new situations, in which unwanted changes are enforced on some members of the society and unforeseen effects encountered by others, pose fresh organizational problems. So the stage is set for further efforts at change. The essence of the dynamic process lies in the continuous operation of the individual psyche, with its potential of unsatisfied desires—for more security, more knowledge, more status, more power, more approval—within the universe of its social system. The paradox is that the efforts at satisfaction, if successful, tend to modify that system, and that the repercussions of such modification upon other individuals tend to render it irreversible.

The object of this chapter is to illustrate how such processes occur in the kinds of societies which the anthropologist usually studies, and to discuss the significance of the effects.

The processes of social change can take their initiative from within a society, or they can be stimulated by external forces. Except where such forces take the form of physical violence they can be regarded as having in the first instance the character of catalytic agents. They may be material goods, such as the pig and the potato, muskets, or clothing. They may be practices, such as literacy; or institutions, such as Christianity. But they release forces hitherto held in check, and facilitate changes, while themselves remaining unaltered. Soon, however, these may themselves suffer modification. Their agents

may consciously or unconsciously interpret to the local
people the social processes involved. They may themselves
become influenced by the situation. They may get, for instance, a " frontier psychology "—having the concept, say,
that the indigenous people have as their role the provision of a
" natural labour force " for them.

Little information has been accumulated as yet by anthropologists on the subject of autonomous change. I shall deal,
then, here with changes produced through external influences.

The economic aspect is so important in studies of social
comparison and social change that it is convenient to begin
from it. From this point of view the societies which have
been the primary concern of the anthropologist so far can be
described as of the peasant type. It is in the study of the
impact of Western culture, in particular the Western industrial
system, on non-European peasant communities that social
anthropology has made one of its most striking recent contributions.

The term peasant has primarily an economic referent. By
a peasant economy one means a system of small-scale producers, with a simple technology and equipment, often relying
primarily for their subsistence on what they themselves produce.[1] The primary means of livelihood of the peasant is
cultivation of the soil. This is not merely a physical attachment; the peasant is not a landless labourer but someone who
has an individual or collective right or claim to the land. It
is this close economic and social—even sentimental—attachment to the soil that is historically one of the main distinguishing features of a European peasantry. But it is convenient, for our discussion outside the European field, to
extend the term peasant more widely, to cover other types
of small-scale producers, such as fishermen or rural craftsmen,
who share the same kind of simple economic organization
and community life. One might argue that there is almost

[1] It has been estimated that in the peasant communities of Eastern
Europe the peasants earn more than half their income in food; produce
sold on the market averages less than 50 per cent as compared with 70–80
per cent in Western Europe (Royal Institute of International Affairs,
Agrarian Problems from the Baltic to the Ægean, London, 1944, p. 46).

as much difference between the European pastoral and arable peasant economic systems—e.g., between the *Alpwirtschaft* and lowland agriculture—as there is between an Oriental cultivator and his brother fisherman, who may in fact be by part-time occupation a peasant agriculturist as well.   Such a small-scale productive organization, built upon a use of or close relation to primary resources, has its own concomitant systems of capital accumulation and indebtedness, of marketing and distribution.[1]   The necessary relation of this peasant economy to particular types of social structure gives a characteristic shape to life in peasant communities.   Indeed, it may be said that there is a range of peasant societies.[2]   For instance, a system of peasant production is closely linked with forms of intimate co-operation between members of a family, most of whose services contribute to a common income.   The residential and working group is often larger than the simple family of parents and children.   It may take the form of an extended family of several generations and wider kin ties. It may even act as a joint family with common property ownership and income sharing among a group of brothers or cousins and their descendants.   Even in Europe such a large social unit still existed until recently in the patriarchal *zadruga* of the Balkans.[3]   Outside Europe, in the peasant communities of Africa, Asia, and Oceania, such large kinship units with

[1] Cf. " The middleman is, indeed, the inevitable product of a society of peasants and small craftsmen, and, because he has exceptional opportunities of preying on it, he is always unpopular, whether he is the English brogger of the fourteenth century or the Irish gombeen man or the Indian buniah of our own day.   Yet, failing a system of agricultural co-operation, he is as essential as he is unpopular, the one link between the small man and the market" (Eileen Power, *The Wool Trade in English Mediæval History*, Oxford University Press, 1941, p. 48).
[2] Robert Redfield prefers the term "folk cultures" and has given illuminating analyses of changing peasant societies in his *Folk Culture of Yucatan* and other works.   His study of the Maya, *A Village that Chose Progress*, re-examines the community of Chan Kom after a period of seventeen years, and presents the changes that took place during that period.   (A).
[3] Vera Ehrlich-Stein, "The Southern Slav Patriarchal Family," *Sociological Review*, vol. XXXII, pp. 224–41, July–October, 1940.   See also *Agrarian Problems*, op. cit., p. 50.   Although decreasing in numbers, the *zadruga* was still to be found a few years ago in parts of Yugoslavia and Bulgaria.   (More generally, *zadruga* means simply cooperative unit.)

production functions are extremely common. With such integral co-operation in economic matters normally goes also a specific type of social and ceremonial life, giving to marriage and funeral rites, fairs and dance festivals, magical and religious practices, music and other forms of art, their " folk " character.

Such small-scale peasant communities have organization, codes, and values which are felt by them to be deeply important. The people have been conditioned to these things since childhood, and feel that they are basic to their corporate existence. Their institutions, partly because so many of the same people tend to be involved in all of them, are closely interrelated, so that change in one affects the others. Hence, changes which are initially economic tend to have repercussions through the whole of the community. This has been particularly marked with the coming of industrialism, foreshadowing the destruction or radical re-shaping of their social structure.

Industrialism or the industrial system in this connection does not mean simply the effects of the establishment of factories in a peasant locality. With the installation of machinery and rise of a wage-labouring class divorced from owning means of production come some of the most marked social changes. But it is rather the gross ramifications or total set of connections of industrial enterprise that are significant. Necessary market relations are created far away in the search for raw materials and for disposal of industrial products. New uses for man-power are stimulated, from road construction to wharf labouring, quite apart from work in warehouses or industrial establishments. In this broad sense the fingers of the industrial system today stretch around the world. They penetrate to the heart of Africa and to the most remote islands of the Pacific. In the Solomon Islands, for instance, with few resident Europeans, and almost unknown to the outside world until the southward drive of the Japanese brought them into the news, there is no industry worth the name—save for a little gold-mining. But for over half a century, as labourers on sugar and copra plantations within and outside the islands, people of the Solomons have helped to supply our Western demands for raw materials. The

effects on their economy and community life have been
profound.[1]

What are the main incentives for the peasant to enter the industrial orbit? Why does he not calmly refuse to be concerned?

One important reason is rural poverty. Faced by the
virtual impossibility of all members of a growing peasant
community making a living at the level they wish, from their
limited resources of land, temporary or permanent migration
of some of them may be a necessity. This would seem to be
the case in some high-density rural areas, such as in parts of Java
or parts of Eastern Nigeria. Disproportionately large urban
centres in some of the West Indian islands seem to exist, in part
at least, as an overflow from crowded peasant holdings. In
Chinese rural areas the progressive deterioration of economic conditions in villages in the coastal provinces drove large numbers
of peasants into the cities in the years before the war. And as
in England the enclosure of common lands at the outset of the
industrial revolution had a great deal to do with the rapid creation of an industrial proletariat, so there is a certain parallel

[1] The reactions of European peasant economy and society to the industrial revolution have been carefully examined by historians. Outside
the European field the material is still very incomplete. Among the many
works by anthropologists on this theme may be mentioned:

Robert Redfield, *Tepoztlan, a Mexican Village*, Chicago, 1930.

L. Schapera (ed.), *Western Civilization and the Natives of South Africa*,
London, 1934.

Monica Hunter, *Reaction to Conquest*, Oxford, 1936.

H. I. Hogbin, *Experiments in Civilization*, London, 1939.

F. M. Keesing, *The South Seas in the Modern World*, New York, 1941.

B. Malinowski, *Dynamics of Culture Change*, New Haven, 1945.

Godfrey and Monica Wilson, *Analysis of Social Change*, Cambridge,
1945.

Clyde Kluckhohn and Dorothea Leighton, *The Navaho*, Cambridge,
Mass., 1946.

I. Schapera, *Migrant Labour and Tribal Life*, London, 1947.

K. L. Little, *The Mende of Sierra Leone: A West African People in
Transition*, London, 1951.

H. I. Hogbin, *Transformation Scene: The Changing Culture of a New
Guinea Village*, London, 1951.

Sol Tax (ed.), *Heritage of Conquest (Middle America)*, Glencoe, Ill.,
1952.

E. M. Spicer (ed.), *Human Problems in Technological Change*, New
York, 1952.

W. E. H. Stanner, *The South Seas in Transition*, Sydney, 1953.

in South Africa, where the compression of the Tswana and other Bantu groups into inadequate reserves facilitated the furnishing of African labour for European industrial enterprise.

Other pressures may operate in special cases. During the war in China the Japanese seized and destroyed factories in the areas they occupied. When the Chinese Government established new factories in Free China they had to seek new labour, skilled and unskilled, to man them. Among the older skilled workers, especially those with families, the prospect of higher wages for the support of their dependants, and of greater savings, was an important inducement. Among the younger skilled men, coming from the industrial centres on the coast and in central China, a dominant motive was the patriotic one of refusal to work for the Japanese and desire to help their country in her struggle against the invader. Among the comparatively unskilled workers, drawn mostly from rural areas, it was the prospect of escaping being drafted for military service that seemed to weigh heavily. There were other factors too. A number of these unskilled factory workers were the sons of land-owning families. They received money

---

Elizabeth Colson, *The Makah Indians: A Study of an Indian Tribe in Modern American Society*, Manchester, 1953.

Audrey I. Richards (ed.), *Economic Development and Tribal Change*, Cambridge, 1954.

McKim Marriott (ed.), *Village India*, Chicago, 1955.

J. C. Mitchell, *The Yao Village*, Manchester, 1956.

V. W. Turner, *Schism and Continuity in an African Society*, Manchester, 1957.

F. G. Bailey, *Castle and the Economic Frontier*, Manchester, 1957.

W. Watson, *Tribal Cohesion in a Money Economy*, Manchester, 1958.

S. C. Dube, *India's Changing Villages*, London, 1958.

N. Nash, *Machine Age Maya: The Industrialization of a Guatemalan Community*, Glencoe, Ill., 1958.

A contribution of interest has been made by novelists, who have expressed various aspects of the disintegration suffered by peasant communities and the psychological difficulties of the people, as the result of contact with the industrial world. For example:

Elspeth Huxley, *Red Strangers*, London, 1949—deals with the Kikuyu of Kenya.

Samuel Y. Ntara, *Man of Africa*, London, 1934—deals with the Chewa of Nyasaland.

Gregorio Lopez y Fuentes. *They that Reap*, London, 1937—deals with a Mexican village.

from home to supplement their factory wages, but they entered the factory because they thought the work would be comparatively light and carry some social prestige—more so than the well-paid work as rough labourers on railway construction in which many poorer farmers, equally anxious to escape the army, had engaged. Other workers, again, entered the factory in the mistaken hope that their work there would get them useful political contacts and improve their social status. Others yet again did so to evade pressing economic or social difficulties in their home community.[1]

But the factory or the mine can beckon too. There can be a definite attraction for the peasant in linking himself with the industrial system. In many cases one might talk of the magnet of industrialism. Urban experience in itself is often a lure. It means more varied amusement, more personal freedom from home ties, and a sophistication about many matters of which the rural dweller is ignorant. The African or the Solomon Islander is no less sensitive to the appellation of country bumpkin than is his European counterpart. But one of the most patent incentives, especially perhaps in the less differentiated societies, is the demand for the material goods which participation in the industrial system, or in the production of raw materials for it, can yield.

This type of demand has operated for as long back as historical records go. The peasant in Indonesia today relies upon the outside world for his household china and most of his cloth. But his forbears were noted by William Dampier 250 years ago as being eager for trade in similar commodities. Dampier, in line with his profession, was moved to reflect on the relation between trade and civilization : " . . . the more Trade, the more Civility; and on the contrary, the less Trade the more Barbarity and Inhumanity. For Trade has a strong Influence upon all People, who have found the sweet of it, bringing with it so many of the Conveniences of Life as it does." However, after speculating whether even " the poor Americans "—meaning the Indians—might not be allured to

---

[1] Kuo-Heng Shih, *China Enters the Machine Age*, Cambridge, Mass., 1944. The analysis was based primarily on a study of one factory, in Kun Ming.

it, he adds, prophetically enough, that this might not be to the increase of their happiness ". . . For with Trade they will be in danger of meeting with Oppression: Men not being content with a free Traffick, and a just and reasonable Gain, especially in these remote Countries: but they must have the Current run altogether in their own Channel, though to the depriving the poor Natives they deal with, of their natural Liberty: as if all Mankind were to be ruled by their Laws." [1] In this Dampier had in mind the Dutch restrictive measures on trade by other Europeans in the Indies. But his central theme, of the attraction of trade, and of the people of remote countries being drawn thereby into a system which they cannot control and which takes charge of their lives, is as valid today. It is even more valid, because of the greater range of the industrial system, its more insistent demands for raw materials, its more effective marketing organization, its more developed forms of communication and transport. It may not be entirely true to say that effect of contact with the industrial system is to create irreversible situations. During the depression of the thirties some South Sea islanders had to revert from calico to bark-cloth. Now in the South-West Pacific deserted airstrips which are going back to jungle are symbolic of deserted natives who are missing the trappings of American civilization. But the major effects are permanent and cumulative. Among the Malay peasantry or the African peasantry, the bicycle, the motor-bus or motor-lorry, and the sewing machine have come to stay, just as steel tools have replaced those of stone and shell in all but the most remote parts of New Guinea. The effects of this process are profound.

These new material goods so much in demand by the peasant are not merely an addition to his existing stock. They are to some extent replacements, obviating the need for spending so much time and labour on the original articles, or on the goods produced to obtain them. To some extent they cause

[1] William Dampier, *Voyages and Discoveries* (1st ed. 1699), p. 82; see also pp. 48, 49, 94 (London, 1931). Daniel Defoe, possibly taking his cue from Dampier, in much of whose track he makes Robinson Crusoe follow, in the *Farther Adventures*, makes much the same equation of barbarism with lack of trade (*Robinson Crusoe*, Everyman ed., p. 369).

modifications. When rather more than a century ago the Maori of New Zealand began to receive axes, adzes and other steel tools in quantity in return for dressed flax, pigs, potatoes, timber, they abandoned most of their ordinary stone adze blades of basalt and greywacke. But they did not throw away their more valuable blades of greenstone or jade. Some they kept as heirlooms in their original form, others they worked with much labour into pendants and other ornaments. In particular, they fabricated numbers of those curiously contorted anthropomorphic neck ornaments known as *heitiki*. The tool substitution thus had the effect of multiplying the quantity of ornaments in circulation and affecting their value. When the people of Tikopia received steel tools they likewise abandoned their ordinary working blades of giant clam shell, though they kept some of the larger ones, which they have continued to use for religious purposes. Like the Maori and other Polynesians, they favour the adze as a woodworking tool, doing even fine dressing of timber with it. So when given plane-irons they make an interesting modification. Instead of using the iron in a plane, as a smoothing tool, they haft it and use it as an adze blade, as a chopping tool. Another ingenious *ad hoc* adaptation I myself observed was when the Tikopia saw my discarded toothbrush handles, which looked rather like turtle-shell, took them and worked them in hot water to form ear-rings by the same method which they use with the natural material.

Some of these new material goods are incorporated into the existing technological and economic organization. Others may make radical changes in the economic and social system. The introduction of the plough to Bantu cattle-owning agriculturists, for instance, has changed the character of their agricultural life. Traditionally, tending the cattle has been the work of the men and tending the farms has been the work of the women. The yoking of cattle to the plough has altered the division of labour between the sexes; ploughing, being employment of cattle, became the work of men. The main implement in cultivating was formerly a short-handled, broad-bladed hoe, which kept fields few and small. The plough opened the way for the production of crops on a larger scale, for sale if there was a market, or for conversion into beer if there was not. In parts of Kenya ploughing has become a regular occupation, the owner hiring out his plough and team of oxen with driver for a fee per acre. Ownership of ploughs by wealthy Africans has also led to a new disparity in the distribution of land, since such men are able to break up large areas and plant them with maize, or wheat, or wattle, and thus take possession of common land to the detriment of other people without such capital resources.[1] In Bechuanaland a woman had her own fields and controlled the crop she reaped from them, usually storing it at her parents' home. Her husband was dependent on this. Under the modern system this still holds. But a man with oxen and a plough often cultivates one or more fields of his own, keeping and doing what he likes with the crop. His greater independence is one of the tokens of the growth of individualism and weakening of the economic side of kinship ties which has come to most peasant cultures with increasing contact with the industrial system.[2] Apart from such adaptations, the material goods of civilization create new wants [3] and additional ways of using labour. The introduction of calico instead of leaf or grass skirts leads to the use of needle and thread, and ultimately to the sewing-machine; the need for transport brings the motor; the coming of the motor lorry means a need for a road wider than the ordinary bush path, and for culverts, bridges, and ferries. The use of machinery means also some organization for its repair, and at one stage or another some education is demanded even to read labels and instructions. So the stage is set for a conscious demand

[1] C. K. Meek, *Land Law and Custom in the Colonies*, p. 97. Oxford University Press, 1946.

[2] I. Schapera, *Native Land Tenure in the Bechuanaland Protectorate*, pp. 133–136, Lovedale Press, S.A., 1943; cf. E. Jensen Krige and J. D. Krige, *Realm of a Rain-Queen*, pp. 40, 41, 55, Oxford University Press, 1943; Monica Hunter, *Reaction to Conquest*, Oxford University Press, 1936.

[3] Cf. the view expressed by the trader Joel Polack in New Zealand in 1840. " . . . However simple the wants of the people may be, yet no sooner are they possessed of one article of European manufacture, the possession of it begets additional requisites." J. S. Polack, *Manners and Customs of the New Zealanders*, vol. I, p. 187, London, 1840.

for further types of goods and services, and also for basic institutional changes. This demand is a very real one. Over most parts of Africa today the Government is interested in developing social services. Yet often it is not so much the Government which is pressing the peasant to adopt improvements in his way of living; it is the African peasant himself who is clamouring for more roads, more schools, more doctors and dispensaries. The basic problems are : Who is to provide the organization to secure these things and who is to find the cost? This in turn leads to another consideration—a review by the more thoughtful people of the means of political representation best calculated to achieve their wants in a technically efficient way. Such transition from calico to political consciousness is not inevitable. But it indicates the complex set of factors in interaction, and something very like it has taken place throughout Ghana and Nigeria during the last half-century.

Entry of goods from the industrial markets means that new types of price must be paid. In the very simple types of society, direct labour services—such as porterage—are one way of giving payment. Provision of raw foods, such as fruit, fish, or coconuts, is another. In addition to these classic methods, so often recorded by travellers, craft labour is employed. Elementary trade goods of the " curio " type are detached from the household store or specially made. The Tikopia, isolated in the Solomon Islands, offer mats, fans, clubs in return for pipes, fish-hooks, cloth, beads, and knives. They barter rather by gift and counter-gift than by setting fixed rates of exchange or by haggling. The Yami of Koto-sho, in another isolated island east of Formosa, have been in somewhat similar straits for metal tools and cotton cloth and thread. They adapted clay and wood models of chickens, goats, pigs, and human beings, which they used to make for amusement, to purposes of trade. Under Japanese tutelage (before the war) they exchanged these for money, and with the money bought the article desired. This was really a kind of indirect barter, because they did not use money generally. Until recently they were at the stage of beating out coins flat to make disc ornaments—as a century ago in

FAREWELLING THE DEAD

No corpse lies in this grave; it holds only burial clothes (pp. 62 *et seq.*) of a lad lost at sea. Sweet-scented leaves give savour to the nostrils of the spirit.

A MODERN MAORI FUNERAL

Kinsfolk round the coffin, sheltered under a tent to avoid putting houses under taboo. The village meeting-house, with carved timbers, near by.

INTERCULTURAL
ECONOMICS IN
MALAYA

Malay craftsmen in a Kedah coastal village have built a boat for a Chinese owner in his own style.

MALAY PEASANT
PLOUGHING RICE
LAND

Strenuous work of a Kelantan cultivator on a small holding.

New Zealand the only use the Maori had for a sovereign was to make a hole in it and hang it in a child's ear, and even then a shilling was preferred because it was a more pleasant colour.[1]

This simple adaptation of craft labour is not of great magnitude. The great mass of African, Asiatic or Oceanic peasants get the material goods and the services they want from the external world by the export of some agricultural product, the export of their labour, or the provision of new services for the commercial market.

A wide range of peasant products is supplied to the external market for industrial use. Some include surpluses from domestic consumption like the palm oil of Nigeria and the coconut products, especially copra, from Ceylon and the South Seas. Others are grown solely for the world market, like the vanilla from Tahiti, rubber from Malaya and elsewhere in South-East Asia, and the cocoa from Ghana—new products which are not in use by the local people at all.

The line between subsistence production, production for a local market, production for export, is easy enough to draw in theory but difficult in practice. A Malay will, with the help of his wife, cultivate enough rice for himself and family, grow vegetables after the rice harvest to supplement the family diet and sell in the local market, and have a small area of rubber trees which he taps to sell the product to a Chinese dealer for export. This mingling of activities has its advantages, by spreading the risks. In the production of rubber for the world market the peasant is favoured by his low overheads, especially his low labour costs, since he can use family labour at convenient times which can usually be fitted in with other work. He may be technically less efficient than a plantation, and his product is often of less good quality. But he has been quick to benefit by proper instruction. The difficulty of his rubber production is its price dependence on the world market of high variability. Hence in a time of depression his cash income drops heavily, and his standards of living suffer. But though he and his family may go short of luxuries, and

[1] E. R. Leach, " The Yami of Koto-sho," *Geographical Magazine*, October, 1937, pp. 417–34; cf. F. Maning, *Old New Zealand*, p. 2, London, 1863.

perhaps even of dried fish and of cloth, his growing of rice and vegetables ensures that they will not be really short of food.   In an all-round fall of prices his diminished income from rubber should still suffice, but it is rare for the prices of staple consumption goods such as food to fall relatively as low as those of such raw materials as rubber.   His subsistence agriculture, then, serves as a kind of backlog for his economic system, and concentration on the export crop alone would result in an unbalanced system of production.

Production for the world market has been an essential element in providing a large part of the peasant's cash income and raising his standard of living.   But until a system has been evolved of effectively controlling the prices of raw materials on world markets so as to ensure a reasonable long-term security for the producer, the peasant has a serious problem in deciding what time and energy he should put into export production as against subsistence production.

Contact of the Oceanic or African peasant with the industrial system has resulted not merely in changes in the production of goods but also in the direct use of man-power.   Under the peasant regime itself labour is often furnished to others for a price.   It is usually recompensed by food or by counter-services, though money payment is becoming more common, as, e.g., in Malay rice-harvesting.   In commercial agriculture, as on the Ghana cocoa-farms or on the Uganda cotton-farms, the seasonal hiring of African labour by African employers has become a distinct feature of the changing economy. Here there is no community tie between the parties, and new forms of contract emerge.   But from the social and economic point of view the most important aspect is the export of labour to European enterprises such as plantations, mines, and public works.   In global terms, the numbers so employed in the Pacific are not large, being in 1939 rather less than 100,000, of whom about half were in New Guinea.   Accurate figures for Africa are not available, but a rough guess at the number of African wage-earners south of the Sahara might give a figure of about seven million.[1]   Many of them, however, are only partially dependent on wage labour for a living.   Wages for all

[1] Cf. Hailey, *African Survey*, 1957, pp. 1359–61, for some data.

except the small proportion of skilled labourers are low—
often only 10s. to 20s. per month in cash, with food, housing,
and some other amenities usually provided.   But increase of
personal wealth is only part of the attraction.   Incentives to
work include: the wish to collect enough money to pay tax,
to buy cattle to hand over to the relatives of a woman one
wishes to marry, or to furnish one's wife and family with
clothing, furniture, and other household goods; curiosity to
see the white man's world, with its variety of new experiences;
and desire to increase one's social prestige by having worked
abroad.

With such a range of incentives, it is not surprising that the
economic and social relations of the peasant have been deeply
affected.

An impression still prevails in some European circles that
not only is the African peasant independent of paid work for
his subsistence but that he is as a rule reluctant to stay away
from home for more than six to nine months, lest he drop
out of the agricultural cycle.   This does not accord with most
findings by anthropologists.[1]   A sample of about 200 workers
at the mines in Broken Hill, Northern Rhodesia, of an average
age of twenty-four and a half years, had spent on the average
eight and a half years away from their villages, in a number
of jobs, with visits back to their homes only about once every
three years.   A survey made in 110 villages in Nyasaland,
where about four-fifths of the men had been away to work
at one time or another, showed that average length of absence
from home in such cases was three and a half years.   This
situation may be fairly representative of much of East and
Central Africa.   Moreover, one may speak of many of these
men not as migrant labourers, but as temporarily urbanized,
or semi-urbanized.   It was estimated that at Broken Hill in
1940 about 70 per cent of the men might be put in this
category, having spent over two-thirds of their time in town

[1] E.g., Major G. St. J. Orde Browne, *Labour Conditions in East Africa*,
Colonial No. 193, pp. 5–6, London, 1946.   Cf. G. Wilson, *Economics of
Detribalization in Northern Rhodesia*, Pt. I, p. 42, Livingstone, 1941; Margaret
Read, " Migrant Labour in Africa ", *International Labour Review*, XLV,
p. 620, Montreal, 1942.

since first leaving their village. Another feature is the comparatively high proportion of young men apt to be away at work from a village—in the Nyasaland villages mentioned, for instance, the area with the lowest average had 24 per cent away. This was near European settlement and in the heart of a fertile tobacco country, while that with the highest average, 43 per cent, was far away from direct European contact. One of the most striking features of the African labour flow is the immense distances—often many hundreds of miles— which the labourer will travel for employment.

The effects of all this upon the peasant economy and culture are very marked. On the one hand, transfers of wealth by the labourers to their homes help to raise the rural standard of living. From workers at Broken Hill between one-fifth and one-sixth of their earnings went in gifts to their wives and kinsfolk in the villages or was taken back by them. Nearly two-thirds of this amount was in the form of cloth, and much of the rest in cash. Moreover, the experience of the labourers in the urban centres and on the mines of good housing and food, plenty of soap and water, and a variety of shops and other services tends to set rural standards too, though it is suggested that these are less flexible in food than in other consumption goods.

On the other hand, the absence of perhaps one-third to a half of the young male population at work tends to disturb the balance of the farming economy very seriously. It throws an undue strain on the older men and on the women. Cultivation is thus often badly done, or circumscribed, and food suffers. A young man whose duty it is, as among the Bemba, to lop trees for his father-in-law's garden, or as it is among the Chewa, to hoe for his wife's parents, goes to work on the copper mines instead. He sends back money which in theory pays for a substitute. But in fact his father-in-law spends it on a hoe or on some article of consumer's goods that he wants badly. The young man has fulfilled his obligation, but the cultivation suffers.[1] Again, relations within the family are affected. Prolonged absence of the husband leads often to

[1] A. I. Richards, *Land, Labour and Diet in Northern Rhodesia*, p. 133, Oxford University Press, 1939; Margaret Read, *op. cit.*, p. 628.

breach of the marriage tie. The children lack a father's care and authority, and the mother misses his help with them. Younger women awaiting husbands from the young men away at work get restless; they may even drift to the towns or engage in irregular sexual relations in the village. The migrant men often have acquired more education than their wives and have seen better standards of living, while their womenfolk behind in the villages are content with more primitive home conditions. This in turn leads to family friction. Politically, there is often a cleavage between the returned labour and the village heads, still old-fashioned and suspicious of the new ways, or less enterprising and active to cope with changing conditions and new needs.

One may conclude, then, that the technological advance which has taken place and the consequent economic and social changes cannot be represented as a simple progress towards integration at a higher or more complex level. Even technologically, the relations with the industrial system are in some respects merely peripheral. The new skills learnt may be difficult or impossible to turn to community account.

There has been rather a redistribution of skills and a revaluation of resources, social as well as economic. Traditional experience and traditional rights are at a discount. Young men gain at the expense of their elders—they are quicker to learn, more mobile. Initially, women lose at the expense of men. Tied more to the home, they are able to participate less readily in the new opportunities. But later, as the changes grow more radical, they get their chance, and are enabled to throw off the shackles of the traditional system also, and gain at the expense of the men. Those with rights over services only are apt to lose in regard to those with rights over material goods.

But various forms of recrystallization are possible here.

The price paid by the peasant for his more intimate contact with the industrial system is, then, more than an economic one in the narrow sense. In the last resort, paying a price means orienting one's activity in a given direction. The transfer of goods or of money, or the provision of a service in payment, all mean that activity has been oriented thereto at some

H

time. Part of the price may be even mental or emotional orientation—involved, say, in loss of status. The peasant pays a social price by suffering disturbance of his traditional institutions, by modifying the patterns of his social relationships, and reorienting his activities to meet the new circumstances.

A simple example from peasant family life comes from Fiji. A Fijian woman had twins, and the mother's milk was not sufficient to feed them both. In former days an additional nurse would have been borrowed from among the village women, as part of the intricate pattern of services based on the kinship and neighbourhood ties of the small community life. In the last few decades the practice of feeding such babes on cow's milk has become fashionable. To get this milk the father of the twins worked in the rice-fields of an Indian cattle-owner, in return for the use of a milch cow, for about six months. Harassed by this and other economic obligations incurred to Indians to provide comforts for his family, he was unable to fulfil the traditional obligation of preparing a feast for his new-born children when the birth took place. He made the feast ten days late.[1] Here the structure of family obligations includes two traditional elements—the obligation to see that the children were fed and the obligation to provide a birth-feast for them. But the structure of economic arrangements is different, and the father's allocation of time and effort is very different from the traditional pattern. Formerly he could have got the wet-nurse and given the feast on the same day, and paid the price of both at leisure in appropriate services. Now milk and feast at the right time proved incompatible objectives. Part of the price the father had to pay, then, was realization of not having fulfilled his duty, and fear of possible scandal or criticism through his delay.

More complex changes in relationships are involved when the contacts of the peasant with the Western industrial system begin to affect his land. Where expropriation of the peasant has occurred, by wholesale purchase of his lands, as with the Maori of New Zealand, or by mere disregard of his claims, as with the Kikuyu of Kenya or the Sioux and some other Indian

[1] Buell Quain, *Fijian Village*, p. 353, Chicago, 1948.

tribes of the United States,[1] radical re-alignments of social and economic relations have followed. In some cases pressure on the remaining land has led to a much sharper definition of individual and small-group interests, to a resort to new courts and other external sources of law in order to explore and support claims, and to an increased tempo of buying and selling land among the peasantry themselves to meet the new economic conditions. In other cases recognition of land shortage has led to increased assertion of group rights, a closing of the ranks to prevent any single individual from reaping an advantage

[1] Examples of expropriation of the lands of American Indians are given in : Bruce Nelson, *Land of the Dacotahs*, Minneapolis, 1946; F. M. Keesing, *The Menomini Indians of Wisconsin*, Memoirs, American Philosophical Society, X, Minneapolis, 1939, especially Chs. VI and VII; Clyde Kluckhohn and Dorothea Leighton, *The Navaho*, Harvard, 1946, pp. 8-12. In Kenya at the beginning of the century grants of land were allowed by the Government to Europeans in the apparently empty highland area, which nevertheless was claimed by Africans for grazing and potential cultivation; further white settlement was later permitted on some lands specifically set aside for native reserves. By 1944 about one-twentieth of Kenya, or 7 million acres, had been alienated for European settlement; of this about 1,300,000 acres are suitable for cultivation and about 864,000 acres were actually under cultivation, by about 2,000 settlers. Africans had about 33 million acres in reserve lands, and also about 77 million acres of poor, sparsely inhabited country in the Northern Frontier District and other isolated areas. The estimated African population was $3\frac{1}{4}$ million (it was $5\frac{1}{4}$ million by the census of 1948). The average density of the African peasantry, at nearly twenty to the square mile, was about ten times that of the Europeans, even including the large number of the latter who were not engaged on the land. Specific density of Africans in the Kikuyu reserve was given as 283 per square mile even in 1933, with local densities of over 1,000 per square mile reported recently (C. K. Meek, *Land Law and Custom in the Colonies*, pp. 77, 79, Oxford, 1946).

Among the Maori of New Zealand a situation of comparative wealth in land a century ago has turned into one of pressure and comparative land hunger. By the Treaty of Waitangi in 1840 the Maori acknowledged the sovereignty of Queen Victoria and were confirmed in the ownership of their lands—amounting to about 28 million acres in the North Island alone. Half a century later, partly by war and partly by sale, these North Island Maori had lost some 17 million acres, or 60 per cent of the whole. By 1911 they had only some 7 million acres left: today, it is less than 4 million acres. Much of this is inferior land, and some of the land is leased to Europeans. The Maori population at the 1951 census was 115,676. See I. L. G. Sutherland (ed.), *The Maori People Today*, New Zealand, 1940, pp. 116 ff.; and *New Zealand Population Census*, Vol. VI, Wellington, 1954.

over his fellows.   Where compression into reserves has taken
place, social relations have often been exacerbated.   The
authority system has been affected through people being
forced on to the lands of another group, with their pride
of ownership left behind them.   In a peasant community
many values other than economic are based on land.   Title
to the soil so often gives title to political authority, superior
status in the community as a whole, and rights to ritual
leadership.   Reputation and prestige depend to a large extent
on a judicious use of the produce of the land, in spending
on public works and feasting, as well as on saving.   Little
wonder, then, that deprivation of lands, whether through
confiscation or through unplanned sale, has been a potent
influence in the armed revolts against Westernization which
have characterized the Maori and the American Indian,
and that suspicion of such deprivation has for long been
a deterrent among the Ga and some other peoples of
Ghana to the introduction of systems of land survey and
registration.

Even where there has been no substantial cession of land to
foreigners, increasing contact with the Western world, particularly in its industrial aspects, has led to far-reaching changes
in group and class land rights and in the social relations
involved with them.   Where a market could be found for the
products of the land at a level of income hitherto unknown,
elaborate and acrimonious attempts at establishment of land
claims have tended to arise in the absence of a strong central
authority to control the situation.   In the Gold Coast Colony,
for instance, the land claims of chiefs of different types have
been stimulated partly by royalties to be obtained from
concessions to mining land, and partly by the profits to be
derived from cocoa cultivation.   As a result, there have been
frequent disputes, sometimes dragging on for years, between
representatives of different " stools " or chiefly titles.   Their
expensive litigation has enriched their lawyers and impover-
ished their children.   Moreover, traditional relations between
superior and inferior chiefs; between chiefs and their people;
between kin groups and between villages, have been distorted,
and new, often confused, patterns have been created.   Some-

what similar reorientation of social relations has occurred among some sections of the Maori of New Zealand. But a different system of representation of communities by their chiefs, and the ability to inherit land through either parent, have meant friction between individuals rather than between chiefs or local groups as such.

In the kingdom of Tonga, in the Western Pacific, such a channelling of social relations into litigation was avoided through the assumption of unitary control by a powerful ruler at a comparatively early stage of contact with the Western world. In what was formerly a system of land-holding by hereditary chiefs, with but nominal allegiance to a central ritual head, the Crown has assumed ultimate ownership of all the land of the kingdom. Great nobles have been given estates, or confirmed in possession of their hereditary lands, but only as major tenants, not final owners. Every male Tongan is entitled by law when he becomes a taxpayer to receive a residential plot of land in a village or town, and an area for cultivation in the countryside, for which he pays a small rent. Whereas formerly the common people occupied land at the discretion of the chiefs, now they do so at the discretion of the Crown. The Crown takes responsibility for granting allotments to individuals on the estates of the nobles, and collecting the rents, which are then paid over to the major tenants. Differences in concentration of population in various parts of the kingdom, inequalities in inheritance of land rights, the pull of the towns on the young people, and attachment of people to the homes of their fathers, have led to some unevenness in land-holding. But the system has preserved the lands from alienation to foreigners, and from undue exploitation by local capitalists. The peasantry have kept a real stake in the land. A relevant factor in the operation of this system has been that in Tonga the Crown is essentially the Sovereign, and that the Sovereign is also now the hereditary holder of highest rank in the traditional status system of titles. The Tongan peasantry thus combine in a complex but unified system a set of administrative relations with the modern State and a set of social relations with a traditional ruling chief. In this system the expansive powers of the nobles to take advantage of modern economic developments have been largely curtailed.

This situation stands in contrast to that of Uganda, which has also a ruler crystallized from the traditional system of chieftainship, but where administrative measures in regard to land took a different form. On what are known as the *Mailo* lands the rights of the chiefs under the traditional feudal tenure were crystallized by the Government into a proprietary tenure approximating to one of freehold type. This was foreign to African custom. It was due to a common European misconception that a chief was the " real owner " of lands, or primary right-holder, with final right of disposal over them, and not in the position of a controller or manager or trustee on behalf of the people of his tribe or clan. When the chief, then, became the legal proprietor of these estates, the people settled there cultivating the land became his tenants. The former social and political relations between them tended to be modified. Economic relations tended to assume primary place. When commercial crops became important—coffee, tobacco, and especially cotton—the chief became simply a receiver of rent. But, unlike the Tongan noble, he was free to charge what he could exact, and to dispossess his tenants when he wished. This situation was later met by legislation fixing rents and limiting eviction. From the profits of cotton cultivation, too, the peasants have remedied their difficulties to some extent by purchasing part of the lands they till. But the structure of their relations with the chiefs has shifted on to a different plane.[1]

Apart from changes effected in the relations of peasants as communities, or as social classes, contact with the industrial system and Western culture tends to result in significant changes in the relations of individuals within smaller groups.

In many peasant communities land, though worked by simple families or individuals, who were entitled to the usufruct, has been held and inherited as the property of groups of kinsfolk. They had an over-right in its disposal. It commonly was not regarded as saleable or transferable to any

[1] C. K. Meek, *ibid.*, pp. 132–33 and 133 n.; L. P. Mair, *An African People in the Twentieth Century*, London, 1934, pp. 164 et seq.

individual outside the group or to any other group as a whole. Such a proscription has often been based upon religious sanction, such as a persisting interest of the group ancestors in the land which fed them and on which they lived. With the growing importance of the cash income to be derived from the sale of crops, and a limited amount of good land available, land has come to acquire a commercial value. When the crops are of semi-permanent character, such as rubber, cocoa, palm products, there is a definite interest in securing as firm a hold over the trees as possible. There has thus been a strong tendency for individuals and families actually cultivating such land—as distinct from the larger group having more general rights over the land—to assert their rights of possession to the exclusion of other members of the group.

An instance of this is given by developments of the ownership of rubber land in parts of Malaya. In Negri Sembilan, on the West Coast, the traditional custom is that rights to ancestral land are inherited by women. Alienation of land is by decision of the matrilineal kin group, not by any individual right-holder. No man, even a husband or brother, could own or sell a piece of ancestral land. But when rubber first came into vogue as a crop, the land on which the trees were planted was usually cleared straight from the jungle by the labour of men. It was not really ancestral land like the rice swamps, which had been cultivated for generations. So the practice grew up that such rubber land was treated differently; it was controlled by the men who had put their labour into it, and it could be inherited by their sons. Here, then, was one effect of the new commercial crop. But there were other effects. Previously there was little inducement for land to be disposed of to other people. Now the practice of sale began, to Chinese as well as to Malays. Disturbed at the actual or potential loss of land or of cash to the group, and also by the threat to the interest of future generations who might be left landless if the process continued, there was a strong movement to have such rubber lands declared ancestral lands by modern law, and so to bring them under control by the kin group. The result was a struggle of several sets of principles—of the individual versus the group; of men versus matriarchy; of the labourer on the soil against him who looked on it as a resource in perpetuity.

The issues were not always so clear-cut; there was much argument among the Malays themselves as to what was the correct custom in these new circumstances. Into this argument entered another element—religious values. The Malay as a Muslim respects the *Shari'a*, the system of rules and interpretations which give guidance to the Faithful in most of the affairs of life, and which have a sanction ultimately resting on belief in divine revelation. Human custom is admitted as valid so long as it can be shown to fall within the sacred law, but the formal scope allowed to it is narrow. The *Shari'a* makes provision for the rights of women, but on the whole its emphasis is on male activity and rights. Hence in Malaya the tendency has been for the religious authorities to lean rather towards a definition of land rights in broad patrilineal terms than towards the maintenance of a local custom which gives pre-eminence to the status of women as land-holders. But one result has been a searching of minds and a clash of views in regard to what is the most appropriate role for custom to play in a modern Muslim State. Here, then, starting with the contact of the peasant with a new market situation, we arrive at a redefinition of religious values.

It has been simplest to enter this analysis of social change by showing the workings of the economic impulsion, in particular some of the implications of the peasant's demands for new material goods. But there are other significant demands as well—for literary education, for some secure social conditions, for a new religion. Sometimes these things are wanted primarily because they are thought to lead directly to increased material prosperity, or because they are regarded as an index of higher status. Historically, the educational facilities so generously provided by Christian missions in Africa and elsewhere have been an important factor in giving them a religious clientele. " Rice-Christians," as converts have been called in China when they joined the Church for the sake of being fed, are common enough, if the term be understood in its widest material significance. With many of the peasantry of Oceania or Africa conversion has been not so much a search for a better way of life as a search for a way of getting a better living.

A conventional view of a peasant society is that the wants of an individual in it are very limited. This may be expressed in two ways: by saying either that he is part of a static self-perpetuating social system, or that he is culture-bound in his desires as well as his activities. More careful observation leads to the opinion that the peasant has a highly expansible set of wants. What has been holding him back so far in their satisfaction has been his limited means. Moreover, it seems that a powerful incentive for him to try to gratify these wants is the possibility of raising himself and his dependants in the status system. This system may not be highly elastic in the traditional form of peasant society, especially where it is linked with political control and embodied in a structure of here-ditary rank. When a new economic possibility arrives, such as the advent of a new market for agricultural produce or for the services of middlemen, some individuals show more initiative, energy, and skill than others in taking advantage of it. The measure of this is seen in changes in the status system. Sometimes it is in the position of chiefs, who, given an initial advantage by their qualified controls of wealth in the traditional system, forge ahead and rivet these controls more firmly on the body of the people, or turn to their own use the income derived from the new avenues for employment of the wealth. Sometimes it is new men who come out of the ruck—men who under the traditional rules had not enough chance to develop their peculiar gifts of organization, but who can plan and execute on a wider scale efficiently. In a non-hereditary status system they may find adequate scope for their ambitions. But where the traditional scheme is not open to them, new status systems are gradually created, parallel to or in opposition to the old one. Very commonly in these changing peasant societies a new aristocracy of wealth arises side by side with the old aristocracy of birth. It pro-ceeds to secure its position in the historical manner, by in-vesting where possible in the traditional tokens of status, including that banner of respectability, the right to marry the daughters of the old aristocracy. Social convection draws in individuals and groups other than those initially affected. Yet the process of fusion may be incomplete, especially if the old aristocracy have ritual functions as part of their social endowment. A process of differentiation takes place. New groups arise and old groups alter their social role. Individuals are offered alternative allegiances in some of their social relations, particularly their economic relations. And with these contrasts in modes of possible action come contrasts in moral evaluations.

Practically all social change has an economic aspect. This is represented basically by a re-orientation of resources in goods or labour power, so that they serve different ends than before. Yet such a re-orientation is not simply with the wish to get more wealth, in a kind of morally neutral atmosphere. The African or Oceanic peasant takes to growing a commercial crop, to individualizing his land-holding, to investing in a plough, motor-lorry, or a motor-launch with the idea that such activities are right, and that the fruits of them are justifiable. Normally, the fruits are material and easily observable. And the justification is apt to be given by reference to the advancement of the individual himself, his children, and immediate kinsfolk, who benefit, rather than that of the community as a whole. The strength of the evaluations falling outside the immediate quantitative estimates of economics is seen by two types of situation: where community activity is engaged for no apparent economic results; and where activity which would lead to economic results is inhibited by evaluations of a strong counter-type. Conditions of social change such as we are discussing here tend to bring out the factors in operation, because of the contrast between the traditional peasant patterns and those of the new situation. Two examples will illustrate this.

The first is taken from the South-West Pacific. Here, since the war, certain new organizations of native peoples have arisen in the Solomon Islands, New Guinea, and elsewhere. They have different characteristics in the various parts of the region, and are known by different names. But despite their variation in form, they have a certain functional similarity.

They are essentially reactions by the native people themselves, without European prompting, to the new forces introduced through contact with the West. They express on the one hand native dissatisfaction with existing conditions. On the other hand, they are attempts to get an adjustment. This adjustment is sought through native means. The attitude here is complex. There is no rejection of the material equipment of the West—it may be even sought by elaborate, bizarre means. But it is recognized that the native share in the distribution of such desirable goods has so far been inadequate in native eyes. Since Europeans have played such an important part in regulating that sharing process hitherto, the tendency is to reject their co-operation in the new movement, and to rely on native organization. Such is the line of argument at the rational level. But other than rational elements enter into the situation. It will be borne in mind from what has been said earlier that economic gains are rarely regarded as being ethically neutral. They are conceived as being of the nature of a right accruing to the possessor, or to the would-be possessor. They are regarded as morally defensible, and the effort to obtain them is infused with moral fervour. These new native movements are handled with an enthusiasm which far surpasses any desire for immediate gain to the individuals concerned. Moreover, the values of the organization are conceived as applying to corporate unity : it is the good of the community which is an ostensible object of the activity.

The results have been surprising to European observers in several respects. In the first place, these observers were taken aback by the strength of the movements. Unsuspected secrecy in some areas, open wild enthusiasm in others, equally demonstrated the hold that these movements had on the native population. Fanaticism could be a description of the phenomenon in some cases. In the second place, there has been surprise at the spread of the movements. Some areas were not affected, but in others the organization proved to be widely rooted, and linking together in a complex network of relations native groups without previous known co-operation. Even those which had mutually non-intelligible dialects and had to use " pidgin " English as a medium of communication joined forces. Thirdly, there has been remark at the degree of organization involved. It had not been thought that the handling of large numbers of people in concert could have been done so efficiently by native leaders, that the administrative models of courts and councils could have been so aptly followed, and that public order could have been so effectually preserved. This was especially notable in the movement in the Solomon Islands protectorate known as the Marching Rule. But a fourth element, not necessarily so surprising, has been in some ways the most spectacular. This has been the extraordinary economic operations of some groups, particularly in what has been termed the Cargo cults of some of the New Guinea natives. The people concerned were affected by the war in a number of ways. Not least was their appreciation of the vast wealth of the Europeans, and the manner in which this could be poured out from ships and aeroplanes when supplies were needed for the fighting forces. Brought into contact, even if only peripherally, with this mass of resources, and then deprived of nearly all use of them again with the cessation of the war, these New Guinea people have tended to regard them as being symbolic of a new way of life. They have conceived the idea that they want such resources for themselves, not through European intervention and not through war, but primarily through their own efforts. They can see no immediate way of attaining this end, save one—by relying on certain elements of their traditional beliefs. They believe the faith that can move mountains to be theirs. They believe that in one way or another, whether through the help of their ancestors or the help of their magical performances, they can constrain ships and aeroplanes to come and land supplies, as before, to meet their wants. So those in the coastal villages have built wharves out into the sea, ready for the ships to tie up, and those in inland villages have constructed air-strips out of the jungle for the planes to land. And they have waited in expectancy for the Second Coming of the Cargoes, as Christians once waited for the Second Coming of the Master.

This can be looked on, pityingly, as mere delusion. But

to regard it as an example of religious mania, as some observers in the Solomons regarded the Marching Rule as the result of Communist agitation, is to miss the point. The Cargo cults are a dramatic instance of misapplied productive effort, it is true. The time and energy that went into the construction of the wharves and air-strips are likely to have yielded concrete results if applied to agriculture, or to a situation where there were ships and aeroplanes to arrive. But the anthropological analysis goes deeper. Here is an instance of incompatibility between wants and the means of satisfaction. Blocked on the one side by inadequate resources, lack of training, and lack of opportunity from creating the desired goods for themselves, and on the other side by lack of knowledge from realizing the necessary technical and economic steps required before the goods can come to their shores, the New Guinea natives have turned to fantasy. They seek their satisfaction in an imaginative projection. But they bolster it up by elaborate work. In one sense, then, this work is not ineffective. It is in itself part of the satisfaction sought. It is part of the symbolic validation given to the idea that the things wanted are morally justifiable. Part of the message of the air-strip or the cargo wharf to the observer is—" What we want is right." It is part of an affirmation of native claims, native community solidarity, native values, in the face of what is conceived to be an impassive, unsympathetic, or hostile outside world. One inference, too, that can be drawn from such movements is that forces of political organization, initiative, and authority exist in the new system to a degree hitherto unsuspected. In some cases this has been perceived by the European administrations concerned, and attempts are being made to harness these forces for the native community development (cf. Appendix).

Such protest movements, revolting against the trend of affairs in order to find a new adjustment to the pressures vividly felt, if obscurely understood, have their analogies in the earlier history of the Pacific, and also in other parts of the world. But more general, though less dramatic, in the life of the peasantry has been a failure to weld effectively the values of the new system of social and economic relations with those surviving from the traditional culture. They have what may be called a dual frame of organization. An illustration of this can be taken from the Maori of New Zealand, who in some ways have had a more successful adaptation to Western civilization than most other non-European peasant peoples.

The Maori in former times had a tribal type of society, each tribe being based on a system of ramifying kin groups with strong local allegiance and definite land rights. The status system included a class of gentry, headed by kin-group and tribal leaders—the chiefs—and the system had provision for the holding of status by women. The common people were defined in terms of genealogical distance from chiefs rather than by membership of a totally separate class, and their kinship ties with their chiefs made for strong loyalties towards them. Tribes and even sub-tribes had a marked sense of group solidarity. Disputes and warfare over women and land were common. There was no single political authority for the whole country. The Maori formerly practised a simple agricultural and fishing economy, with considerable hunting of birds and collection of forest fruits. They had elaborate forms of co-operation in work, based largely on recognition of the moral claims of kinship to assistance. The exchange and communal consumption of food played an important part in their social and ceremonial as well as their economic aspects of life. Marriages and funerals, especially of people of rank, were occasions of much public display, speech-making, and entertainment. Their systems of ritual observance were elaborate, and included stringent sets of taboos relating to the persons and belongings of the dead.

The modern Maori still maintain many of the principles of the traditional social structure, though in modified form. But in addition they have adopted much of the culture of the European New Zealanders among whom they now live, and with whom they share to a considerable extent a common economy and polity. Maori political consciousness now includes a concept of loyalty to a foreign Sovereign, the British King. There is also a concept of Maori unity transcending tribal boundaries, expressed in part regionally through Maori representatives in the New Zealand Parliament, and partly nationally in acts of the Maori people as a whole.   This new political articulation has involved a shift in the traditional status and authority structure.   While hereditary chiefs still exercise influence in virtue of their ancient lineage, this is circumscribed, and has no legal backing.   They divide the field in practical affairs with men whose ability, education, and other personal qualities have won them the respect of their fellows.   The Maori economy still depends to a large extent on primary production.   But their bird-snaring and collection of forest products are minimal.   Their agriculture is now farming in general European style.   In fishing they have adopted many European features, including the use of petrol-launches and imported hooks and nets.   Many Maori, women as well as men, have left the land and taken up work in towns or in industry, usually supplying unskilled or semi-skilled labour. But their social mingling with European New Zealanders is incomplete there.   In their own social and ceremonial life they display a strong group consciousness.   Although at marriages, funerals, and other gatherings goods of European style are largely used, these are treated as part of the Maori culture.   The traditional concepts of taboo have been modified in their weight and their incidence, but they still operate (Plate IIʙ).

Against this background the following incidents, which occurred a few years ago, are significant.[1]   A Maori was drowned at sea, and after efforts to recover the body had failed, the elderly women of the sub-tribe of the deceased imposed a taboo on a stretch of fishing coast some fifteen miles long, and on the waters off it for some distance out to sea.   According to the terms of the taboo, no fishing might be done there. The taboo applied to all fishing, by any method, and was intended to apply to Europeans as well as Maori.   The nominal period of the taboo was twelve months, but it was understood that if no breach of the taboo occurred within three months it would be lifted.   Should a breach occur, however, it would last for another three months, and so on,

[1] Reported in the *Auckland Star*, August 14, 1946, and *New Zealand Herald*, August 28, 1946.   A similar incident was reported in *New Zealand News* (London), January 25, 1949.

till the full period expired. The livelihood of more than 200 Maori fishermen was involved. They, however, were understood to be prepared to obey the dictates of their womenfolk and refrain. There was a danger, however, that fishermen from other localities, especially those on European trawlers, might not hear of the ban and fish the area, so prolonging the taboo period, to the detriment of all. The Marine Department of the New Zealand Government, notified of the ban, then made it widely known, asking for the co-operation of European as well as Maori fishermen in observing it. In the other case, more recent, some three miles of the coastline were declared taboo when a young Maori man was drowned, and the taboo was for one month. This period, shorter than that usually fixed, took account of the fact that the body had been discovered soon after death. The imposition of the taboo was notified by Press advertisement to ensure that it would be respected by Europeans as well as Maori users of the coast, and the Marine Department was advised for the same reason.

These ritual observances of one people are conceded by another, not so much from direct respect, but from unwillingness to impose economic hardship on the others by nonconformity. The newspaper publicity, the ban on Europeans as well as Maori, the period of taboo reckoned in calendar months, the entry of a Government Department to help enforcement, are all features involving a wider social horizon than in traditional Maori life. But the taboo on fishinggrounds owing to a death there is in conformity with ancient custom. The central attitude is that of marking the significance of the death of a member of the community by an act of economic abstention.

The dual frame of organization comes, however, in the contrast between the ritual and the economic obligations. In former times, it is true, these two pulled opposite ways—abstention from work through respect for the dead, and pressure to work in order to gain the wherewithal to live. But the rhythm of production was geared to the want schedule of the Maori people in a way which took account of such interruptions to production. They might affect individuals or groups adversely. But the subsequent expenditure and standards of living could be adjusted to the reduced incomes. Moreover, lacking a high degree of specialization, the men of the tribe could turn from the sea inland—from fishing to bird-snaring or other occupation free from taboo. Nowadays Maori occupations are much more specialized, and a taboo throws men out of work in a way which makes it difficult for them to find alternative jobs. And yet their standards of expenditure are not so elastic. There may be regular instalment payments to be made on the launch or on furniture in the house, which cannot be easily postponed and which need a regular income to sustain. The daughter at school may not have to pay fees, but she will need some new clothes. And there are many other expenses which cannot be easily adjusted to a sudden cessation of employment. One frame of organization, the traditional Maori one, consists of respect for ancient forms, a complex social position in the kinship system and local community, a most wholesome fear of offending the women of the group by disobedience to their fiat, and a general religious and moral attitude of avoidance of the scene of death. The other frame of organization consists of a market economy where a man lives largely by selling his produce or his labour in competition with others, a social life in contact with Europeans who do not share and often despise Maori ways, and a set of consumption patterns with many elements pressing for money to spend. The modern Maori is thus faced by the need for choice and decision. Normally as yet in such problems he chooses the traditional Maori frame of organization of his activity.

But there are spheres where the choice is less precise. In the example given, the New Zealand Government supported the Maori attitude of obedience to the taboo, and even attempted to enlist European obedience. In another basic Maori funeral custom, the *tangi*, akin to the Irish wake, the issues are not always so clear. The *tangi* means a large assembly of kinsfolk, many of them perhaps coming hundreds of miles to see the dead, mourn, and make farewell speeches (Plate II). The obsequies may last a week or more, and large amounts of food are assembled and consumed. On several occasions official and

I

unofficial attempts have been made, primarily by European New Zealanders, to have curtailed the size and duration of these gatherings. The grounds given have been drain on foodstuffs, the burden on public transport, or the danger to public health according to circumstances at the time. In other words, though Maori funeral customs are usually tolerated by Government and the white New Zealanders, they are apt to be criticized when they affect the economic position too adversely.

The dual frame of organization here has a social frame, demanding the customary tokens of respect for the dead and sentiment for the kin to be paid in concrete acts, and an economic frame, demanding conservation of resources. Too often in modern conditions the two frames of organization are confused by Maori. This is not usually so at funerals; they regard the ritual obligations as paramount (cf. the primacy of funeral obligations in the Tikopia example, Chapter II, p. 65). Only a severe economic depression like that of the third decade of this century will drive them to reduce their social commitments. But there are other spheres where this confusion is manifest.

Maori occupational behaviour shows this. The Maori in olden times was an agriculturalist, a woodsman, a fisherman, using ingenious but simple techniques, and engaged mainly in production for a small social group. His occupational behaviour fitted his social aims. He cultivated, fished, and snared birds at times and at rates which were adjustable and suited his social obligations. Later, after the European advent, he became mainly a peasant farmer. Here duplication of frames of organization gradually became evident, as production for the external market came to be measured in terms of relative efficiency. There is one frame of organization with its foundation deep in Maori old culture, which regards a farm as a place for a man and his family to live, to put up his and his wife's kinsfolk for as long as they care to stay, and to use as a base from which to operate in attending funerals and other social gatherings and in getting cash from road-work and other casual occupations. So long as current wants are covered, the farm can look after itself, fences and buildings get into disrepair, weeds accumulate, and stock run wild. There is another frame of organization which demands that the Maori farmer shall "make his farm pay" by producing enough to allow for depreciation of capital as well as for cost of manures, seed, and other annual outgoings, and which demands attention to stock and fields and careful balancing of expenditure against income. But to do this means a sacrifice. Work cannot be dropped at any moment to attend a funeral lasting a week. All and sundry kinsfolk cannot be put up indefinitely, eating up the farm produce and contributing little or nothing in work, and their horses and other stock cannot be grazed at will on the striving farmer's fields. The Maori "returned soldier," the war veteran who has fought by the side of his fellow New Zealander in Italy or North Africa, expects that the State will give him equal assistance in setting himself up as a farmer. Yet the State, if it is to make an investment in human enterprise, demands conformity to certain standards of efficient operation, which militate to some degree against Maori social norms. Either system can yield satisfactions, but both cannot operate together without friction. Yet side by side with the attractions of the work of modern farming and the incomes to be derived from it are the attractions of the Maori social system, with its reliance on kinship obligations and its characteristic community life. Little wonder that the dual frame of reference is being commonly confused. The same is happening with the Maori in industrial employment. As pressure on the land is becoming more evident, and the attractions of urban life more bright, many Maori young people are looking to industry for work. For this also they are often ill fitted, partly through inadequate technical training and general education, but partly through being unwilling or unable to meet the requirements of industrial employment by the aid of the norms of conduct they learn in their homes.

I have spoken of the dual frame of organization as if one frame were social and the other economic in character. This is, of course, not adequate, since each has social and economic aspects (see Chapter IV). But the sociability and community emphasis are most overt in the narrow peasant frame of reference, and the resources, income-producing emphasis, is most overt in the broad, "modern" frame of reference. Up to a point also the contrast is between communal interest and individual freedom. But the essential feature is the inconsistency between values in the organization.

Values do not exist as isolated entities—they link as systems, with some degree of integration, for every individual. At the same time, the value systems of different individuals must present some common elements in order that community life can go on. And for values to be capable of influencing choice there must be standards, i.e., elements of relativity, involved. Every organization—that is, a directed system of action—for the accomplishment of a human being's ends can operate effectively only in virtue of a system of values.

Now, it is characteristic of these dual frames of organization that the individual is trying to operate one type of organization with a set of values more appropriate to another type. Take the case of a Maori farmer whose farming is criticized as inefficient. Organization for efficient modern farming in New Zealand demands a set of values incorporating regularity of work, concentration of resources on very limited objectives, alertness to the importance of margins. Moreover, the organization itself embodies certain logical implications of action. If these are disregarded, the organization is rendered ineffective. The purpose of a fence is to restrain stock. If a paling fence is used, it requires repair according to the durability of the timber; if a wire fence, according to the quality of the galvanizing. If this is not seen to, the stock escape, and the time taken to find them nullifies the fencing organization. These logical implications may go unseen through stupidity or lack of experience or lack of training—which is only a foretaste of experience. But they may also be ignored because the system of values of the actor does not impel him to take the necessary action, though he realizes it is required. He prefers alternative uses of his time and energy, because he is operating under a different value system.

There is, of course, always a difference in the personal frame of organization of activity as between different individuals. In the last resort, effort can be only individual, and satisfactions can also be only individual.   Yet for their fulfilment co-operation between individuals is essential.   The personal frames of organization must be superimposed, and be sufficiently coincident for joint action to become possible.   The decision at what point that co-operation is to be instituted is often one of the most difficult decisions for an individual to make, since it involves some measure of sacrifice of personal freedom. There is always a basic inconsistency in social activity at some points, between individual and group interests—that is, the interests of a number of other individuals.   This is the real eternal conflict in the nature of society, far deeper than any conflict of classes, which is only one of its manifestations. Even should the Marxist millennium, the entropy of the classless society, ultimately arrive, this dialectical basis of human activity will remain, for constant personal decision and redecision.

The confusion and apparent failure to weld life in the Maori community successfully to life in the modern industrial state have their analogies in many other parts of the world.   In particular, it is characteristic of the behaviour of people in a simple peasant agricultural system when they attempt to integrate their system into a wider organization which has social, political, and economic ties of quasi-international scope.

To understand social processes and organization in change we need to consider the social values or standards, the way in which these can alter by presentation of new elements in the social environment, and the symbols in which these values are expressed and modified according to circumstances.

To get a closer appreciation of the issues involved, we shall examine in some detail the kind of standards that operate in four aspects—economic, æsthetic, moral, and religious—in these peasant types of society.   This analysis will also cover some of the main problems of anthropology in these fields.

CHAPTER IV

THE SOCIAL FRAMEWORK OF ECONOMIC ORGANIZATION

THE anthropologist is interested in the structure and organization of economic activity for two reasons: most social relations have an economic coefficient; many social relations are primarily concerned with economic values. But the anthropologist is not setting out to discover the principles of economics in the sense of the abstract body of theory which attempts to explain economic aspects of human behaviour at the most general, universal level. His task is to examine how these principles work in specific social or cultural contexts. The principles of economics which are truly general or universal in their application are few. Most of those which purport to be general have been constructed primarily within the framework of ideas of an industrial, capitalist system. This means a machine technology, a monetary medium of exchange, an elaborate credit system using stocks and shares and banking institutions, developed private enterprise, and a social structure of an individualistic, Western kind. The anthropologist struggles with a diversity of types. Many are peasant systems, with money used for a limited range of transactions, a simple technology with hardly any machinery, and methods of enterprise, co-operation, credit, and income-getting very different from those in a Western economy. Some are truly primitive, with no monetary medium at all to facilitate the processes of exchange, distribution, and storage of wealth. The anthropologist's problem, then, is one of applying or translating economic principles in novel contexts. He is even deprived for the most part of the common means of measurement available to his economist colleague. Without money there is no simple means of reckoning prices. Even where money is used, its limited range inhibits easy measurement of the bulk of economic relations. Although the passage of time can be quite carefully expressed, it is rare for any system of regularly spaced units of less than a day to be used. So any close calculation of labour expenditure, as in man-hours, is possible only by field observation. All this has one advantage: that the anthropologist is not so subject to the possible distortion of monetary preoccupations. He is looking at the interplay of " real " units of man-power and materials, output and income, not veiled by the " money illusion " of a Western economy. He finds it necessary to examine the picture of economic relationships in the kind of frame in which the people themselves have set it. What results has he achieved? And what is their relation to the study of economics as ordinarily understood?

First consider the nature of economic organization, in its broadest scope.

Economc organization is a type of social action. It involves the combination of various kinds of human services with one another and with non-human goods in such a way that they serve given ends. This means an arrangement of these elements in a system, by limiting the kinds of relations that can potentially exist between them. Such combination or limitation does not occur mechanically, but by giving values to the goods and services. Choice is exercised in the light of these values. From among the available means those are chosen which seem most appropriate to the given ends. From among possible ends those are taken which seem to be most realizable by the available means. Choice at some level of consciousness is required for most types of action. Its implications for economic organization lie where the emphasis is on disposal of resources. There can be other emphases—on the nature of the social relations involved, or of the action as such. Moral choice or æsthetic choice, for instance, are concerned with actions and relations rather than with use of resources.

Choices are not discrete, unrelated. They form a system, they have continuity. Each is related to the others which succeed it, behaviourally—not only in a time-sequence but in an action sequence. They are related also conceptually, in terms of values—that is, in regard to a series of qualities assigned to the relations involved in action.

In all this, the fact of sociality is vitally important. The choice, the behaviour, the values of any one person are all conditioned by other people. They, too, are exercising their choices. They compete for a common set of resources. By their very existence they are significant elements in the individual's total appreciation of his own position. Relations with them are then assigned specific qualities—values. This is so in part because the actions of these other persons give sense to the conceptual and symbolic system of the individual. His notions of economic reality are confirmed by seeing the type of choice made by others around him. The less any individual acts in isolation, the more he must be responsive to choices, or the expectations of choices, by others. Economic organization is set in a social framework—of relations between persons and between groups, expressed in different conceptual ways and with different emphases, as values, symbols, rules of conduct, patterns of behaviour. To take a very obvious example—the operation of a monetary system. Money is a symbol. It represents in a measurable way some command over goods and services. It can operate effectively only so long as there is general confidence that it is a valid symbol in the economic system concerned, and is so recognized by others. This confidence can be shaken by events arising from within the system—as a very rapid increase in the volume of money in circulation. But it can also be shaken by events from without the economic system—as by a legal pronouncement that this money is no longer valid; or by a new moral conviction of, say, religious origin that it is wrong to use money at all. The confidence of every individual in the monetary system is a matter of delicate adjustment, and is a function of his wider confidence in his fellows. This is maintained not merely by seeing them use money, and seeing the material equivalent for what money he himself uses: it rests also on his belief in the general consistency of their conduct, on his expectations that there will be general consensus of views even in spheres where money is not used. One aspect of this is seen in the demarcation of such spheres. It is only by taking into account the general social framework of relations and evaluations that one can accept the Western exchange codes. One pays money for a meal in a restaurant but not for one in a private house, for a cow but not for a wife. Yet these are conventions of primarily a moral order. There are non-Western systems where money is handed over in return for the private meal, and for the wife, and where both transactions are justified on moral grounds.

It is against this social framework that the anthropologist takes up his economic study.

The basic concept of economics is the allocation of scarce, available resources between realizable human wants, with the recognition that alternatives are possible in each sphere. However defined, economics thus deals with the implications of human choice, with the results of decisions. Choices, wants, and their implications in action involve personal relations, social relations. If social anthropology examines forms of social relations in the more primitive societies, economics examines certain types of social relations—for example, production and exchange relations—in all societies. This is done with a rigour rarely if ever reached in anthropological propositions. In so far as the science of economics can be said to put forward principles that are truly universal, it could have more justification for being called the science of man than has anthropology, which might be called the science of kinds of men.

The relation of social anthropology to economics can really be shown best by examples. The problem is complicated by the asymmetrical development of the two sciences. Whereas some institutional fields of relationships given conventional recognition, above all kinship, are almost wholly the subject-matter of social anthropology, the economic field is already pre-empted. The most significant generalizations—that is, those which explain the widest spheres of action and link very many elements of apparently disparate kind—are the property of economic science. What, then, can be done in the name of economic anthropology?

If we examine economic propositions we see that all but the

most formal and abstract are expressed in terms of institutionalized concepts. There may be no reference to particular commodities, no time and place coefficients. There may be even deliberate avoidance of the monetary expression of relations in favour of expression in output units, investment units, labour units, and other " real " quantities. But the concepts of output involve more or less explicitly stated notions of the business firm as an entity; of an industry as a series of such localized entities using much the same kinds of resources and technical processes and bringing out a comparable product; of the entrepreneur with the specialized function of conducting economic operations in such a *milieu*. The concepts of investment likewise involve notions of a market in which buying and selling are characteristic operations and in which there is sufficient continuity of requirement, in replacement of equipment at least, to allow of reasonable alternatives in choice. Usually there is a far more substantial content in the propositions—they involve ideas of foreign trade, government taxation and expenditure, accumulation of money balances, limited liability in industrial and commercial operations. Moreover, this is set against a specific background of socially oriented notions of community life—involving autonomous national entities; a distinction between public and private services; the operation of government as a legislative as well as an executive machine. Many of these concepts are alien to the kinds of economy the anthropologist has to describe.

This contextualization of economic theory is obvious and necessary. It is primarily Western, not only, as some would argue, because of the need for a theory to give social and moral validity to the series of economic changes which found their outlet in the industrial revolution. The anthropologist is perhaps more prone than most other social scientists to a tacit historicism. Yet even should one accept much of the criticism of such a standpoint, in its more extreme forms, the way in which the trend of economic theory has followed the march of economic fact cannot be ignored.[1] But the cogency

[1] It has probably been the rise of the Soviet and Fascist economies and the prospects of democratic socialism elsewhere, rather than theoretical preoccupations, which has led to the many recent analyses of the economic

of the argument implied in most economic analysis, that the complexities of the Western institutional field offer the most attractive intellectual exercise and the greatest possibilities of mensurational refinement, must be recognized.   One can expect an economist, then, to have only limited sympathy with Radhakamal Mukerjee's complaint of the neglect of non-Western economic forms,[1] which has been repeated by anthropologists.   The role of the anthropologist here is rather that of a watch-dog—to see that no one takes away the reality of the economic systems of primitive peoples by default.   Of this there has been some danger.

But the anthropological function is more relevant from a theoretical angle.   Economic propositions and processes of economic analysis tend always to involve assumptions about social behaviour.   One of the great achievements of modern economic theory is the success with which it has eliminated such extraneous matter, and based its reasoning upon a very small amount of primary data about human existence. The main premisses are: the varied and expansible nature of human objectives of conduct—the multiplicity of ends; the limitation of means for satisfying them—the fact of scarcity; and the need to choose between them—the exercise of preference.   Thus equipped, the economist can afford to ignore the character of specific ends, except by way of illustration.   From this point of view the argument of Herskovits, that economists have neglected the psychological factor in assessing the determinants of value,[2] is a misunderstanding. The " psychological factor " is introduced much farther back,

---

problems involved in central planning and restriction of freedom of individual choice in a socialist State.   And this also, combined with the difficulties attending a programme of investment in technically under-developed countries, may lead to more intensive theoretical investigation of peasant economic systems, including moneyless ones.

[1] Radhakamal Mukerjee, *Principles of Comparative Economics*, London, 1922, vol. II, p. 86.   Cf. also: Raymond Firth, *Primitive Economics of the New Zealand Maori*, London, 1929, pp. 2–4; *idem, Primitive Polynesian Economy*, London, 1940, pp. 23–8.   Cf. Max Weber, *Theory of Social and Economic Organization* (trans. by H. L. Henderson and Talcott Parsons), Edinburgh, 1947, p. 192.

[2] M. J. Herskovits, *Economic Life of Primitive Peoples*, New York, 1940, p. 210 (somewhat modified in his *Economic Anthropology*, 1952).

in the assumptions of demand and choice as such. To investigate the psychological and social determinants of particular evaluations, to chart the value system of a society empirically, are important tasks. But they cannot be imposed on the theoretical economist in a concrete way. When, however, economic theory moves from the realm of pure abstraction to analysis and description of the behaviour of people in any specific society, then additional assumptions must be inserted into the argument. The objection that can be legitimately raised against some aspects of economic analysis is that such assumptions, which should be explicit and based upon empirical study, are often only half-explored and based upon some vague general notions of what is the local norm of behaviour.

In ordinary economic analysis the " impersonal system of markets and prices " serves as a medium by which allocation of resources among different possible uses is arranged, through the competition of users, expressed in monetary terms. The system is recognized to be in fact not one of really free movement. Competition is imperfect; combinations of producers, of traders, restrict fluctuations in commodity prices, and trade unions restrict wage rates. A theory of imperfect competition may take such " frictions " into account in a highly abstract way. But something more is needed if the economic system described is to be part of the real world. Whenever an attempt is made to assess magnitudes, whether in the expenditure patterns of people with small incomes, in the relations of co-operation and rivalry of capital and labour, in the decisions of the directors of a joint-stock company, in the whole sphere of incentives to production, assumptions have got to be made. These need the empirical data which the sociologist and historian should help to supply. Such data provide a basis for assumption as to what people will really do in response to changes in their economic conditions, and, in particular, by how much their behaviour will be likely to vary. Highly technical devices, such as indifference curves, are claimed to rule out the psychological elements of utility or satisfaction from the exercise of preferences. But they have to rely ultimately on some observational foundation—if they are to be anything more than logical manipulations. For the economic propositions derived from them to be capable of reference to reality it is necessary to assume, as Hicks points out, that there are no " kinks " in the curves or that the kinks can be ignored. This means an assumption that there is enough regularity in the system of wants and in the productive system for inferences about possible equilibrium to be made. Just as the older economists based their principle of diminishing marginal utility on some appeal to everyday experience, so also Hicks, after pointing out that this assumption about regularity is the simplest possible, says, " In fact, its accordance with experience seems definitely good." [1] But how does one arrive at the idea that it is good or correct to assume a regularity in the system of wants? Only ultimately from some observation of the behaviour of people.

The implications of this for economic anthropology are clear. Part of the task of the anthropologist is to assist in translating general propositions of economic theory into terms that will apply to the particular types of society in which he is interested, and which do not ordinarily come under the economist's observation. To do this he must expose the social factors which are of most relevance in the preference scales of the members of the society. He must make clear— ultimately, if possible, by quantitative demonstration—the regularities and irregularities in the system of wants. If in a primitive community a fishing-canoe is an important item of wealth, ranking high in the scale of exchange values, then the anthropologist must make clear just what is the position when such a canoe is destroyed on the death of a close agnatic kinsman. He must indicate that this competing use for an item of capital has very definite restrictions placed upon it by social convention. It is not simply a sporadic, incalculable individual act. There is predictable regularity in the complex adjustments concerned with breaking up the craft or saving it from destruction.

In essence, then, the anthropologist accepts as valid the body of economic doctrine. Ordinarily he can absorb only

[1] J. R. Hicks, *Value and Capital*, Oxford, 1939, pp. 24 *et passim*.

a very small part of it into his conceptual apparatus for the study of primitive society. But he attempts to push it farther into the empirical field by securing evidence to give content to economic propositions in social situations where the economist's assumptions about human behaviour must be reformulated. It cannot be said that the results are yet very satisfactory. One reason for this is undoubtedly a lack of clear ideas or formulation by many anthropologists as to the nature of economic data.

Most social relations have an economic aspect. The exercise of choice in social situations involves economy of resources in time and in energy. In this sense a marriage has an economic aspect in all the decisions and relations of daily life, even in sex congress, quite apart from the exchanges of goods and services that may go on. But by a convention the science of economics concerns itself with those fields of choice which involve goods and services, and primarily those which have a price put upon them. In this sense relations between persons in virtue of their association in the production or exchange of these goods and services are " economic " relations. Anthropologists have frequently missed the point of such relations. We need demonstrate only briefly that economics is not technology. To read in the chapter entitled " Economic Life " in a well-known ethnographic monograph such statements as, " To relieve the itch, the juice of the *kabatiti* . . . is applied to the skin " or that " cracked feet are treated with carabao dung,"[1] reminds one how wrongly classified has been much of what is called economic treatment in most of the classical records of field research. Yet even in the examples mentioned a little interesting economic information might have been given about the amount of time and effort spent on collecting and applying the remedies; the frequency with which they were found to be used by the people; whether they were ever borrowed for a consideration; whether there were other remedies easier to come by, but not preferred. Failure to realize the nature of the problems has led to the omission of a whole range of data on output, on costs, on

[1] Fay-Cooper Cole, *The Tinguian*, Field Museum of Natural History, Publication 209, Anthropological Series XIV, No. 2, p. 410, Chicago, 1922.

incomes, on circulation of valuables, and other economic aspects which could have given form and precision to a dreary collection of facts. The castigation which Robbins gave to Alfred Marshall's "spineless platitudes about manures" would clearly be even more merited if applied to some anthropologists who have written under the heading of Economics. Apart from this, there is still a tendency among modern anthropologists to frame their definitions of economics in terms of goods, or material goods, to the exclusion of services. Yet the anthropologist, above all, is in a position to appreciate Frank H. Knight's dictum that the economic magnitude is not goods, but service. A tendency to neglect the basic factor of choice in the allocation of resources betrays an equal unfamiliarity with guiding ideas of the economic discipline.

If, then, economics deals with the principles of the use of resources in general, economic anthropology deals with concomitant social relations, the specific ways in which the principles are exemplified in a range of given social situations. Economic anthropology is an empirical study, and a comparative one. But what social situations are its subject-matter? The definition obtained on this question is no more precise than that of the scope of social anthropology—that on the whole it is the more primitive societies that are the proper study.[1] The first criterion, then, is an empirical one—simplicity of technology. A second criterion, also empirical, is to some extent related to the first, but arises in part from the abstentions of the economists themselves. The tendency of economics is to claim the complete realm of choice in the allocation of resources as their province, but in practice to restrict their analyses to price situations, where there is money measurement. Pigou, for instance, after correcting Marshall to include the operations of a barter economy in the subject-matter of economics, in fact pays little attention to such operations in his analyses. The reason is

[1] Radcliffe-Brown gives different delimitations. In the article on social structure (*op. cit.*) social anthropology is the study of human society, equivalent to comparative sociology. In a comment on Leslie White's views (*American Anthropologist*, 1949, vol. 51, p. 563) he describes the science as the study of primitive or preliterate societies.

that the technical difference is regarded as embodying also a conceptual difference. Further, an evaluation containing moral and possibly æsthetic elements gives approval to the efficiencies provided by a monetary system.[1] Such an evaluative approach to the existence of money as an effective calculating medium of exchange draws strength in contemporary conditions from the conviction of many economists that the price mechanism is a necessary instrument in the economic system of any developed community, and that planning of the major structure of the economy by the State, if ever it can be effective, must employ such an instrument. The close connection of the political and economic arguments means that statements about a moneyless economy by those who are not anthropologists have usually to be read in a special context. We read that co-operation and exchange cannot function effectively without a money system. We are also told that a moneyless economy, which could not orient its production on the basis of profitability, would have to make its decisions as to what and how much should be produced either according to tradition or to arbitrary dictatorial regulation.[2] But we need not make immediate protest. If it were a primitive economy that was under discussion, an anthropologist would have to make two points. First, the concept of what is effective functioning of an exchange and co-operative system depends on what criteria are applied. For many primitive societies, taking the small magnitude of the society and the ends of the people into consideration, a claim

---

[1] Pigou heads a chapter " The Need for Money in Voluntary Private Dealings," Pigou, *Economics of Stationary States*, 1935. Cf. J. E. Meade : " There can be no doubt that money and the pricing system are among the greatest social inventions of mankind. Properly used, they should be capable of giving to each individual a general command over his *fair* share of the community's resources ; of allowing each individual to decide for himself—where private choice is *appropriate*—in what form he will exercise this command ; of allowing initiative to individual producers and merchants to produce what is most wanted, in the most economical manner, in the markets where supplies are most needed ; in short, of combining *freedom, efficiency* and *equity* in social affairs."—" Planning without Prices," *Economica*, new series XV, Feb., 1948, p. 34 (my italics).

[2] Pigou, *op. cit.*, pp. 33, 70. Max Weber, *op. cit.*, 1947, pp. 166, 190 ; and discussion by Edward Shils, *Economica*, new series XV, 1948, pp. 36–50.

Peasant Marketing in Malaya

(*Above*) Petty dealers in fish at Kuala Besut, Trengganu, count the results of a purchase. They combine their small capital, they buy and divide small parcels of fish, with which they jog-trot inland to sell retail in the villages at a few cents profit.

(*Below*) A seller of areca nut (for betel chewing) concludes a deal.

(*Right*) A Malay woman
of Trengganu sells sweet
potatoes, peppers and
spices.

(*Below*) A Yoruba woman
of Ijebu, Nigeria, sells fish,
live snails, cassava, spices
in a similar role.

for effectiveness might well be made. Secondly, granting the difficulties of measuring efficiencies in a non-monetary economy, goods and services are in fact measured against one another, and there is no evidence that efficiency declines without effective check. The problem of decision as to how much shall be produced in a primitive economy is decided in terms of at least four considerations. Dictation by individual leaders does occur, though usually in a modified form of a decision which is basically representative of group interests—as that a feast of a certain magnitude shall be held, and food accumulated accordingly. Again, traditional norms help to decide the level of production—expressed in the form of immediate conventions of day-to-day work. Apart from these two elements, mentioned by Max Weber, a non-monetary economy does provide for a great deal of direct matching of goods and services, in which ideas of comparative worth of time, labour, and other components of preference scales operate. Finally, the concept of technical efficiency in an economic situation is partially replaced by that of social efficiency. The lack of a money index in the comparative rating of goods and services means imprecision. But it does not imply either the lack of rational calculation or an unregulated system of handling expenditure of resources.

Exposition of this last point can best be done by examining more deeply some of the general characteristics of the simpler economic systems, especially by contrast with a highly differentiated industrial system. It should first be made clear that just as the term "preliterate" has little value as an empirical defining character in contemporary conditions, where some system of primary education is creeping into all remote communities, so also the term "non-monetary" is for the most part a conceptual and not empirical criterion for distinguishing economic systems. In the whole Pacific region, for instance, only a few isolated communities on islands such as Tikopia, and in the heart of New Guinea, are entirely without money of a Western type. When the economist talks, then, of the "natural economy" of primitive communities—that is, the obtaining or exchanging of goods and services without using money in the transactions—this is

K

to be regarded as a label—not to the anthropologist an attractive one—for a section of an economic system. Like the term "subsistence economy", it describes an emphasis, a conceptual category, not an economic totality. (It should be clear from earlier analysis that the term "natural" cannot be held to imply an economy springing direct from the uninhibited wants of the primitive individual. These wants are highly socialized, and the exchange system operates in a set of social conventions, often employing also symbolic media.) But where there is a monetary medium facilitating exchanges and serving as a measure of economic activity, the system of transactions in which this medium is used is apt to be restricted. Many exchanges of goods and services take place which fall outside the monetary sphere and yet must be reckoned as an integral part of the economic system. The price system which does exist in such conditions may be, as Weber argues, of a highly traditionalized type, with relative inflexibility in rates over long periods, and considerable resistance on the part of producers and consumers to variation in these rates. This is not always the case. There may be a distinct contrast between the traditional rates for some types of service and the highly flexible rates for others. In the Malay peasant economy, side by side with firmly established conventions of paying harvesters of the rice crop a tenth of what they gather, irrespective of the current price of rice, and of making conventional money gifts at feasts (see p. 194), there is a most sensitive bargaining system in the buying and selling of fish, with prices varying from site to site and hour to hour. Fluctuations in supplies and requirements, and in the expectations of profit, are geared into a mechanism of almost "pure" market relationships. In such peasant conditions the manifestations of a price economy and a "natural" economy can occur side by side. But more important is that economic behaviour in many types of relation, as, for instance, attitudes towards saving or lending, can be equated as between price and non-price systems. Such behaviour is a function of the social structure, with its emphasis on the village community and the kinship group.

A summary of the principal features of the economy of

such peasant systems, whether monetary or non-monetary, outside the immediate Western orbit, would be as follows:

The relative simplicity of technology, with little use of machinery, means the lack of a high degree of economic specialization. With it goes also the lack of allocation of resources to technical development as such. The economic mechanism is not highly sensitive to the possibility of technical change, and such change is slight and slow.

The actual productive unit is small. Even in a large community such as an African or Malay state, where the network of producers may be wide, their combinations at one time and place as units of differentiated function are of limited scale.

There is no constantly expanding market for capital, ever seeking fresh avenues of investment, though capital goods exist, and there are effective notions of their use and maintenance.

Correspondingly, there is no widespread entrepreneur system ever seeking to create new demands. Entrepreneurs usually play some part in the organization of goods and services, but they normally plan to fulfil traditional wants, and they are not restricted to this occupation.

The system of control of capital goods follows different conventions from those with which we are familiar in a Western economic system. The social limits to accumulation differ, by providing more specific and more regular institutionalized avenues for disbursement, as by a feast; or by prohibiting certain kinds of increment—as Muslims are forbidden to take interest from their fellows. Traditional means of levelling out or mitigating inequalities in the possession of capital exist, as by enforced lending on request—with the sanction of public disapproval on refusal—or by the recognition of communal rights which are basic to the whole social order.

In terms of personnel, the agents of production are often not clearly separable in practice. Instead of the separation familiar in the scheme of a capitalist economy—of entrepreneur, workmen, organizing manager, capitalist—the provider of the major capital is commonly a manual worker himself. Other workers may put up some of the capital, directly or indirectly, severally or jointly, as by contributing food to the undertaking.   This makes for a different scheme of economic relationships.   It tends to obviate friction between the parties. It also allows for different expectations as to the outcome if change in circumstances should affect the rewards of production.

Partly as a result of this, the organization of production tends to be based not merely on a system of cash rewards, where money is used in exchange.   Wage relations as such may not exist.   The workers may get their return by simple profit-sharing, and may be drawn to contribute their services by a range of incentives, including kinship, or ties of loyalty to a chief.   The ties between producers tend to reach out beyond their common interest in the act of production and its rewards alone.   A production relationship is often only one facet of a social relationship.

Emerging from this, the system of distribution of the results of production tends to be a complex one, and not easily separated into a classical economist's scheme of rent, interest, wages, profits—granted that this formal division is now breaking down in modern economic analysis.

The peasant system may be much simpler, as, for instance, by rewarding all the agents of production together at a common meal or feast.   Or it may be much more complex, and assign to each a reward which is calculated in accordance with his social contribution rather than his economic contribution.   For example, take the building of a house in the simple community of Tikopia.   The workers comprise a few skilled craftsmen and a number of ordinary assistants. The former get special payment in bark-cloth, mats, and other valuables in recognition of their skill, though not directly proportioned to the relative amounts of time they have put in.   The assistants get their payment at a common meal which they share with the skilled builders.   Any man who comes along gets his share of the meal, no matter how little work he may have done.   As a special section of producers, come the husbands of the sisters and daughters of the men for whom the house is being built.   They each bring to the work a bundle of firewood and some coconuts or other raw food. This is their contribution to the meal, in virtue of their marriage obligations, which extend to attendance in a similar capacity at all social events of the group into which they have married. They have also to act as cooks for the occasion (cf. also p. 59). In their turn, they also receive as reward a portion of the cooked food in due course, and possibly other goods too.

The principle recognized by the economist, of reward proportioned to total productivity, is not easy to recognize here. Such a principle does exist in this type of system. But its operation is conditioned by other factors—social factors. In such circumstances economic relations can be understood only as part of a scheme of social relations. What I have said about the peasant society studied by the anthropologist is very much what the historian has described in other language for the economic life of the Middle Ages. One can translate this into various propositions. One may say that in such a peasant economy economic ties are personalized—that is, relationships as economic agents depend on the social status and relationships of the persons concerned. Put another way, labour is given as a social service, and not simply an economic service. Its reward is therefore apt to be calculated in terms of the total social situation, and not merely the immediate economic situation. Economic means tend to be translated into social ends.

Contrast this with economic relations in an industrial system. In the latter the individual has normally a high degree of anonymity, of impersonality in the economic situation. Even if he is not merely a number on a pay-roll, it is his function as an energy factor, a provider of capital, or of organizing capacity that is of prime importance. As such it is his specific industrial characteristics, not his total social characteristics, that matter. He is deemed to be replaceable. It is the magnitude and quality of his contribution to the economic process, irrespective of his personal status or position in the society, that defines him. In primitive communities the individual as an economic factor is personalized, not anonymous. He tends to hold his economic position in virtue of his social position. Hence, to displace him economically means a social disturbance.

Another general characteristic, linked with this, is the overt entry of group elements into individual choice. In a Western economic system the role of an individual may be affected by his group position. A worker's choice of employment is guided by his wife's attitude to the conditions of his work, its cleanliness, occupational risks, or security His choice of whether to work or stay at home if he is ill is governed largely by the family reaction to his condition. But in a large range of decisions in economic aspects of his behaviour a person is guided by the immediate advantage to himself. His choice is made in consultation with others concerned directly in the economic process, but not with those external to it. But in a primitive system personal choice operates more overtly in a social, not merely economic, *milieu*. In the smaller scale communities it may be even difficult to find outsiders; all the members are involved, in one way or another, in an economic situation, as co-holders of resources, co-producers, or co-sharers in the rewards of production through various social channels.

The contrast can be seen still further in the relations between economic and moral standards. In our modern Western society they often clash or their inconsistencies are unresolved. "Business is business" and "love thy neighbour" are normally parallel lines which never attempt to meet, and the State or voluntary organizations have to bridge the gap. In a peasant society business is often keen enough. But since the relationship is often more than a purely economic one, provision for moral obligations can be made within the economic framework itself, which is integrated with the social framework. Hence what appears to be a paradox—that in an African or Oriental peasant economy there may be no unemployment problem, no radical class struggle, no gap between the hungry and the well-fed.

It is important, then, in economic anthropology to examine the economic role of a person in a particular situation against his social role, and against that of the system of groups of which he is a member. Economic anthropology deals primarily with the economic aspects of the social relations of persons. The factors in economic process are considered not as abstract entities, as units of labour or capital or purchasing power, but as social entities, in terms of the relations of persons controlling or using these units. The economic anthropologist has a dual role : to analyse and classify the processes of combining goods and services in circumstances where money does not enter largely into the combination system; and to examine the way in which the necessary relations involved in such handling of goods and services affect the system of social relations. As an adjunct to this the anthropologist can help to provide for the proper social contextualization of economic propositions.

One can see that the generalizations offered here are very far from the kind of proposition which the economist is apt to use when he talks of primitive economic systems. Quite a lot of economic theory is still in the " nuts-and-apples " stage when it comes to assumptions about a non-monetary economy. In line with this is the treatment of " Crusoe economics." Crusoe is taken as the illustration of the isolated economic man. But the modern economist is often more profoundly read in Lewis Carroll than in Daniel Defoe. " Alice " he quotes to some purpose. But he often seems curiously unaware that Robinson Crusoe is less remarkable for his economy of isolation than for his adventures into trade and colonization. And when Robinson's economic ventures came to nought it was mainly—as he says himself—because of his failure to take into account his own human frailty and the complexity of other men's motives! It is true that Robinson Crusoe and the Marshallian savage are only expository devices. They are not intended to mirror real life. But they carry with them some of the implications of crudity which the Westerner is only too prone to attribute to his primitive contemporary. If the economist does not distort the ethnographic image, he does at times seem to behave as if there were no reality to furnish one.

Much of my argument so far has been necessarily abstract. It can now be taken up more concretely. One of the central themes in understanding an economic system is the nature of the incentives which move people to action. A brief consideration here of incentives in the use of labour and in the use of capital in some primitive and peasant economic systems will show how many economic incentives are culturally defined and often of a symbolic character.

To the economist of a quarter of a century ago the nature of incentive in industry was not unimportant, but it was treated as being outside his immediate concern. He did not necessarily assume that the only incentive that mattered was money. But he did assume that the main element that mattered for his purposes was money, partly because it was the easiest to measure. In more recent years problems of incentive occupy a prominent place in discussions of output, by business men and economists alike.[1] There is much difference of view as to how far in modern industry the level of output of wage labourers is dependent on the relative weight of such factors as the amount of the money wage, the amount and nature of outlets for spending, the amenities of the work, or the compatible character of managing and employing agencies. One point of view is that the size of the wage-packet remains the most important factor still in the incentive to work. A more sophisticated opinion stresses not the amount of the money wage, but the availability of the consumption goods to be bought by it. Here the wants of a man's wife and

[1] See: Lionel Robbins, " The propositions of the Theory of Variation [i.e., Laws of Supply and Demand] do not in the least involve the assumption that men are actuated *only* by considerations of money gains and losses. They involve only the assumption that money plays *some* part in the valuation of the given alternatives. . . . Money may not be regarded as playing a predominant part in the situation contemplated. So long as it plays some part then the propositions are applicable."—*Nature and Significance of Economic Science*, London, 1932, p. 90.
    Cf. S. Moos, " Laissez-faire Planning and Ethics," *The Economic Journal*, vol. LV, 1945, pp. 17–27. " One of the foremost tasks facing the economist today is an investigation into the problem of incentives," etc. Sir Sydney Chapman, " The Profit Motive and the Economic Incentive," ibid., vol. LVI, 1946, pp. 51–56 : " The mistake of identifying monetary actuation with personal initiative lies at the root of the error I have been trying to expose. Initiative . . . in the social system (it) is the motive force. The one-sided ' economic incentive' theory was sometimes advanced to account for its operation in business matters. But nobody who had pondered over the matter could suppose for a moment that the thought of what paid one best was the primary fact and strenuous application merely the product or an expression of it " (p. 54).

family are held to be an important determinant. Again, it is argued that at present levels of prices the ordinary working man is not much interested in further increments to total money wages. What he wants, it is said, is a weekly income of a certain definite size to meet his usual requirements, and he is not willing to work to get more. In effect, these latter views tend to minimize the importance of the opportunities for saving as incentives in modern conditions. Some empirical research has been carried out to try to determine the relative importance of these and other propositions. But the results so far seem to be applicable to particular rather than to general industrial conditions. An example of interest in this connection is an inquiry into restriction of output in an American factory, conducted by a group of anthropologists who worked there for many months as "participant observers." Their general conclusion was that output restriction has been looked upon hitherto far too much as a technical and economic problem to be solved by devices such as production control and incentive pay. But basic to the whole problem of output in that factory was the idea of the workers about the differences between their goals and those of the management, and the conviction of the importance of group loyalty within the workers' organization. The problem seemed, then, to be one primarily of social relations, not economic relations.[1] Such results may do little more than confirm existing impressions. But they reinforce the need to give some assessment of this sociological element among the factors composing entrepreneurial costs and expectations.

For the peasant and primitive economic systems which he has studied the anthropologist has accumulated a great deal of qualitative data on labour incentives in production. With the possibilities of money measurement largely absent, he has had to concentrate on the more direct objectives of work. He has shown how the individual's work in such conditions is

[1] O. Collins, M. Dalton and D. Roy, " Restriction of Output and Social Cleavage in Industry," *Applied Anthropology*, Summer, 1946, vol. 5, No. 3, pp. 1-14. Some observations on incentive in production are to be found in: Raymond Firth, " Anthropological Background to Work," *Occupational Psychology*, London, 1948, vol. XXII, pp. 94-102. (A).

motivated by his conceptions of the wants of his family, of his obligations to his kinsfolk and the community in which he lives, of the chances of gaining prestige in socially prescribed and valued ways, of the dictates of a magical and religious system.   Even where monetary rewards for labour are largely current, he has noted that work may be undertaken for other than money symbols.   For instance, to revert to the Irish peasantry referred to in the first chapter—there is a form of non-monetary co-operation known as *coor*, in tasks such as mowing, turf-cutting, or potato-planting.   No wage payment or other cash equivalent is involved.   The help is given as part of the reciprocities of kinship relations—to a second cousin, an uncle, or other member of an extended kin group.   The expression in English is that So-and-So " has a right to help," meaning that he has an obligation to do so.   In an industrial community such rights are not likely to be of great importance in the scheme of production relations.   But in a peasant community they may account for a substantial part of the agricultural services.   In the olden days in Ireland a working team of wider scope, called *meithal*, was drawn from the community in the same way to mow and harvest for the village priest or for an old couple without children ; or to re-settle an evicted family.   Here, too, the contribution was given by each person as a social service, without reciprocity being sought.   As with the *coor*, the incentive was of a social, even of a moral, kind, and the material element did not overtly appear.

The principle is not precisely that of the old slogan, " From each according to his ability, to each according to his needs." It is crossed by another, " From each according to his status obligations in the social system, to each according to his rights in that system."   Putting it another way, powerful incentives to work lie in the individual's membership of a social group. He dare not relax lest he lose many of the benefits of membership.   In distribution, the apportionment of the rewards for work, short-term effects can be distinguished from long-term effects.   In the short run it is the impact of the social obligation that is most marked, the frequent rendering of the service without apparent equivalent return.   In the long run contributions and rewards may be assumed to even out. The system operates because, in addition to the immediate social satisfactions gained, some material reward is often eventually obtained. Concretely, the work which A does for B as a social obligation is paid back in the long run by gifts which C makes to D. Here B may be the father-in-law of A, D the son of A, and C the brother of B. Or B and C may be the brothers-in-law of A, and D the son of A. The recognition of the long-term trend towards equivalence of service is one of the most important incentives to work in a primitive or peasant society.[1] In societies with strongly demarcated kin groups, such as exist in most of the primitive field, one may speak figuratively of vertical, lateral, and diagonal service relations. In a system with patrilineal lineages, for example, there are vertical service relations between father and son and between other people of different kinship grades in the same group. Lateral service relations occur between people of the same kinship grade, in the same group, as brothers: or in different groups, as brothers-in-law. Diagonal service relations occur between people of different kinship grades in different groups, as between mother's brother and sister's child. The combination of such service relations is one of the most important networks in the economic organization of such a type of community. It represents one of the exemplifications of the principle of basic compensation which is a fundamental aspect of social organization.

This brings out also the importance of the moral imperative of much economic activity. Behind a person's work, mirroring the allocations of his labour, are obligations bearing as it were a moral electric charge. Positively and negatively, his conduct is regulated by the right and wrong of giving and of receiving, of paying a material equivalent for one type of service and a verbal equivalent for another type, of using one kind of object for food and of avoiding the use of another superficially as good. Even in our own Western society there are strong conventions as to the propriety, amounting

[1] Some of the effects of this were worked out well by B. Malinowski in his *Argonauts of the Western Pacific*, London, 1922 ; and *Crime and Custom in Savage Society*, London, 1926.

to the morality, of work and the return that should be made for it. Work in itself in general is regarded as good, and idleness as morally wrong. Most people have definite ethical views about others giving " a fair day's work " for the pay received. With the fixing of hours of work in many occupations has grown up the idea that " overtime " is a concession, and that it is a matter of right, not merely economic demand, that entitles a person to get pay at more than average rates. And many religious people, while supporting the morality of work in general, regard it as immoral to do work on the Sabbath—though they are not all agreed as to what activity comes under that category. There is also the convention that certain kinds of work, known as " personal service," demand a special acknowledgement over and above ordinary wage-return. Most people seem to give tips not because they expect better service or because they themselves think it morally right, but out of deference to the moral views of others, including the recipients. Examination of industrial disputes would probably show that moral indignation plays a considerable and very real part in exacerbating the issues between the parties, and that concepts of moral justice rank side by side with economic pressures and legal requirements in effecting a settlement. Far more than we ordinarily suppose, economic relations rest upon moral foundations. If it were not so, Communism in the industrial field would be without one of its most powerful weapons. In a primitive society the moral design is very different from that in a Western society, and the pattern of economic relations is therefore supported at different points.

One of the points of difference is the use made of status concepts. In the West we have learnt from Veblen and from the behaviour of industrial magnates the role of " conspicuous consumption " as a motivating force in economics. This is one of the facets of status acquisition. In a Western society the process is comparatively unsystematized. Lavish entertainment and public gifts may lead a man to honours. But they are not recognized as constituting a ladder in themselves, giving their own title to the donor. In primitive and peasant societies there is much variation of practice. But the tendency is for feasts and other forms of large-scale consumption and display to be schematized, set in a series each with its own name, and each giving in succession a right to the feast-holder to take a specific title of honour, to wear certain reserved ornaments, to build a more lofty house than his fellows have, or to exercise other privileges. The *potlatch* of the Haida, Tlinkit, and other Indians of the American North-West coast; the Feasts of Merit of the Chins of Burma; the *Pai* of the Chinese Shans; the *anga* of the Tikopia; the *gawai* of the Borneo Dyak are all examples of the allocation of large-scale resources in goods and labour with primary reference to status yields. This involves not merely the use of surpluses above daily requirements. It involves the creation of surpluses for the purpose, the orientation of the energies and wealth of the feast-holder and his community for months or even years in advance. Such a system is bound in with the obligation system discussed earlier, of kinship and other bonds, which are given economic expression in the preparations for these feasts. But the status incentive is of much wider application. Some of these large-scale consumption occasions confer no particular title or insignia on the donors. But these feasts are a means of heightening their prestige among their neighbours, or at least of maintaining their status by rendering an equivalent for past services. Moreover, in the general conduct of affairs, in the everyday handling of resources and the application of labour to enterprises, maintenance of status in the eyes of others is important.

It is this which explains the great measure of conformity to obligation which occurs. It can be argued that in a small-scale personalized economy such as we have been discussing there are many opportunities of shirking work. The kinship system and other structural arrangements will ensure that no man starves. Is it not true that a sense of insecurity is a necessary drive to induce a man to work and give of his best? But in such an economy it is taken for granted that most people will fulfil their obligations. This normal expectation is based largely upon the status factor. If a man does not do his share of work, and especially the tasks which fall to him individually because of his kinship and other social obligations, then his reputation suffers. Apart from direct stimulus by taunts and jeers, a lowered prestige in the eyes of others is apt to wound his pride. And desire for prestige in the positive sense may well lead a man to proceed to excess in fulfilment of his obligations. (Stakhanovite methods in the Soviet economy have utilized this principle.)

The material incentive must be considered in conjunction with other criteria. The Bemba of Northern Rhodesia have not been very keen cultivators in the past. This has been due in part to the lack of a tradition of good gardening, a lack of good leadership, and a lack of workmates owing to the absence of many young men at the mines. Poor nutrition is perhaps also partly responsible. The practice among these people is that agricultural work for someone else gives a legitimate claim to food. But distinctions are made on the basis of nearness of kinship. A close kinsman will continue to be fed even though he be a wastrel and do practically no work at all. A young son-in-law risks not only his meals but even his bride if he should turn out to be incorrigibly lazy. A distant kinsman has service and material reward equated as closely as possible; he has to earn his food by his work to such a degree that the line between a co-operating kinsman and a temporary labourer is a fine one.[1]

The interweaving of incentives can be seen in a case where money is largely used in the economy as a reward for work. In one Canadian Indian community it was noted that the incentives to work included prominently a recognition of the need to settle one's debts in order to be able to get supplies to go trapping with in the following autumn; the desire to provide for one's family; the unwillingness to excite community disapproval by neglect of family obligations. All these could be expressed in ordinary monetary terms through the money earned. On the other hand, the prestige element operated in the exhibition of a fear of failure and the shame attendant on it. If the chances of success were very dubious, then this tended to result in a slackening off of work and exaggeration

[1] A. I. Richards, *Land, Labour and Diet in Northern Rhodesia*, Oxford, 1939, p. 143.

of the risk factor to a degree almost irrespective of the rate of return. The tendency for the Indian was then to select work which promised a ready success, which was likely to evoke favourable public opinion, and which was in general significant to his immediate value scheme. The Indian was correspondingly unwilling to work for the Hudson Bay Company, since not only did he judge the wage rates to be too low, but the work tended to lack meaning in his scheme of values. It included in particular a concentration on routine and a conflict with his leisure season which did not fit his other social and economic patterns.[1]

In discussing economic incentive the anthropologist is sometimes tempted to deny the value of material inducements and to stress to the exclusion of them the non-material factors. This is a mistake. In many cases the incentive to work is primarily the desire to get food and shelter, granted that in every case the form that these things take is culturally defined. In other cases the incentives, whether status-seeking or other, are given expression in material terms. But when allowance is made for this, granted that there are prospects of equal return to courses *a* and *b*, why is course *a* consistently chosen rather than course *b*? And, granted that course *a* offers prospects of greater return than course *b*, why is course *b* nevertheless consistently chosen? At this stage of the study the answer can be given only in reference to social and moral standards lying behind particular economic systems. Some indication of it has been made already. The questions can be looked at further in reference to some aspects of the use of capital, in particular as regards the taking of interest.

Throughout most economic discussions it is implied that to obtain the use of capital some interest payments are necessary. It is also held that receipt of interest is morally justified. The basic point I wish to make is simply this. The ideas about capital and the way in which it should be used and rewarded are not merely economic concepts; they are also social concepts. They are not rooted in the nature of economic activity itself; they vary from one society to another.

[1] John J. Honigman, " Incentives to Work in a Canadian-Indian Community," *Human Organization*, 1949, vol. 8, No. 4, pp. 23–8.

First consider the concept of interest as such. Just as
Marxism revolts against capitalism in general, so mediæval
Christendom and Islam revolted against interest specifically.
But the West, forced by the expansion of its economic programme, has come to justify the taking of interest, and, in fact,
always did distinguish in practice between common usury and
the results of an apparently productive investment of capital.
Islam, on the other hand, still carries the moral law overtly
through into the commercial sphere. The fulminations of the
Koran against " the devourer of usury " are regarded in many
Muslim circles as being as valid today as they were 1300 years
ago. The word used in the Koran for interest or usury is
riba, meaning increase in anything, or addition—that is, the
additional amount which a debtor pays to a creditor in consideration of time to use the money. According to Moslem
jurists, *riba* is the extortion of wealth without legal or lawful
consideration. And the taker of *riba*, its giver, the scribe of
the deed, and the witnesses to it have been pronounced by
the Prophet to be alike cursed in their sin.

What, then, are the arguments for this forbidding of interest.
Islam does not forbid the giving of credit in general. The
essence of its objection to the taking of interest is that the
creditor receives an increment on his loan and that this increment is a fixed periodic sum. If, on the other hand, one puts
one's money into a business as a partner and takes a profit by
sharing in the risks of the undertaking, this is legitimate; the
increment on one's money is uncertain. One may get no
increment, and indeed may lose one's capital invested. As
Imam Razi, a well-known Muslim scholar, writes: " The
creditor's deriving a profit from every investment in business
is uncertain, whereas this ' additional amount ' from the debtor
to the creditor is certain." [1]

Now, these words of the Egyptian scholar are almost
identical with those used to me by a Malay fisherman, and
those of R. H. Tawney in speaking of the mediæval prohibition on pure interest. The Malay fisherman argued that if
one lends money on a boat and takes half the weekly earnings

[1] Quoted from Imam Razi, *Tafsir Kabir* (Cairo, vol. II, p. 58), by A. I.
Qureshi, *Islam and the Rate of Interest*, Lahore, 1945, p. 52.

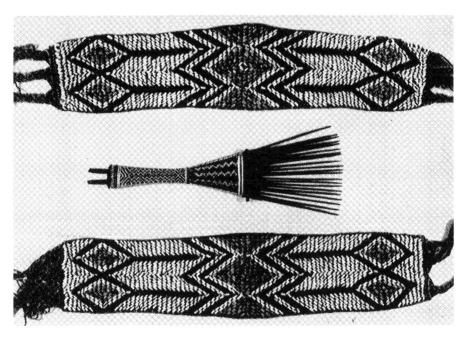

PRIMITIVE VALUABLES

Shell bead anklets and a rattan plaited comb from Malaita, Solomon
Islands.

PATTERN ON PENDANTS

Pubic ornament of pearl-shell from Western Australia (p. 177), with
meander design; and breast pendant of clam-shell with turtle-shell fret-
work, from Santa Cruz, Solomon Islands.

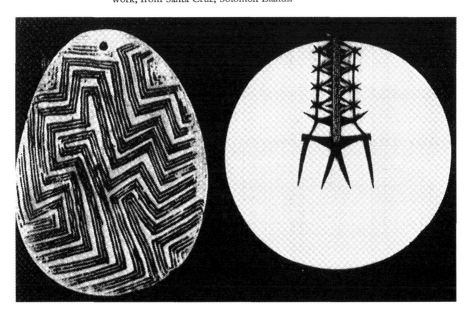

"Protection against Sorcerers"

Two views of a wooden figure, 4 ft. high, brought from Fumban, French Cameroons, by the Mission Labouret in 1934. The scanty information given in the title is all that is recorded about this figure, which may well have had a ritual function.

of the boat in return (quite apart from principal) this is not a "tax on money" or "the child of money" (i.e., interest), "because it is uncertain." One week the provider of capital may get a good increment on his loan, the next week he may get nothing. To the Malays, then, the process is one of profit-sharing and not of interest-taking. Now compare Professor Tawney. "The essence of usury was that it was certain, and that whether the borrower gained or lost, the usurer took his pound of flesh. Mediæval opinion, which has no objection to rent or profits provided that they are reasonable . . . has no mercy for the debenture holder. His crime is that he takes a payment for money which is fixed and certain and such a payment is usury."[1]

The coincidence, of course, is not fortuitous. The Egyptian jurist and the Malay fisherman approach the subject of economics from opposite angles, but they both share a simple faith in the rightness of the Koran. The mediæval churchmen built on different religious foundations. But the same basic social and economic conditions apply in both cases. Both societies have an essentially peasant basis to their social structure, and trade rather than industry as their major outlet for economic enterprise. What Tawney says of the mediæval West, "That the doctrine of interest received its character in an age in which most loans were not part of a credit system but an exceptional expedient, and in which it could be said that he who borrows is always under stress of necessity," would seem to apply largely to the contemporary East as well. The prohibition of interest, then, is not just the result of an arbitrary moral attitude about the use of money. It is linked with a type of society in which the use of money in certain ways is apt to result in clearly perceptible personal hardship, and in the drying up of that fount of compassion which should remain fresh in every human being.

In modern Islam, as in mediæval Christendom, these doc-

---

[1] R. H. Tawney, *Religion and the Rise of Capitalism*, London, 1926 (Pelican edn. 1938), II, chapter, i, "The Sin of Avarice." Cf. Max Weber, *The Protestant Ethic and the Spirit of Capitalism*, Eng. trans. by Talcott Parsons, London, 1930, p. 202. Raymond Firth, *Malay Fishermen: Their Peasant Economy*, London, 1946, pp. 169–76.

L

trines have not passed without either challenge or evasion.
The Christian story is well known. In Islam there are two
parallel movements, both responsive to the economic situation,
but in different ways. One is that of plain side-stepping of
the Prophet's injunctions. I knew of cases in Malaya where
lenders of money secretly stipulated and received a fixed
increment on their loan. Or in order to be able to defend it
before the courts, if necessary, they lent a smaller sum than
was written down for repayment on the document agreed to
by the borrower. The courts, which disallow any case brought
where there was a bargain for payment of interest, would
have no evidence that less than the agreed sum for repayment
had in fact been handed over. On the other hand, some
Muslim modernists argue for a more refined interpretation of
the Prophet's views. Some Muslims defend the taking of
interest and say that what the Prophet really disallowed was
" usury." This is combated by the more orthodox, who
argue that usury is commonly regarded as an exorbitant rate
of interest, but that ideas as to exorbitance vary greatly at
different times and there is no essential difference between the
two concepts. Another view is that simple interest is allowed,
but not compound interest. But this again is regarded by
most Muslim jurists as very specious. Many modern Muslims
of the educated class regard even ordinary interest on bank
deposits as illegitimate for them.[1] It has been said rather
ingeniously that although many of them do in fact accept the
addition of interest to their bank deposits, this is to be regarded
as " a personal weakness " analogous to that of not saying
one's prayers regularly at the prescribed times. A strictly
orthodox view of the role of banks in an Islamic State would
be that they can function provided that they pay no interest
to depositors and charge no interest to their clients—in other
words, they would treat all deposits as Western banks treat

[1] I am indebted to Mrs. Barbara Fisher for the information that in 1901,
the first year in which Savings Banks were opened in Egypt, of 4,197 total
Egyptian depositors, being largely Muslims, 390 Muslims refused interest on
their deposits (presumably on religious grounds). For the most part the
depositors were urban residents (and therefore likely to be more sophisticated than ordinary peasants). (From H.M. Agent and Consul-General's
Report, 1901, in *Accounts and Papers*, 1902, vol. CXXX.) (A).

current accounts, and depositors would use them for security, and not profit.

The prohibition on *riba* was also extended by the Prophet to such transactions of exchange whereby quantities of gold, silver, wheat, barley, dates, and salt are exchanged for more or less of the *same kind* of commodity. Trade in general is encouraged, but this prohibition puts a bar on concealed interest-taking and direct dealing in futures. But here again there is a difference of opinion among the learned men of Islam. Some wish to extend this prohibition in modern times to all commodities. Others, holding to the letter of the law, argue that one may not reason by analogy, and that it is only the six commodities specifically mentioned by the Prophet which are so affected.

A sophisticated view of the orthodox Muslim position in which many of the points just made are examined in detail has recently been put forward by an academic economist who has been economic adviser to the Government of the Nizam of Hyderabad.[1] His thesis is briefly that many of the ills of capitalist society are mainly due to interest and that Islam has made a contribution to the solution of world ills by the definite prohibition of interest. He quotes Western historical precedents in support of his contention. Aristotle's comparison of money to a barren hen which laid no eggs is cited; likewise the mediæval objections to interest. To him, as perhaps to others, the age of faith has given place to the age of science, but not necessarily to that of reason. He defends the position further by arguing somewhat ingenuously that Western economists are not agreed on the nature and theory of interest, that Keynes and others have regarded the rate of interest as a highly conventional phenomenon, and that the rate of interest in Western countries is progressively becoming lower. Hence it is theoretically possible and practically by no means out of the question that the minimal rate of interest may be a zero rate. His general conclusion is that that which Islam has forbidden on religious grounds should be abandoned on economic grounds. The certainty, regular accumulation, and lack of expenditure of effort characteristic of interest-taking

[1] Anwar Iqbal Qureshi, *Islam and the Rate of Interest*, Lahore, 1945.

militate socially and economically against it. To him, as to most Muslims, the proper method of using capital is the partnership system in which capital co-operates with labour, and gets a profit on the joint result. This profit should be allocated in an agreed proportion—one-third, one-quarter, etc. —of the joint product, and not as fixed percentage of the principal sum invested. This is the Muslim *mazarebat*, the profit-sharing enterprise.

Islam has thus not illegalized all transactions which produce income without labour. In fact, in addition to the profits of co-partnership, it allows rent from houses and agricultural land. What it objects to is a situation where only one party bears sacrifice or the risk, and the other remains immune, or practically so.

To a nineteenth-century audience such arguments would have sounded like the sheerest idealism, or a sentimental antiquarianism. Today perhaps we are not so sure. We do not accept the fiat of Mahomet as an argument for not charging interest. We accept the view that it may be necessary to give interest in order to obtain the use of capital. But we have seen that the rate of interest in itself is not necessarily a measure of the willingness of people to lend money, provided that the security is sound. And we can conceive of social circumstances in which loans can be made—or perhaps should be made—either at a rate so low as to be called uneconomic or even interest free. It would be difficult for a nation which has had the advantage of lend-lease from the United States during the war and of Marshall Aid after the war, to argue otherwise. And I think it is undoubted that the practice of making interest-free loans of smaller magnitude either as a general social gesture, or in order to assist economic recovery or expansion to the ultimate benefit of the lender, is a practice which has increased during the present century.

Our concern, however, is not with the possibilities of an interest-free economy as such. It is with the basis of choice in this type of economic action. What we have shown is that, faced by prospects of apparently equal return, the good Muslim prefers profit to interest, a share in the risks of an undertaking to a passive usury; moreover, he is prepared in some cases to forego return on his capital. No absence of monetary incentive is implied by this, but a positive desire for conformity to moral and religious ideals.

This bears on the problem of rationality in economic action. Rational behaviour involves the adaptation of means to a recognized goal as closely as possible in terms of the available knowledge. In the economic sphere in particular it has been interpreted, as by Max Weber, to mean the deliberate systematic adjustment of economic means to attain the objective of pecuniary profit. It will be clear from discussion earlier in this chapter that many of the economic actions of primitive peoples, including their feasts and other large-scale consumption efforts, appear to lack an immediate rationality. But they do in the long run meet the ends of material gain. Even where this is not so, rational conceptions have not been abandoned. Their scope has only been extended to embrace the social system, and not merely the economic system. The economic system has no intrinsic meaning for an individual. It derives its evaluations ultimately from his interpretation of social concepts. Situations continually tend to arise, then, in which some sacrifice of economic benefit is judged necessary to maintain or raise one's social status, or to help give reality to social ideals which one thinks are important. Economic activity is subordinate to social ends. It is only by studying those ends that one can see how particular economic systems work. Failure to do so may impair the effectiveness of many of the attempts now being made to stimulate the productive organization of primitive and peasant peoples by process of investment from the Western world.

In this field of problems the social framework may be conceived as a system of choices in situations where the emphasis is other than on the " prudent allocation of resources." This framework affects choices in the economic sphere in several ways. To some extent it limits the number of combinations of his resources open to any individual—social and moral values inhibit his range of action. On the other hand, by providing him with well-recognized norms of conduct it aids him in selection of fields for the use of his resources. Many of them, for instance, he puts into strengthening the position of his family. Moreover, it aids him to some degree in prediction. He knows in advance how the exercise of much economic choice by other people will be made, and this allows of easier planning of his own choices. Social codes give him clues to what other people will do. But what is particularly important is that the social framework confirms his choices, and gives them that basic meaning without which the economic process could not continue. The economist is apt to think of the social framework as consisting mainly of the controls exercised by law—e.g., in regard to the holding of property, in minimization of force or fraud. The anthropologist thinks of this framework as essentially one of values giving meaning to the economic system.

In succeeding chapters we shall examine more closely the nature of some of these values.

CHAPTER V

THE SOCIAL FRAMEWORK OF
PRIMITIVE ART

THE values of art are in strong contrast to those of economics. It is commonly held that economic activity is a necessity, but that art is a luxury. Yet we can assert empirically the universality of art in man's social history. Palæolithic man ten thousand years or more ago had his statuettes and his cave-paintings, of which some still preserved to us are of such æsthetic mastery and dynamic skill that they evoke the admiration of modern artists. Even in the hardest natural environments, art has been produced. The Bushmen of the Kalahari desert have had their drawings of animals and men, in an austere though vivid style. The Eskimo have their etchings on ivory of men hunting, dancing, drumming. The Australian aborigines have simple rock carvings and paintings of animals on rock walls, geometrical designs painted on bark or graven on shell, and a variety of elaborate patterns of ceremonial decoration with feathers and down and fur. It is easy, then, to refute the idea that at the primitive stages of man's existence the theme of subsistence dominated his life to the exclusion of the arts. But there is the question as to how far the arts are in fact regarded by the people who engage in them as a contribution to subsistence. How far does the evident preoccupation in art with the animals, birds, and other items of the natural environment suggest that primitive man is concerned with magical values, totemic values—to preserve his life in general, or to maintain it by giving aid to him in his control of nature in securing food? The problem may be put another way. How far do sculpture or painting of this kind mean the recognition of art as a separate category of ideas, or only as a department or even by-product of social or economic activity?

A work of art makes a selection of elements of experience, imagination, and emotion. It does so in such a way that its formal expression and arrangement call up in us special kinds of reaction, evaluations based on feeling tones which we call æsthetic. When a work of art is judged æsthetically—and it can be judged from economic, political, or religious points of view—it is considered primarily in relation to its formal qualities: its arrangement of lines, mass, colour, sound, rhythm.

No great amount of direct investigation has been made of the æsthetics of the non-European peoples who have conventionally been termed primitive. But there is strong indirect evidence that they share the same kind of æsthetic sensibilities and judgements as Western peoples. The effective colour contrast in designs on the plaited combs, shell-bead bracelets and anklets, or the pearl-shell inlaid bowls and canoe-prows of the Solomon Islands; the scroll-work and other curvilinear motifs on Maori rafters, canoe stern-posts, and gateways, or on Massim shields, lime spatulæ, and other woodcarving; the delicate contours of the bronze heads of Ife; the elaborate plane surfaces of many types of West African masks; the intricate patterns of African drum rhythms; the nuances in the verbal imagery of much Polynesian poetry, all indicate a sensitivity to æsthetic criteria. This view is reinforced by the fact that when we look at most series of such objects, all of the same kind, hardly any two are alike: there is some variation, however slight, in every one. They are not just copies from a central model, like some Bavarian or Swiss peasant wood-carving made for the urban tourist market. They are individual works of art, each with some significant arrangement of elements which has demanded an æsthetic solution of its own by the maker (Plates VI; VIII).

Western appreciation of the æsthetic qualities of much of this material has been slow. One can distinguish three main reasons for this.

The first has been simple unfamiliarity with the content of much of the primitive work, and the lack of a sufficiently analytical æsthetic theory to allow the relevant principles to be disentangled. This has been especially the case with primitive music. Some negro rhythm has filtered through into Western jazz. And when Maori, Hawaiian and other Polynesian melodies become heavily diluted by Mission hymnal and other Western influences, they can be very popular, as has happened also with negro American " spirituals." But the great bulk of the music of Africa, Oceania, and the Orient is a closed book to all of the Western world except a few scholars. The songs of the Australian aborigines use such unfamiliar melody and have an idiom of production that is so harsh to ordinary Western ears that most white Australians would deny them the name of music at all. Yet they have a recognizable scale structure and use the same main pitch relations as those on which European music is built.[1] The effect of unfamiliarity can be easily recognized if it be remembered that Oriental music of a highly sophisticated character such as the *gamelan* music of the Javanese, or the vocal and instrumental music of the Chinese, produced by peoples who cannot be classed in the primitive category, is still largely unappreciated and almost entirely not understood in the West. The most lively appreciation of primitive art forms has probably been in the case of what has been called, not too happily : " oral literature " —myth, legend, epic, and song. Primitive traditional tales have for long been popular, because their narrative style, drama of episode, and completion of sequence are akin to Western practices of story-telling, and their unfamiliar idiom gives only an added charm to the recital. Hence the popularity of Sir George Grey's collection of tales from the Maori of New Zealand, published under the title of *Polynesian Mythology* about a century ago,[2] and of other collections of primitive folk-tales.

---

[1] About thirty years ago a set of three gramophone records was issued by Columbia, from Edison phonograph records made by the Board of Anthropology of Adelaide University. These records have a commentary by Professor Harold Davies, indicating their musical interest. More recently, records of Australian aboriginal music have been made by various expeditions.

[2] Published under the title of *Nga Mahi Nga Tupuna* (The Works of the Ancestors) in Maori in 1854 ; this was issued in translation as *Polynesian Mythology* in 1856. Subsequent editions included a cheap reprint in 1906. Grey published also a book of Maori songs, in Maori, as *Nga Moteatea*,

The second reason for the lack of Western appreciation of primitive art has been the often unconscious view that the primitive was racially inferior, and as such incapable of producing any cultural achievements of any significance for the West. There is no need here to spend time in controverting such myths. But some elements of this attitude have been perceptible in the persistent attempts to equate the art of the primitive with that of the child, and to stress other developmental themes when considering it. They have been perceptible again in the argument which raged early in this century as to whether the Maori and other primitive peoples were capable of perceiving the colour *blue*. It had been noticed that blue was rarely seen in the colour composition of Oceanic and other primitive peoples, and words which represented the colour in an isolable way were also few. It was held by some savants, therefore, that this was due to some deficiency in the primitive sense equipment. (The controversy is reminiscent of the argument carried on by German scholars as to whether the distortion of the human form in the paintings of El Greco was not due to his being astigmatic!) The truth seems to be that there is no significant difference to be observed in the colour sense of primitive peoples. The absence of blue in their art is due primarily to the relative scarcity of this pigment by comparison with the relative abundance of white (kaolin), black (charcoal), red (hæmatite), yellow, orange, brown (turmeric and other vegetable dyes), and to the infrequency of blue objects in their natural environment.

The third reason for the refusal to recognize æsthetic sensibility in the primitive has been due to a confusion of categories of judgement. Moral and religious criteria in particular have interfered with the appraisal of art. When the wooden and stone anthropomorphic sculptures of Polynesia were regarded by the Christian missionaries and their followers as primarily " idols of the heathen," there was not much chance

New Zealand, 1853, with the fore-title of " Poems, Traditions, and Chaunts of the Maories." Reissued in a revised form by Sir Apirana Ngata, it was published by the Board of Maori Ethnological Research, 1928–29 (new ed. pt. I, with translation by Ngata and Pei Te Hurinui Jones, 1958).

of their getting a fair æsthetic trial.[1] If it is to the missions we owe today some of the most important primitive art objects from Polynesia and elsewhere, it is due less to æsthetic reasons than to the fact that these things were preserved and sent home in triumph as spoils by the victors in the battle of faith (Plate VIIIB). But if the missionary be allowed to mingle his moral with his artistic judgements, the same should not be said of the modern art critic. One of those who welcomed the French *Fauves* in the early years of this century, and defended the æsthetic quality of their then novel vision, has admitted the expressive quality, the simplicity and directness, and the technical dexterity of West African sculpture. Yet, afraid of the submission of Western artists to what he regards as African ideals, he has said, " Even the best of them (the sculptures) take us down to the animal—never up among the angels. Therein lies the danger of their influence. . . . There is time yet for us all to become savages." [2]

A more sensitive critic, Eric Newton, praises the marvellous æsthetic quality of primitive art. " Never perhaps in the history of art has form been more closely dovetailed with content, or style so firmly rooted in an attitude to life." But the content, he finds, is repellent. Behind the dignity of the masks and carved bowls " are terror, cruelty, and a pathetic acceptance of the Unknown—everything, in fact, that Renaissance humanism detested and tried to get rid of." (It is a moot point, I would think, whether Renaissance humanists had any particular aversion to terror and cruelty—the Medici, the Borgias, Benvenuto Cellini, at least would seem hardly to have borne out the argument. But this is not our issue.) Masks are described as having " cunning eyes," " fiercely

---

[1] An analogous situation has been delicately exposed by Osbert Lancaster in a discussion on architecture : " . . . with the advent of Mr. Ruskin, whose distinction it was to express in prose of incomparable grandeur thought of unparalleled confusion . . . the whole theory of architecture had become hopelessly confounded with morals, religion and a great many other things with which it had not the least connection." (*Pillar to Post*, London, 1938, p. xii.)

[2] Frank Rutter, in a review headed : " Africa in the West End," in *Sunday Times*, February 3, 1935. Cf. Sir Michael Sadler, *Arts of West Africa*, London, 1935, pp. 4–6.

protruding lips," " frowning brow and predatory beak." This content, this emotional atmosphere which these objects are regarded as carrying with them, are attributed to their ritual preoccupation with disease and death, with drought and catastrophe. " The spirit behind it is always the same. It is that of a trapped animal trying to escape by means of magic." [1]

This setting of primitive art upon a magical base is a question that will occupy us later. But as regards the particular emotional content attributed to these objects, it should be clear that in such cases this is injected by the observer. It is not necessarily a true expression of the original artist's attitude, nor of the interpretation of the object by the people of the artist's community. To give one's own emotional reaction to a work of art is legitimate; to argue that this reaction is a test of the æsthetic quality of the work is questionable; but to infer from it anything about the original conditions in which the work was created is unsafe in the extreme. Whatever be the chances of a correct diagnosis when both art critic and artist share the same culture, they are reduced to a minimum when the former is an intellectual of the contemporary West and the latter an anonymous sculptor of some primitive community. This is particularly relevant when it is remembered that rarely can the work of the primitive artist be accurately dated, to know if he has ever been subjected to direct or indirect European influences.

One element which has militated against the acceptance of much primitive art as a congenial form has been its non-naturalistic character. The bodily distortion, elongated face, glaring eyes, and gaping mouth of many human figures have alienated the Western observer. We are accustomed to our own conventions, and forget that a portrait of a person on canvas, because of its two-dimensional translation, is a naturalistic reproduction in only a limited sense. But it has been precisely the non-naturalism of much primitive art that has led it to find favour in some quarters.

The reaction of Western artists to primitive art has been interesting. Many have ignored it, or stigmatized it. But

[1] Eric Newton, in a review headed " Darkest Africa," in *Sunday Times* December 29, 1946.

some, including the most vital, have found in it a source of inspiration. Since about the turn of the century Gauguin, Matisse, Picasso, the German Expressionists, and others have looked to the formal qualities of primitive art, especially of negro sculpture, to help them in solving their own technical and conceptual problems of a non-naturalistic order. More recently surrealists and allied artists have held primitive art in high regard for its symbolism. Concerned with art as primarily an expression of the artist's emotion, especially of elements from below the threshold of consciousness, surrealists find in primitive painting and sculpture an attitude to man and Nature given in a condensed emotional form which appeals to them. Stimulated by the suggestions they get of tension and release of the human spirit, of supernormal presences behind the conventional appearance of reality, these artists have been led, it is argued, to explore their minds in a revolutionary manner. We are not concerned for the moment with the adequacy of the theories of art, especially primitive art, implied by this. It is sufficient to note that there is a cross-cultural bridge here, thrown over by the modern Western artist. In his continual search for stimulus to his own creation and expression he has recognized a significant æsthetic quality in the primitive work.

I believe that there are universal standards of æsthetic quality, just as there are universal standards of technical efficiency. An object, whether it is called a work of art or not, can be judged by these universal æsthetic standards, which are primarily those of its form. But we inevitably supply this form with some content, some meaning derived partly from our knowledge of the social context of the object, and partly from many obscure intellectual and emotional associations of our own. We also to some extent endow the object with our own patterning. In this subtle linkage of form and content, often involving the perception of new relations, lies much of our æsthetic pleasure. Such æsthetic activity, indeed, is a kind of new creation at an unexpressed level. All we know of primitive peoples, from their myths, dreams, ceremonial, economic, religious, and other behaviour, leads us to credit them with an essentially similar basic psychology to our own. But similar psychological impulses can emerge in very different art forms because of different social conditions. Art is one of the high points of individual expression, a vehicle for conveying intense and refined human emotions, which can be recognized as of a universal order when they are isolated. But all art is composed in a social setting; it has a cultural content. To understand this content it is necessary to study more than general human values and emotions; they must be studied in specific cultural terms at given periods of time. Even in what is broadly called primitive art, it is usually possible to identify the cultural region, and sometimes even the community, from which an object comes. To assign it to any particular period is usually more difficult. Archæology gives almost the only guide to relative age, and datings made without its aid, on the basis of style alone, are to be regarded as a rule with suspicion.

It is this element of cultural content in art that has admitted the anthropologist to the field. On the one hand, he has collected objects of primitive art as cultural material, thus performing an important sub-æsthetic function. Apart from his use of the material for the study of primitive technical processes—of weaving, use of wood-working tools, etc.—he has aided modern Western artists themselves to see the æsthetic quality in things outside their ordinary range of experience. On the other hand, it is on his shoulders that the task of interpreting the meaning of these things has largely fallen. To fulfil this task in any proper sense involves attention to two major problems. The first problem is the effects on the society of producing and using the art objects. The second problem is the nature of the values which are expressed by the formal characteristics of the art objects.

These problems may be put in another way—what does art *do* in a primitive society? The social correlates of art have two aspects. On the one hand, the creation—the actual making, and use—of objects of art affects the system of social relations. On the other hand, the system of representations conveyed by the objects of art, in particular the system of symbols, corresponds to some system of social relations. Analysis of these is our main theme.

We may begin considering these problems by reference to some general questions.   Let us first re-define the notion of primitive, as applied to the field of art ordinarily studied by the social anthropologist.   The work of the anthropologist in the sphere of art has been, of course, almost wholly concerned with what is termed primitive art.   The term " primitive " in this connection refers, properly speaking, neither to chronology nor to style only.   When we talk, for instance of primitive Greek art, of the Italian primitives, or of the American primitives, we are referring in each case to art that is distinguished primarily by being earlier in time, though it usually also bears the character of lack of sophistication.   But the primitive art studied by the anthropologist includes not only that which is of greatest antiquity in human culture but also much that is contemporary or near-contemporary.   In its treatment it is sometimes crude, but most of the work cannot be described as lacking sophistication.   It has behind it a long stylistic tradition, and expresses great capacity in handling design and symbolism within the limits of the material. The idiom may be unfamiliar, but this is another matter. The distinction of primitiveness cannot be made simply in terms of a radical difference in the tools employed.   The Maori wood-carver of pre-European days, for instance, appears to have used spade-chisels and skew-chisels of the same generic types as those used by a modern European craftsman, although they were in stone and not in steel.   And though many cultures did not use the drill, and others employed it with a stone point, the essential principle of boring is the same.   While mechanization is the mark of civilized industry, it has small vogue in civilized art.   By contemporary primitive art we mean, therefore, the art of people whose general technology is pre-industrial.   The essential point, then, is this.   When in the æsthetics of the West we talk of the primitives, we are thinking of the beginning of a process; the primitives which an anthropologist discusses are, if not the end of a process, at least a long way along the road.

By the end of a process one means either when an art dies out completely or when such a revolutionary change has occurred in the culture as to destroy the *raison d'être* of a par-

ticular type of art. For example, now that nearly all Polynesians have been Christians for more than a century, images
of the old heathen gods no longer form part of their art
creation. It is true that in a few cases one finds a transference
—as, for example, a black Madonna in Maori style (Plate VIII).
But this is rare. Of course, a great deal of the primitive art
still persists in such conditions, either in traditional or in
modified form, to serve the continuing needs of the people
for decoration and symbolic expression.

The influence of new technical conditions is interesting and
in some respects surprising. Modern sculpture lays great
stress on the way in which the essential qualities of the different
media—wood, stone, clay, metal—must be given expression
in the finished work of art. But the technological factor goes
farther, in regard to the tools also.

To take an extreme instance, from outside the primitive
field. A traditional Chinese painter works with a definite
theory about the use of the ink-brush. It is charged, so to
speak, with the æsthetic spirit of the artist at the moment of
its application to the paper. It should accomplish its task in
a single sweep, with no re-touching. Such a technique and
ideology of brushwork is admirably suited to the painting of,
say, bamboos in Chinese style. But it is not so easy to maintain when a Chinese painter takes to European material,
working with oils on canvas. One expects such painting,
then, to show not simply differences due to the change of
medium alone, but also to the change of the way in which
any medium is viewed. In essence what has happened is not
simply the production of a different kind of work of art
because of a technical change; the change has also been a
social change. Oils and canvas are European products—for
the painting world—and the use of them implies not merely
technical experimentation but also experimentation in a new
civilization. With their acquisition comes also the acquisition
of new ideas and, it may be, new emotional attitudes to old
ideas. It is along these lines that we can explain what has
often appeared as a paradox in more primitive cultures. In
the traditional system in many of these cultures the technical
equipment of the artist was of the simplest. In wood-carving,

THREE ANTHROPOMORPHIC
POLYNESIAN SCULPTURES

(*Above, right*) "Black Madonna"
by a modern Maori carver.
Many traditional features are
retained (*see below and Appendix*).

(*Above, left*) Hawaiian figure of
a god, obtained from a sacred
enclosure and brought to England by the London Missionary
Society.

(*Below*) Maori Ancestor. This
massive gate carving in traditional
style, over 6 ft. high, depicts
Putiki, an ancestral chief of
Arawa tribe.

White Man through African Eyes

Painted clay figure, almost life size, of European, set at table against frescoed wall. This is part of Mbari house of Oratta, Agbara group, of the Nigerian Ibo.

Ibibio Sculptures

These statuettes from Eastern Nigeria are about 2 ft. high. They are similar to memorial figures set up for a chief.

tools of stone, shell, or bone were used, and some of the finest results in primitive sculpture and decorative art have been produced by such crude implements. With the coming of Europeans, steel tools, prized for their keenness and durability, came into use. Yet in many cases the quality of the art declined. This seems to have been due partly to the fact that with the introduction of the improved tools came also new incentives to divert the artist—very often the commercial incentive of selling his work for money. New ideas also arose about the part which that art should play in his own life and the life of his people.

With a change in his religious views, for instance, came a lessening of the conviction that an important purpose of his art was to support and convey religious ideas. The primitive artist had hardly anything like the theory of æsthetic dynamism lying behind the use of the Chinese brush. But his tools were often used in an atmosphere of ritual observances—no Maori wood-carver, for instance, could ever allow cooked food in his neighbourhood when he was at work, lest he and the work be defiled by this common substance.[1] With this removal of many ritual and social sanctions for the work of the sculptor or the weaver, the result often has been slipshod execution and poor conception. Design has lacked balance, boldness, and originality, as if the heart had gone out of it. Even where technical competence has remained, the work has tended to be dull and flat.

Yet modification or entirely new developments introduced through European stimulus are at times just as interesting as the traditional forms of art. For example, some of the Ibo people of South-Eastern Nigeria construct elaborate series of clay figures, almost life-size, as part of a ritual task to avert some catastrophe from their community—it may be epidemic disease. Under the leadership of a priest, a group of young people may spend weeks on the task. This clay modelling, often accompanied by fresco work, shows a wide range of motifs and a variety of applied colour. The traditional figures of the Earth Goddess, with elaborate patterns painted

---

[1] So strongly is this traditional attitude implanted that some modern Maori carvers have also kept this taboo, though they have neglected others.

M

on in white, yellow, and brown, are set side by side with modern scenes. Amazingly vivid groups of Africans manipulating clay sewing-machines sit side by side with Europeans playing cards at a table. The clothing of the figures, the chairs, the table, the bottles, glasses, and cigarettes of the players, are all carefully modelled and crudely coloured, revealing a close observation and a power of handling the material in a plastic way (Plate IX). In mood, they show a cool detachment of presentation of the human figures in actions which amount at times almost to satire. This kind of simple descriptive art is produced in conditions where the social structure of the village is still relatively unaltered by European contact, and where traditional sanctions still operate to safeguard the style and standards of the work. There is an enlargement of theme, but the primary values of the work have not been disturbed.

Even where the structure and sanctions of the traditional society have altered considerably, a vital art production may exist, through the development of new sanctions and interests. In various peasant communities in parts of Africa, among the Maori of New Zealand, among some Malay groups, in Mexico, and among some North American Indian tribes, new art sanctions have been provided in modern workshops and schools. These try to weld together commercial standards of craftsmanship, effective business methods, elements of good design, and a remnant of traditional motifs and techniques. Their success, which has been very variable, has depended largely on the enthusiasm and skill of the teachers, and also on their ability to estimate the demands of an actual or potential market for the work produced.

Another development by Africans and other people of peasant environment is the use of the techniques of European painting and sculpture under the influence of educational authorities. Much of this work is crude and amateurish and follows European conventions fairly closely, in theme and style, as well as in actual technique. But from among African student painters enough work has been produced to allow the emergence of specifically African concepts to be seen. Cultural characteristics, including symbolic characteristics, reveal attempts to express the old and new forces which the African is encountering in his daily life.[1]

This raises the question of how far in primitive art, and in the art of primitive societies in change, political attitudes can be detected. In the ordinary primitive community there would seem to be practically no political art, no art of revolt. The class structure, where it exists, is accepted, and the art is used, as far as its themes go, to represent and support the position of chiefs and other men of rank, not to criticize them. One reason for this is, as explained before, that the common people are frequently bound in a net of kinship with the leaders of their society, and consequently feel a sense of identification with them, even at a distance. There is therefore no particular incentive for an artist to express directly or indirectly in his painting or carving a theme of status resentment. Rather is he impelled to portray the common ancestor, to give material form to the symbols which represent the common group. His art forms reinforce the bonds of the community rather than make manifest and challenge the oppositions within it.

When the primitive community changes under European influence, however, a different situation is to be expected. One of the outstanding features in societies in Africa, for example, is the political and social dominance of Africans by Europeans in many fields. In British Colonial territories this has been lessened by recent constitutional changes, but not removed. It is a dominance, an asymmetry of social relations which is deeply felt by Africans themselves—perhaps the more so because of the largely unconscious bland acceptance of it as natural by many Europeans. A frontal attack on this situation is to be expected by African artists. At present, however, all that can be seen is the rather critically humorous note that has crept into the depiction of Europeans when they appear in songs, in the plastic arts,[2] or in the rare novel by an African writer.

[1] An interesting analysis of some aspects of this situation has been given by Mrs. K. M. Trowell, " Modern African Art in East Africa," *Man*, 1947, 1. In this, reference is made *inter alia* to the striking wooden sculpture " Death," by Gregory Maloba.

[2] See, for example, the collection of material in Julius Lips, *The Savage Hits Back*, London, 1937.

There are several reasons for this. The range of art teaching in these African communities is as yet limited. At present so much of the pupil's attention still goes on the acquisition of the vast new field of European achievement suddenly opened to him. Moreover, in many cases personal loyalty to the European teacher is strong; teacher and pupil are united, a structure of æsthetic interests, against the body of the uninitiated. In a generation or two, when Africans have fully mastered all that Europe and the Americas have to offer in æsthetics, then one may expect the artist's eye to turn inwards once again, and African nationalism, or other political movements, to become manifest in wood or on canvas.

The recognition that art may express political tensions and that such tensions are likely to find some æsthetic expression does not mean simply an acceptance of Marxist theories of art. Lenin's view was that art belongs to the people, and should be understood and loved by them. Its social role, therefore, is to serve them as a force of unification in their struggles and of elevation of them in their development. Marxist theory recognizes a primary distinction between realistic art, which reflects the productive intercourse between man and Nature, and idealistic art, which attempts to conceal such relations by presenting concepts of a religious or other delusive character. So long as society is divided into classes, the struggle between them is represented in the history of art by the clash and interaction of these two art traditions. Marxist criticism in art consists, then, primarily in identifying these principles in the various art movements and estimating the way in which works of art reflect the objective truth of the class struggle and of proletarian achievement, by imagery which is intelligible to the masses and has the power to bring conviction.

Considering such a thesis simply from the point of view of our study of primitive art, we see certain difficulties. The tradition of realism is regarded as being natural to a non-class society. Most primitive societies cannot be said to have more than an embryonic class structure. Many must be categorized as without class division, as Marxist argument indeed agrees.   Yet the art of these societies is distinguished not by its realism but by its non-naturalistic, symbolic, often religious, character.   A clear example is given by the art of the Sepik river natives of New Guinea.   The society is of a highly individualistic classless type.   But the sculpture, for example, shows a wide range of distorted forms, with exaggeration and fantasy of marked kinds, and totemic and other spirit values prominent.   The art is one that is comprehensible to the ordinary people, in that the symbolism is not foreign to them.   It has meaning for them as a traditional mode of representing significant elements of their universe.   These elements—crocodiles, birds, women—have significance not only because they are found in the natural environment; they are also associated with the social groups in which much of the individual's life is lived.   Here, then, is a non-realistic classless primitive art.   If it be argued that, after all, the art is realistic, since it expresses important productive relations of the people with Nature, then this suggests the inadequacy of the bipolar classification into realistic and idealistic.

On the other hand, if it be argued that such Sepik art expresses a struggle, then it is not a struggle in class terms. Where the symbols are those of kin-groups, then their carving and display illustrate and crystallize the opposition of these groups.   The continued struggle of such groups to maintain themselves socially and economically and to enhance their status is brought out in the art of their members.   Moreover, it is not only opposed elements in the group field that are involved.   Tension and struggle exist between individuals, even within the same individual.   This tension may arise for many reasons, including inter-personal rivalries in age-sets, men's clubs and secret societies, family jealousies, and conflict of experience from which moral lessons can be drawn. Granted that the creative activity of the artist is not a purely individual phenomenon, but stands in some relation to his perception of significant forces in the social world around him, such forces can be seen at all levels of group behaviour.   His reaction to them, or representation of them, may be very direct, and easily comprehensible to all the public in his social world.   Or it may be indirect and obscure, couched in imagery that requires long training and great insight to understand. But there is no simple equation which will express these differences of artistic creation and value in terms of concepts of realism and idealism or of the class struggle.

It will be realized that primitive art, being defined primarily on technological grounds, does not constitute a unity. It has a great diversity of themes and styles, even within a recognized broad cultural region, such as West Africa or Oceania, or even Australia. Some of these differences have been described in terms of the form of the designs used: geometrical, zoomorphic, anthropomorphic, and so on. Others have been described in terms of the quality of the representation—naturalistic against conventionalized; static against dynamic; formal as against emotional. The concepts indicated by such terms are essentially derived from Western thought, with its historical preoccupation with the antithesis between classical and romantic attitudes. These elaborately worked-out systems of ideas and art forms are not applicable to the art of primitive communities, and the terms mentioned can be used with no more than an immediate descriptive meaning. The styles which they are used to categorize are aggregates accumulated by the study of the Western observer. They are not necessarily at all a coherent expression of a common æsthetic attitude, backed up by explicit theoretical analysis and defence, as is common with Western art styles. It is not surprising, therefore, that there has been little success in trying to equate stylistic differences in primitive art, expressed in such terms, with crude differences in the geographical environment, or in the type of social structure. It may be tempting to regard a " static " style of primitive art as correlated, for instance, with a type of society in which a rigid system of inheritance and other rules inhibits the economic and social mobility of the individual member; and a " dynamic " style as correlated with a more elastic system of social opportunity. A more plausible hypothesis, however, is that the art of a society with a less rigid system of rules is likely to display a greater range of variation in style and motifs, a multiple symbolism, rather than a more dynamic quality as a whole.

Now let us examine more closely the social relations involved in the production of a work of art in a primitive community. Primitive art is highly socialized. To begin with, in many respects it is the handmaid of technology. One of its great applications is for the adornment of objects of everyday use—spears, pots, adze handles, fish-hooks, boats. In Western culture most people seem to think of art as something that no ordinary citizen has in his home—or at least has only in imitation, since he cannot afford the real thing. The statue or painting belongs to the Art Gallery, the book of poetry to the library, while music comes from the radio or the concert-hall. In a primitive community, art is used by the ordinary people, in embellishment of their domestic implements, and in their ordinary social gatherings.

As part of this situation, the primitive artist is first and foremost a craftsman, from whom art flows as an extension of his craft activity. By this is meant that he is essentially the constructor of things for material use which are also regarded as giving enjoyment. He does not make things simply for the æsthetic satisfaction to be got out of looking at them. Even songs, as a rule, are not composed simply to be listened to for pleasure. They have work to do, to serve as funeral dirges, as accompaniments to dancing, or to serenade a lover. And in each case concrete results are sought, for which the song is intended to pave the way. In the community of Tikopia, for instance, which has been mentioned earlier, funeral dirges appear as part of the social organization from three points of view. First, on any formal occasion they are not sung indiscriminately, but by groups of people who stand in specific genealogical relations to the deceased person. Secondly, these relations are given collective expression by the choice of the song. These dirges are classified in kinship categories of application—dirge for a father, dirge for a mother, dirge for a grandparent, etc.—to which the opening words of the song usually give the clue. The mourning group of the moment chooses a dirge most suitable to their collective relationship. Thirdly, chanting the song is not simply an æsthetic act nor a performance of piety—it is an economic act, too, and as such earns some material recompense. Yet the performance is not devoid of conscious æsthetic standards.

There is much appreciation of the merits of a song and of its performance. Moreover, the name of the composer is often attached to it, so that renown through the generations is part of the reward of success as a versifier.

The terms of payment for the work of the primitive artist bring out the social context still more. In every society, as far as we know, work of recognized æsthetic quality brings some access of reputation to the creator. But the degrees of social status and material privilege by which this reputation is expressed have great variation in different societies. In many societies a man is expected to contribute his æsthetic skill without material reward, and to get his compensation from the plaudits of the crowd, or from their obvious wish to use what he has made. He is paid for the article as a craft object, irrespective of the quality of artistic elaboration he has given it. In some, where a heavy concentration of population allows of fairly extensive division of labour, specialist craftsmen on practically full-time work are apt to get some remuneration proportionate to the quality of their art. Such would seem to be the case with stool-makers and other wood-carvers, and with weavers in various parts of West Africa. Most commonly, however, the artist-craftsman is only a part-time or leisure-time worker in this activity, and gets his living ordinarily by farming or fishing. In such conditions he may execute a piece of work to order, as the specialist often does. But he may often restrict his work to fulfilling specific social obligations. In such circumstances his art and his income as an artist operate not as a function of a free market but of a particular socially defined market. An example is the construction of the elaborately carved slabs with avian and other designs, used by the people of New Ireland as part of their funeral rites. These slabs are essentially a form of mortuary art, with intricate symbolism and associated mythology. But an important feature about New Ireland society is that it is divided into two halves, matrilineal moieties, so that a person belongs to that of his mother. His father, his wife, and his children belong to the other moiety. When he dies, the mortuary slab should be made for him by one of his kinsfolk from the opposite moiety, i.e., his father's kin; and be paid for by kin from his own, i.e., his mother's moiety. This means that art creation in New Ireland society is very heavily tied up with the kinship system. It is interesting to note that this does not seem to have inhibited the artists. They have produced a great range of *malanggan*, as these mortuary carvings are called, of highly developed fantasy and elaboration, as well as great technical facility.

All this means that the primitive artist and his public share essentially the same set of values. It means that, in contrast to what is generally the case in Western societies, the artist is not divorced from his public. This organic relationship between art and work, and between artist and community, has had its reactions on both sides. The development of certain branches of primitive art may have suffered through it. It may be argued, for instance, that intellectual analysis in which the artist is consciously aware of sensation and experience different from that of his fellows is necessary for an adequate development of painting. It is certainly in this sphere that primitive art seems weak. The same is true to a lesser degree of primitive poetry. Where there is possibility of combination of a large number of elements, then the intellectual and emotional separation of the artist from his community seems to bear most fruit. Where, however, the æsthetic problem is one of handling and shaping something from a solid mass as it is in sculpture, or where the motor activity of the individual can be used rhythmically in relation to that of his fellows, as in the dance, the primitive artist can bear comparison with the civilized even by the canons of rigid æsthetics.

The essentially social character of primitive art is reflected in forms themselves. There is almost entire absence of landscape. What depiction of landscape does exist appears as subsidiary material in hunting scenes and the like. Figure sculpture also receives special treatment. Renderings of human and animal forms in which the proportions and expression are what we would regard as life-like are very few. Even those figures which have been treated by European critics as portraits, and in fact are identified by personal names in the culture of the people concerned, are highly conven-

tionalized. Identification of them as being the portrait or
this or that chief rests upon the recognition of a particular
symbol incorporated in the portrayal rather than upon perception of individual personal characters in the physiognomy.
The wooden "portrait" figures of the great leaders of the
Bushongo people of the Congo have often attracted attention
(Plate X). Yet all have a family likeness which is a product
of æsthetic convention and not, it may be presumed, of their
close physical resemblance. The identification of a carved
wooden figure of a Maori ancestor may rest upon the fact
that it was decided to give the figure this specific name, appropriate to the name of the house in which it stands. Or, like
the noted ancestor Tamatekapua, who used stilts in order to
steal the breadfruit of a fellow chief, the representation is
carved with and identified by such tokens. In general, primitive figure sculpture is concerned to bring out certain social
attributes of the figure or to express through it certain sentiments which are of importance in the culture of the people.
To this end no exaggeration or distortion is amiss. Figures
of gods have large glaring eyes and gaping mouths which, it
would appear, tend to emphasize the awe in which they are
held. Other figures enlarge and emphasize the sex organs in
token of the virility and power of the beings they represent.
To pin down the expression of any particular emotion to
these figures is often impossible. But throughout the realm
of primitive art one is struck by the way in which special
prominence tends to be given to eyes, to nose, to mouth or
teeth (Plates VII, VIII, IX)—which suggests symbolism.

All this is not an abortive naturalism, the failure of the
primitive artist to recognize proportion and perspective. Its
analogies are too wide for that. Romanesque art, Hindu art,
and the art of many modern Western painters and sculptors
display the same essential characteristics. The art of, say,
Picasso, Epstein, Modigliani, has a certain manifest content
which has drawn upon the primitive for inspiration. But it is
not a mere copy; it is the outcome of the artist's own personal
conviction about the treatment of his material, which has led
him to that particular source for stimulus. A European ivory
carving which foreshadows the art of the Middle Ages has been

described thus: "There is in this carving an almost deliberate protest against realism. The sculptor makes it clear that he has no confidence in formal beauty and naturalism. He disregards the laws of Nature; he shows that he is not interested in such things as three-dimensional space and the anatomy of the human body. For these he substitutes other values. His concern is the abstract relationship between things rather than the things themselves."[1]

Save that for "abstract" the anthropologist would substitute "social" relationship, this might have been written of much primitive non-European sculpture.

Art necessarily implies selection and abstraction from reality. It was for long a convention in European art that this selection should be made with a view to presenting the elements in a way which could be taken to represent the agreed physical proportions of a subject. What the primitive artist does in many cases is to select and represent what may be termed the social proportions of a subject—that is, its relation to the rest of a social structure. One of the most obvious examples of this kind of treatment is the making of some human figures in a sculptured or painted scene larger than others. This is done not in accord with the rules of perspective, nor with their relative physical size in life, but with their social importance. Such a device appears often in Oriental and mediæval Western painting. Sage, saint, or Emperor not merely occupies the centre of the design, but also dominates it in physical proportion. The universality of this device is one indication of how the selective vision of the primitive artist is expressed through a social medium, but not one that is peculiar in its psychology.

In discussing primitive art it is essential to consider its symbolism. In a broad sense, symbolism may be said to exist when some components of the mind's experience elicit activity and values ordinarily associated with other components of experience. From this point of view almost all language and almost all art would be symbolic. But it is useful to consider symbolism also in a narrower sense. A dis-

[1] Ernst Kitzinger, *Early Mediæval Art in the British Museum*, London, 1940, p. 14.

tinction may be drawn between a sign and a symbol.   A sign is an object or an action that represents another entity in virtue of some intrinsic or integral relation perceived between them. A symbol, on the other hand, is an object or action that represents another entity in virtue of some arbitrarily assigned conceptual relation between them.   In both cases there is a referent, and something representing it, and the association between them is a mental one.   But with the symbol, referent and representative are in a relation which is less easily perceived, since the two elements of experience concerned are much less general in their association—they may be even peculiar to a single individual.   To take a simple example. Heavy dark clouds are a sign of rain; an integral relation has been perceived to exist between them by common experience. It is not part of common experience that a snake should be taken as representing rain.   Yet in Australian aboriginal mythology and art a giant snake, known as the Rainbow Serpent, stands for rain.   He represents rainbows, rain, and water in general, and is associated also with notions of the fertility that follows the coming of rain in those arid lands. The relation here is not an integral one, but one that has been arbitrarily assigned in the aboriginal culture, and that is maintained by elaborate myths.   There is no means whereby a Western observer can infer from his own ordinary experience what the Rainbow Serpent has as a referent, except by drawing on the concepts of the aborigines for whom its relations have the significance of rain.   Here, then, is a symbol of rain. Most symbols are culturally defined.   But some are private, or nearly so, to the experiences of single persons.   In discussion of art, it is a question how far a purely private symbolism should be admitted.   For a symbol to be æsthetically relevant it must be presented with attention to its formal characteristics. Without this formal element its presentation has psychological interest, but not æsthetic interest.   Now, the presentation of a purely private symbolism in the name of art raises the difficulty of recognition of the formal characteristics, as well as of identification of the referent.   I would argue that there must be some element of shared recognition in the symbolism in what is presented as a work of art for it to be accepted

as material for æsthetic judgement.   A view such as that of
André Breton, that the work of art must refer to a purely
interior model, cannot be accepted unless it implies that such
a model is a re-shaping of elements of common experience,
or a presentation of new elements in such a way that they can
acquire public significance by their formal relations.

By no means all primitive art is symbolic.   Much of it is
simply descriptive, using signs, in the sense in which we have
just defined them.   Many motifs employed by the primitive
artist are simple line arrangements of a " geometrical " order,
with no allusive significance.   Or they are conventionalized
representations of natural or cultural objects, the reference
being a direct one to them without any further significance.
Most of the scroll-work in Maori or Massim art, for example,
has no symbolic character.   On the other hand, the simplicity
of a design in itself is no clue to its nature.   Highly symbolic
designs in Australian aboriginal art are the simple line meander
arrangements of a kind of " Greek key " pattern which represent the wanderings of venerated totem ancestors, and which
have most elaborate cycles of sacred stories to explain their
meaning (Plate VI).

The range of symbolism in primitive art is wide, and the
associations which give the meaning of the symbols are often
recondite.   The sense of mystery which Western observers
often feel when they look at primitive art is largely due to
their ignorance of this symbolism.   But, however intricate,
the symbols of primitive art are rarely private symbols; they
are shared by groups of people, either members of a clan or
secret society, or members of the society as a whole.   In this
respect the symbolism has an important social function.   It
is not simply a matter of common interest and knowledge;
it serves as a vehicle for the expression of values which are
significant for the social relations of the people.   A symbol
may do this for the whole society, as the Rainbow Serpent
may express for an entire Australian tribe the values to their
life of water and its implications.   Or it may be sectional in
its application, having part of its importance from the way in
which it helps to define and stress the status and values of a
particular group as against those of other groups of the same

type. Much totemic art has this function. The art of the Indians of British Columbia and other parts of the north-west coast of America has much of this totemic character. For example, the beaver, as one group emblem, is represented on totem poles, tobacco pipes, and many other objects. The presence of this animal may be difficult to identify in a design, since the artist is apt to dissect the subject and distribute the parts around the field without regard to their normal anatomical relations. Or he portrays merely some of them, as crucial indices. So it is sufficient, if the figure has a short fat nose, or large incisor teeth, or a broad tail with cross-hatched markings on it, to recognize it as a beaver. Again, much of a beaver's activity is concerned with timber, so if a stick is held by the figure in the design, that also signifies a beaver. Moreover, the beaver may be given a human face, in token of its human affiliations. Here, then, is a complex piece of symbolic art, in which a carved representation of a nose, teeth, a tail, or of a stick, symbolizes an animal; the animal symbolizes a human group; and this relation is itself symbolized by depicting the animal with a human face.

By providing a symbolic expression of some of the values of group alignment, art can thus serve as a rallying point for the attitudes of the group members. To use Tolstoy's argument, though not accepting the moral connotation he gave it —" Art is a means of union among men, joining them together in the same feeling." This is, of course, true to only a limited degree. Its group referent is often only sectional. Like any other set of symbols, the æsthetic object can stimulate opposition as well as union.

Realization of the importance and the role of symbolism in primitive art helps to clear up a confusion. It is often held that such art is magical in its origins and in its primary objective. The view receives some support from the inference that palæolithic paintings of bison and other animals depict some of them with arrows and bleeding wounds, suggesting that this was a means of trying to secure success in hunting by ritual means. It is supported also by the way in which many ritual objects in contemporary primitive life are given æsthetic elaboration. But it is a mistake to think that all

primitive art is concerned with ritual.   This view owes something, one can imagine, to the tendency to romanticize and
see mystery in that which is merely strange.   It will be
realized from what has been said in this chapter that there is
a great deal of purely mundane decorative art in primitive
communities.   What is meant by "magical" may well be,
in fact, what we have shown as symbolical.   But the symbolism, while having magical associations in some cases—that is,
attempting to control by ritual means—is very often in other
cases part of the complex way in which social groups are
defined and their relative status asserted and delineated.   To
say that the primary objective of most of primitive art is to
produce an effective social symbolism would be nearer the mark.

   This view of the magical character of primitive art has its
analogies in the stress sometimes laid on the importance of
the religious stimulus to art through the ages, in the total
field of civilization.   Mulk Raj Anand has explained that art
for Hindus has been simply a way of illustrating the central
truths of religion and philosophy.[1]   Eric Gill has gone
farther, in maintaining that art in its very essence owes its
existence, its very being, to philosophy and religion.   As
these lose their hold on men's minds, it is argued, so the works
done in response to them show vulgarity, extravagance,
fancifulness, grandioseness, and all the other signs of deca-
dence.   But this use of the concepts of religion and philosophy
as a basis of art rests ultimately on throwing the net so wide
as to include almost any relation of the artist with reality.
The importance of religion cannot be denied in supplying
both a stimulus to artistic creation and a rich body of content,
both subject-matter and symbolism.   The history of European
and Oriental art has demonstrated this, and the lesson has been
pointed out in sociological terms by various art historians,
including Yrjö Hirn and Émile Mâle.[2]

   [1] Mulk Raj Anand, *The Hindu View of Art*, London, 1933, p. 169 and
pp. 14, 16, 18, 26.
   [2] Yrjö Hirn, *The Sacred Shrine*, London, 1912 (Sweden, 1909).   Émile
Mâle *L'Art Religieux du XIIᵉ siècle en France*, 5th ed., Paris, 1947, and
related volumes—abridged in English as : *Religious Art from the Twelfth
to the Eighteenth Century*, London, 1949.

But it is difficult to establish the degree to which religion influences æsthetic life. It would seem, indeed, that those who have maintained that all art is religious at bottom have confused history with necessity. Religion may supply one important factor in co-ordinating and stimulating the ideas and emotions of the artist. But ambition, a political ideology, a burning desire to explore the nature of things, coupled with what Herbert Read has described as the peculiar possession of all genuine artists—the ability to express, the technical skill to transpose mental images into linear signs—may also play a part.

One difficulty in accepting the view of the essentially religious nature of art is that its corollary is to judge the merits of the art by that of the religion. If one is a Christian the temptation is to argue that an art which is by Hindus, or which deals with Hindu subjects, is necessarily inferior. Eric Gill, moved as much by his profound sense of craftsmanship as by his Catholicism, does not make this error. But to him good art or bad art manifests itself to the degree that clarity of purpose or the lack of it is expressed in the form. "Look after goodness and truth, and beauty will take care of itself," is one of his *dicta*. It is good advice to a craftsman, but not to a critic. It was this confusion of moral judgements with æsthetic judgements which ruined so much of late nineteenth-century English painting.

Art is a patterning not merely of the seen, the images of the contemporary external world. It is also a patterning of the unseen. But this unseen is not a spiritual world, in the religious sense. It is the emotional and intellectual organization of the artist's personality. One may argue that good art—that is, art which is economical of the elements it uses and yet is capable of suggesting new relations—should be the outcome of a personality with a well-integrated structure. Yet one immediately thinks of Chatterton, Rimbaud, Gauguin, Van Gogh, and many others whose lives seem to indicate a fundamental lack of adjustment. But in order to produce their art in effective form they must have had to focus their powers at a certain point, to integrate various elements of their personalities so as to crystallize their ideas and emotions

BUSHONGO SCULPTURE

This wooden figure, 2 ft. high, is a conventionalized memorial to a chief
of the Bushongo, a Congo tribe.

SPEEDING THE SOUL

A Tikopia funeral rite. Spirits of the maternal ancestors of the dead are thought to bear off the essence of this offering, together with the dead person's soul, to the afterworld. The material goods are put back into circulation.

in coherent, powerful media. In a way, art creation is an expression in pattern form of the artist's vision of himself. Yet this must not be interpreted to mean simply a resolution of his own difficulties. Primitive art has not just the spirit of " a trapped animal trying to escape by means of magic." It is not simply "creation in order to subdue the torment of perception." Primitive man is not simply obsessed with timidity and doubt in the face of the world, with the fluctuating images of which he can cope only by fixing them in the absolute, permanent forms of art.[1] There are elements of all this there. In primitive art, as in all art, there is expression of a need for security and certainty in face of the perplexing problems of human life. But there are three points to be borne in mind in considering the theoretical interpretation of primitive art. The first is that for the resultant work of art to be effective there must be not merely conflict and tension, doubt and anxiety and frustration, but also a resolution of these in the personality. The chisel or the brush alone is not a solvent. Some fusion of the elements, or some hierarchical order in the stimulus they give, must be arrived at for æsthetic creation to take place. The second is that with many primitive artists the organization of the elements of their personality takes place in the events of their daily life, and is not focused on their æsthetic creation alone. It is probably true to say that their anxiety, doubt, and timidity are shown as much as anywhere in the fulfilment of their economic and social obligations connected with their place in the status system of their society. It is there, above all, that they resort to magic. By contrast, their æsthetic expression can be relatively serene, since it is less highly competitive. (In a community where neither his public reputation nor his income depend primarily on his art, the primitive artist can afford to be less exercised than in our Western society, where the specialized function of the artist helps to breed tension in his approach to his art.)

The third point is that the primitive artist does not stand

[1] See Eric Newton, *loc. cit.*; Herbert Read, *Art Now*, London, 1933, pp. 114–15 (with quotation from Worringer, *Form in Gothic*, London, 1927, p. 29).

N

alone. His public are with him in a way which is not the case in Western society. His themes are traditional, he is creating in order to fill a specific social demand, to express common values. His inner conflict, if such there be, then, is resolved in advance to some degree. The solution is provided by the traditional symbols which have already formed a considerable part of his experience. He may question their validity, but they provide him with some answers. Each art form, visible in wood or stone, or made known in song or other medium, is a permanent reminder of how other individuals have found a resolution of their wants, tensions and imagination, in terms of traditional values which are at the same time an assertion of personal human faith.

CHAPTER VI

MORAL STANDARDS AND SOCIAL ORGANIZATION

MORALITY is a heavily loaded term in popular speech today. It is apt to be treated as a set of negative attitudes—a bunch of "thou shalt not's," epitomized for many people in the Ten Commandments. To some, it implies a sober restraint, a straight if narrow path. To others it implies a cold constraint, a fettering of the spirit which would be free. When questions of morality are discussed, one of the commonest references is to sex conduct. This is in part still a Western inheritance from the nineteenth century, when ideals of the solid domestic virtues in the bourgeois family needed the prop of decorum, if not prudery. But many moral judgements are positive. Over the whole range, comparatively few are concerned with sex.

By the moral attributes of an action is meant its qualities from the standpoint of right and wrong. Morality is a set of principles on which such judgements are based. Looked at empirically from the sociological point of view, morality is socially specific in the first instance. Every society has its own moral rules about what kinds of conduct are right and what are wrong, and members of the society conform to them or evade them, and pass judgement accordingly. For each society such rules, the relevant conduct, and the associated judgements, may be said to form a moral system. Examination of these moral systems, particularly in those societies of a non-Western kind which are still technologically and economically undeveloped, is part of the work of social anthropology. The anthropologist hopes to reach some more general principles as the result of his comparative study. But his analysis is directed to finding out what is common to conduct in different kinds of societies. He is not concerned directly with questions of ethics—the abstract, philosophical examination of the bases of right and wrong in general, the assumptions on which such notions are founded, the problem of the existence of intrinsic good and evil, and their relation to human conduct and human destiny.

For the anthropologist, the terms moral and immoral relate to social actions, to social relations. They imply the attribution of certain special qualities to such actions and relations. This does not mean distinguishing actions by content quite in the same way in which the terms economic or religious do. We commonly speak of exchange as an economic action, or worship as a religious action. There is no corresponding category of moral actions *per se*. Morality refers to the qualities rather than to the substance of actions. Practically every economic or religious action, for example, has a moral quality. Moral judgements in any society are notable for the ease with which they tend to be uttered. They cost so little; they demand no sacrifice of resources and almost none of energy. It is not surprising, then, that they are pervasive, and this is important for social organization.

The pervasiveness of moral judgements may be easily realized by a little consideration of affairs in our modern Western life. Except in the purely technological field, simple unevaluated description of social action is rare. Some judgement of its propriety in terms of right and wrong is usually stated or implied. In the minutiæ of everyday life there is plenty of material for such evaluation. Commendation or criticism is continually being formed on the way in which a man behaves at work, his treatment of his colleagues, the way a woman keeps her home, the way she acts in a shop queue, how they spend their income, how they bring up their children, how they let their dog react to their neighbour's cat. It is very similar in any more primitive society.

To many people these will not at first thought seem to be matters of morality. Yet the rightness or wrongness of the social action is being judged, often fiercely. Many of the ordinary terms used to describe behaviour in such situations bear a moral stamp on the face of them: a bad-tempered, wrong-headed colleague; an ill-mannered queue companion;

a good housewife; a right-thinking mother; a badly brought up child—such are the small change of moral judgements, which build up to a large sum as the daily process of social contacts goes on. In the broader sphere, the moral issue is equally well to the fore. Moral approbation is continually being sought by the more articulate agencies. Many industrial enterprises, and all newspapers, on their own showing exist primarily to serve the public and justify their profits by their righteousness. If the actions of government in a democracy are presumed to be in the public interest, those of government in a modern autocracy proclaim this interest as their sole property. Political and economic power, when it emerges nowadays as simple naked force, is unhappy until it is clothed in some form of moral justification. Even war, though the apparent antithesis of moral conduct, raises the moral banner. It is a just war to punish the guilty, it is argued, or its violence is doing evil that good may come. The onus of immediate moral evaluation of what a soldier does is normally removed from him in the name of military duty. Obedience to his superiors in the organization is regarded as a moral obligation of great stringency, and relieves him from censure when he commits many acts of destruction for which he would otherwise be called to account. In modern times there has grown up a concept of international law, which is regarded as having operative rules even in time of war. Yet in the trials of "war criminals" in recent years it has seemed to many people that the real basis of judgement has been less legal than moral. However watertight be the formal proof of "crimes" against civilization, the effective standard of judgement underlying the whole procedure has appeared to be the recognition of offences against a moral code of behaviour commonly believed by large numbers of civilized people to be right, even in warfare. In religion, above all, the moral element is apt to predominate. To many people the real defence of Christianity as a world religion of proselytizing value, and the justification of its historical role in Western culture, lie in the superiority of its moral standards.

To be capable of such a range of application, moral judgements must clearly be of great importance to social action.

They are so not merely as side-line comment, but as part of the springs to action. The existence of moral standards involves not merely an acknowledgement of the correctness of the judgements of right and wrong as they are passed. There is also a conviction that it is proper that such judgements should be passed at all. A person's conduct tends to be guided, then, not only by actual judgements given by others, and by his expectations that similar judgements will continue to be given, but also by his own evaluations and by his recognition of the validity of how others might judge were they in a position to do so. A large element in what is called conscience is a highly formulated version of this latter recognition. Along these lines, it may be argued that the moral system of society is one of the most vital elements in maintaining the continuity of social action. As has been shown in previous chapters, technical and organizational situations carry with them to some extent their own continuity—a process, once begun, implicates the actors, so that it becomes difficult for them to stop except at stage-points. But in many types of social action such inducements are not very obvious, and alternatives are present. Here moral criteria often provide the thread of continuity, assist decision in one direction rather than another.

From the empirical point of view, in studying social processes, what are the essential elements in the exercise of moral judgement? There is the recognition that conduct is measurable by certain standards, commonly known as those of good and bad, right and wrong. These standards are regarded as not emanating from the person giving the judgement, but from outside him; they are external, non-personal in their origin. Linked with this, as Durkheim has pointed out, they are invested with a special authority; they are credited with an intrinsic virtue which demands that they be obeyed. The felt necessity of obedience to this authority is termed *duty*. Yet this moral obligation is not of the order of mere yielding to superior weight. These moral standards have the character of being thought desirable in themselves—the character of *goodness*. Given this, the elements of authority and desirability, moral standards tend to be regarded as absolutes.

Moreover, when moral judgements are applied, although they are given intellectual expression and presented in reasoned form, they are emotionally conceived. The common statement " I know what is right" would be more accurately put " I say what I feel to be right."

What can be said about the source of these moral standards, and of the workings of moral obligation, from the point of view of a social anthropologist? The answers depend largely on his personal background. But in themselves they are of sociological interest and provide a useful contrast of possibilities. The commonest answer probably in the history of Western social thought is that the source of all morality is God, that He provides both the absolute desirability of the standards and the unquestionable authority for following them. On such a view the distinction between right and wrong is absolute, universal. Often linked with this is the idea that moral purpose is inherent in the nature of the Universe, and of human life. As one modern writer has put it, his philosophy in a few words is that " history is the working out of God's purpose." [1] Since by definition the nature of God is good, and the good is the eminently desirable, it would be clearly an obligation laid upon us to follow this purpose. The problem lies primarily in identifying it. On this and similar views the moral rules to be found in different types of society are various forms of approximation, according to the perception or ignorance of the members of the society, to the absolute criteria springing from the central divine source. At the opposite extreme from this are the various views that morality is a thing of circumstance, of pragmatic value for an individual or for a society at a particular period, but lacking any absolute character of external necessity, any validity of universal principle. In Westermarck's conception of ethical relativity, for instance, conduct can be judged to be right or wrong only within its own social setting.

The anthropologist does not explore the ultimate correctness of views on such fundamental issues. But he is interested in the framework of ideas they use. On the one view, morality

[1] A. D. Ritchie, *Civilization, Science and Religion*, London, 1945, pp. 176, 185 *et passim*.

is seen as a handmaid of religion—a necessary offshoot from the divine nature. It is human by endowment and social by practice, but its origin is sought beyond man and society altogether. Empirically, such a view gives firmness and strength to a moral system, aiding conformity. But it also necessitates more elaborate adjustments when there is wrong-doing. To break the moral rule is also a religious offence, a sin; and this calls for remedial action on two planes: of relations with man and relations with God. On the other view, morality is essentially a social product, concomitant with the activities of man as a social being. This view disregards the powerful sanctions of religion, and foregoes also an easy answer to many problems of human existence, such as the nature of human purpose. But it makes easier the task of applying moral rules and obviates the need to operate on two fronts, the human and the divine, at the same time.

Whatever be his personal opinion on such ultimate issues, as to the source of moral judgements, it is clear to the anthropologist that, in the immediate sense, for every individual in society these judgements are socially formed and generated. Durkheim stressed this point, even to extremes. He argued that the term moral cannot be applied to a purely egoistic act. Individuals alone cannot furnish moral ends. These can arise only through a group of associated individuals, a society. It is society, then, which constitutes the ultimate good for its members and which exercises the ultimate moral authority. To this the comment must be that " society " as such is a concept rarely present to its members, even in a highly intellectualized community life such as that of Western Europe; its nature and authority are normally perceptible and interpreted only through the actions of other known individuals. The moral authority of society, then, is vague and amorphous. The moral rules of a society may be clear-cut. But their application to particular social actions may be difficult to determine with any exactness, and individuals tend to interpret them in accordance with their own special interests. Hence the social processes of moral formulation, moral transmission, moral interpretation, are not those in which " society " and " individual " are parties, in which the goodness and authority of the one are directly manifest to the other. Rather are they processes of filtering through of opinions, in which individuals are parties, with all their personal bias. If the comparative studies of anthropologists, exemplified in Westermarck's classic work on moral ideas and in the use L. T. Hobhouse made of material from primitive societies, have brought out the social correlates of morality generally, the intensive studies of psychologists have shown the social influences in the growth of morality in children. By direct inculcation of notions of right and wrong, by increase of understanding of social situations of which it is not a part, by experimental extension of moral terms to describe the behaviour of toys and animals, the child gradually learns the nature of moral concepts and their range of application. Close observation reveals the sensitivity of the child to judgements on its conduct. It shows, too, the tendency to reflect and imitate such judgements in commenting on the behaviour of others, to seek occasion to employ the new operational terms as they are learnt. Over and over again in the course of each day do the social agencies in its neighbourhood impress the moral stamp on the mind of the child. But here again " society " must be regarded as only a remote abstract idea, even for adults engaged in training the child. For the child itself, to recall Durkheim's thesis, the goodness and authority of the moral law are simply personified. In the crudest situations, commonly, the goodness of society is that of the mother; the authority of society is that of the father. The sense of moral obligation, then, is a social product, spreading outwards in its application from the family, until it embraces the full range of adult norms of judgement in community affairs.

What the anthropologist does in the study of moral systems is to examine for particular societies the ideas of right and wrong that are held, and their social circumstances. He studies the terms in which they are expressed; their range of application to different kinds of actions. He studies also the degree to which these ideas are put in rules and the extent to which the rules and moral ideas in general operate as sanctions in affecting conduct. He looks for the source to which these moral ideas are attributed. He is interested also in seeing how far the moral ideas, rules, and associated conduct can be regarded as a system—that is, what degree of coherence can be seen between them. Further, he studies the moral system of a society, if it can be called such, in terms of its social correlates, endeavouring to see what other elements of the whole social system are particularly related to the moral ones. And in all this he is concerned not solely with the immediate aspects, but also with the extent to which the moral ideas can be identified over a range of societies, and presumably therefore have some general social validity.

In this chapter these problems can be only briefly touched. But consideration of material from some of the more primitive societies, and a contrast of it with Western patterns, will bring out some of the basic moral aspects of social action.

A simple way of introducing this subject is to mention a personal experience. It concerns the morality of giving, which has important problems in all human societies.

When I went to the isolated island of Tikopia I was dependent, as every anthropologist is, on the co-operation of local people for information and for guidance. This they gave, freely in some respects, but with reservation in others, particularly on religious matters. Almost without exception, too, they showed themselves greedy for material goods such as knives, fish-hooks, calico, pipes and tobacco, and adept at many stratagems for obtaining them. In particular, they used the forms of friendship. They made me gifts in order to play upon the sense of obligation thus aroused in me. They lured me to their houses by generous hospitality which it was difficult to refuse, and then paraded their poverty before me. The result of a month or two of this was that I became irritated and weary. My stocks of goods were not unlimited, and I did not wish to exhaust them in this casual doling out to people from whom I got no special anthropological return. I foresaw the time when I would wish to reward people for ethnographic data and help of a scientific kind and I would either have debased my currency or exhausted it. Moreover, I came to the conclusion that there was no such thing as friendship or kindliness for its own sake among these people. Everything they did for me seemed to be in expectation of some return. What was worse, they were apt to ask for such return at the time, or even in advance of their service.

Only in one man did I think I saw disinterestedness. But even he, having treated me with much kindness, at last showed the cloven hoof. Before we set out on a trip one day he said quite frankly that we were going to pass by his sister's house and he wanted for her a quantity of fish-hooks and other small goods. I was disgusted. He, too, shared the general acquisitive attitude.

Then I began to reflect. What was this disinterested friendship and kindness which I expected to find? Why, indeed, should these people do many services for me, a perfect stranger, without return? Why should they be content to leave it to me to give them what I wanted rather than express their own ideas upon what they themselves wanted? In our European society how far can we say disinterestedness goes? How far do we not use this term for what is really one imponderable item in a whole series of interconnected services and obligations? A Tikopia, like anyone else, will help to pick a person up if he slips to the ground, bring him a drink, or do many other small things without any mention of reciprocation. But many other services which involve him in time and trouble he regards as creating an obligation. This is just what they do themselves. He thinks it right to get a material reward, and right that he should be able to ask for it. Is he wrong in this? Was my moral indignation at his self-seeking justified?

So I revised my procedure. At first I had expected a man to do me a service and wait until, in my own good time, I made him a freewill gift. Now I abandoned the pretence of disinterested friendliness. When a gift was made to me or a service done, I went at once to my stores, opened them, and made the giver a present roughly commensurate to the value of that received. Technically, this was a great advantage. By counter-giving at once, I usually satisfied the recipient. His service was not left hanging in the air. And while he was happy to take what I gave him then, I often forestalled by this means a request for something bigger when he would have had time to ponder on and exaggerate the value of what he had done. Again I took the initiative myself. If I saw an interesting ethnographic specimen I made the owner a present of what I thought would be equivalent to the fair value. I then capitalized the goodwill by expressing an interest in the article—an indirect request that the owner usually felt it difficult to refuse.

But more important than the change in my procedure was the change in my moral attitudes. I was no longer indignant at the behaviour of these calculating savages, to whom friendship seemed to be expressed only in material terms. It was pleasant and simple to adopt their method. If one was content to drop the search for " pure " or " genuine " sentiments and accept the fact that to people of another culture, especially when they had not known one long, the most obvious foundation of friendship was material reciprocity, the difficulties disappeared. When the obligation to make a material return was dragged into the light it did not inhibit the development of sentiments of friendship, but facilitated it.

There is another interesting point. In theory I was perfectly well equipped to understand all this from the start. My anthropological reading had made me familiar with the principle of reciprocity. I had even had arguments with a high dignitary of a local Mission, who had maintained that his Solomon Islanders did not have such a materialistic ethic. But it is only by living through an experience personally that one comes to appreciate the issues involved.[1] I discovered on Tikopia the reality of the cultural differences in moral standards and moral judgements on matters such as friendship and making gifts. Such differences are deep-rooted, so that, even when prepared for them, it takes one some time to realize that one's own judgement is culturally dictated, not simply a free objective view. Moreover, if one is prepared to examine the alien moral standard against its cultural background, one can see that it has an intelligibility, a coherence, a function.

What I have shown of the material elements of friendship

---

[1] For a civilized man, the adjustments of war often provide an opportunity of re-formulation of his moral ideas. As one of the characters in a novel by Louis Codet, published after the First World War, said : " There are no truths save those which one has rediscovered for oneself, and when the hour comes."

in Tikopia is intelligible in a society where, as I have shown earlier, no very clear-cut line is drawn between social service and economic service, where there is no sale or even barter of goods, but only borrowing and exchange in friendly or ceremonial form. In European culture we demarcate the sphere of business from that of friendship. The former insists on the rightness of obtaining the best bargain possible, while the latter refuses to treat in terms of bargains at all. Yet there is an intermediate sphere. Business has its social morality. Things are done " as a favour," there are concepts of " fair " prices, and sharp practice and profiteering are judged as wrong. On the other hand, friendship does not necessarily ignore the material aspects. " One good turn deserves another " epitomizes regard for reciprocity which underlies many friendly actions. And if there is no proverb that one good meal deserves another, there is at least a convention of " repaying " hospitality, and not only in words. While hearty thanks may suffice to acknowledge a birthday present, it is common to expect something more substantial as a proper return for a Christmas gift. In many ways we show that on the plane of sociability, as distinct from the plane of business, we regard some kind of reciprocity as a moral obligation. As with the so-called primitive peoples, the fulfilment of the obligation is often associated with questions of status. By doing what is right, one helps to maintain one's social position. By exceeding what is demanded by the moral code, one may even be able to elevate oneself in the social scale. Generosity is often a passport to social success. Where we often differ from the more primitive peoples, however, is in the way we treat words as valuable coin. An African peasant may give fulsome thanks for a gift. But in many other societies the peasant may utter no word, or give a mere grunt of recognition. His appreciation is expressed by some more concrete token. With us, to give no verbal acknowledgement is a lack of manners and incurs moral censure. But to give some material token of acknowledgement may be unnecessary, and even embarrassing to the recipient. Such situations of embarrassment find hardly any correspondence in the more primitive communities. Since the moral code prescribes some material return sooner or later, there is no uneasy jostling between words and more solid return. In return for hospitality, for instance, money is not infrequently handed over. But the transfer is done in prescribed form, with due courtesy and dignity, often in public, with murmurs of interest and approbation. To a European, it would be strange and highly embarrassing to go a dinner-party after a wedding and then hand over a pound note to the host or his representative, who calls out the amount of the contribution loudly so that all the guests may hear, while a clerk sits by and writes it down. Yet this is precisely what happens at a Malay wedding party in the State of Kelantan. It is a good working arrangement, whereby gastronomy, sociability, economics, are all combined in a setting of manners and morals which provide a clear-cut sanction for the elaborate rules. As such, it has become a highly systematic procedure.

There are certain social correlates to the working of such a moral system of giving. One is that it can operate effectively only in a community where there is a high degree of personal knowledge and contact between the members. They must have some confidence in one another's capacity and desire to pay at the appropriate time, or to provide the proper hospitality. There must be expectation that for reasons of status, if not of virtue, there is fair probability that they will fulfil their obligations. Again, there is the implication of continuity of relations. The system does not operate by single isolated acts, but by repetition and rotation, even if over long periods of time. It is a system which is well adapted to a community structure of parallel groups of the same order, such as clubs or clans or kinship units, since such a structure allows of regular calculable rotation of events requiring economic expenditure. But it is not necessarily bound to this. As in Malay peasant society, individual men may act as the pivots of the system, with a less regular recurrence of events. But what is usually characteristic of all such systems is that the individual making or repaying a gift is not acting for himself alone. He represents others as well, commonly the members of his family. Rarely are contributions reckoned on a " per head " basis. They are usually reckoned in terms of families or other socially significant units. Hence the system is one which operates a morality of giving and receiving between individuals, against a morality of relations between these individuals and others with whom they are closely bound by kinship or other complex ties. Gift-making is, then, only one type of transaction in the moral use of resources, which are there not merely for the benefit of the person himself, but of his son, his daughter, and other kinsfolk also. In Malay society the specific obligations of returning hospitality with a gift are not integrated closely with the moral prescriptions of Islam. But the religious approval of generosity to others, including the charitable gift, gives a general cover for the reciprocation. A term for charity, *sĕdĕkah*, is in fact colloquially applied to conventional monetary returns for hospitality.

Now turn from the morality of giving to that of property-holding in general. Here we are faced by a paradox. The savage who is so meanly insistent on a material return for his presents or his hospitality is conversely generous in allowing other people use of his goods. Property is lent very freely. It is wrong to refuse the request for a loan if it is made in correct form and with a small gift as a *douceur*. Some societies in New Guinea and elsewhere even give specified kinsmen, such as sister's sons, definite and far-reaching rights of appropriation, without asking permission, over the property of their mother's brothers. It is right for the hungry to be given food, and for the thirsty to take coconuts or other drink at need. In some societies such as Tikopia one may even go and cultivate someone else's land for a season, without asking his leave. The canons of morality are satisfied if a basket of the produce is given to the owner at the harvest, as an acknowledgement that the land is his. And among Malay fishermen, who set down coconut-frond lures on the fishing-banks, to take fish from someone else's lure without his leave, is not stealing—provided one gives him a share of the money they fetch. These are but a few examples of the ways in which these simple peasant communities place social rights.

There is recognition of theft as a category of social actions in primitive societies. Even among economically simple peoples with little property, such as the Australian aborigines, if a young man takes food without permission from women cooking it, this is stealing. Abuse, threats and fighting may follow. Theft is condemned as morally wrong, even though there is not always any specific legal sanction against it. But definition of theft involves more than the taking of an article without having obtained the permission of the owner, in order to convert it to one's own use. In some circumstances the prior permission of the owner is not needed. If he is a kinsman, the general tie between them may give a moral umbrella to the abstraction of the article—a right to interfere which overrides the specific rights to the sole enjoyment of his property. The taking of an article without the owner's permission is commonly not treated as theft if two conditions are satisfied: that no attempt is made to conceal it; and that the owner is notified as soon as is reasonably possible. Sometimes there is an extra condition—that some equivalent is given in return, or that some other object, however small, is given in acknowledgement of the actual ownership and as an earnest of ultimate return. Here, then, the line between stealing and borrowing is not easy to draw. The classification and the moral evaluation of the act depend in part on the moral evaluation of the ties between the participants—that is, on the rightness or wrongness of their actions in other circumstances.

It can be seen, then, that there is no real opposition between the apparent covetousness of expecting a counter-present for every gift and the apparent generosity of conceding to others a wide range of rights over one's own property. The contrast is a superficial one. There is no need to deny the existence of what may be called the noble motives; freedom in giving may often express them. But in addition to the convictions of generosity being right, there are other sanctions for such moral acts, other forces tending to make for conformity to the rule. It is true that the general notion of giving one's property to others, or conceding to others the right to use it, is regarded in most primitive societies as a good thing in itself. As Durkheim has pointed out, there is something almost mystical in the notion, akin to the idea of the sacred.

But whereas in Christian communities this finds a rationale in the New Testament, in a heathen society it often has no specifically religious referent. Three kinds of sanctions are certainly important. One is the force of tradition, the idea that what has been done in the past is valuable, and should be followed. Another is the desire to maintain or increase status. Prestige, position in the society, depend on generous use of one's goods. The third is the long-term economic sanction—generosity now will pay dividends later on, in indirect if not in direct benefits. All this means that the primitive or peasant makes his property play a dual role; it has to do social as well as economic work. His morality of property-holding and using is geared to this attitude, which is a reflection of his particular type of small-scale organization.

What has been considered so far shows that in these alien forms of society studied by the anthropologist basic moral concepts are often different from those in Western society, but are closely related to the requirements of social action in such circumstances. How far can they be said to constitute a moral system, in the sense of giving a coherent set of judgements on right or wrong in respect of conduct which is apparently regulated by them, to the extent of showing predictable reactions?

Even the brief analysis it has been possible to give here points to the existence of such systems. The observer is not faced by fundamental inconsistencies in moral judgements, or by judgements which, despite all investigation, appear quite unrelated. Further study would reinforce this view. The behaviour of people and their ideas of right and wrong expressed about such matters as land tenure, handling property, telling lies, personal violence, fit broadly into their behaviour and ideas about the morality of relations between kinsfolk, worship of ancestors, use of black magic, respect for chiefs. The existence of a social system necessitates, in fact, a moral system for its support.

But it is necessary to define each moral system empirically for each society. The range of conduct subjected to moral judgement varies, as does the quality of such judgement, its intensity. There are some parts of the field of conduct

o

where variability between systems is most marked. One of these is in the use of the concept of cruelty and the identification of cruel behaviour. In Western thought cruelty is the intentional infliction of pain above the necessary technical minimum to achieve approved ends—as, e.g., in surgery. In torture, pain is also intentionally inflicted; but there is difference of judgement as to whether the ends are approved, and therefore whether even the minimum of pain is necessary. In modern Western civilization cruelty and torture are held in abhorrence, and legal sanctions reinforce the moral disapproval. Even in the West such attitudes are of comparatively recent development. In some primitive societies there is often no category of behaviour expressly recognized as cruelty. It is violence rather than the infliction of pain that is stigmatized. When, as with some American Indian tribes, prisoners were tortured, it seems to have been not so much delight in the infliction and witnessing of pain that was dominant, but the experimental testing out of the reputation of the enemy for fortitude. Red Indian torture was a form of status-trial and implicit competition between representatives of warring groups aiming at degradation of each other. In Australian puberty rites the mutilations, the scarring, the frightening procedures are done not for sadistic motives, but to test out and harden the boy, amid the admiration of his kinsmen for his fortitude. Physical pain is regarded as necessary for social ends. But it is not done as an outrage on the personality. The idea of cruelty does not necessarily enter.

As regards behaviour towards animals, contrast with the West is still more marked. The English are pre-eminent even among European peoples for their animal cults. The variety of institutions for the care of animals, from Cats' and Dogs' Homes to the Royal Society for the Prevention of Cruelty to Animals, has often been remarked upon. Moral indignation at the ill-treatment of animals is intense, and attracts public notice easily. Yet alongside this are apparently disparate attitudes about sport which involve a great deal of both random and systematic destruction of animal life. The inconsistency here is more apparent than real. We protect the animals that are domestically useful to us, serve as tokens of our status, or as emotional outlets. Moral sentiments about animals are thus largely the projection of attitudes about ourselves. Analogous sentiments occur also among non-European peoples. The Hindu respects the cow, and the Jain or Buddhist has certain highly conventionalized procedures to avoid taking life in many other sections of the animal world. Among the more primitive peoples, too, there are many ritual attitudes of respect for totem species of animals, leading to avoidance of injury to them, and having a strong moral support. Among many African pastoral people, cattle are treated with great care, and sentiment for cattle is often strong. There is a well-known story of one Bantu chief years ago who, when it was suggested to him that he should yoke his oxen to the plough, and so improve his agriculture, replied, it is said: " How can I be so cruel as to make them work?" Yet such pride and affection do not seem to degenerate into sentimentality, into indulgence in emotion for its own sake. They do not appear to hamper the relatively free transfer of these cattle for ceremonial exchange. So also with pigs in Melanesia. In many other societies animals or birds are kept as pets. Yet they are usually treated in an astringent, neutral way. They are objects of interest and curiosity rather than of affection. Even children are apt to be quite realistic about their loss. The handling of such animals, or of others encountered in hunting or casual capture, is usually without any tenderness. A child may be seen dangling a bird by the leg on a cord, for instance, and looking on curiously at its struggles, while adults sit by unmoved. The more primitive peoples have been accused of cruelty to animals. It would be more correct to say that they do not deliberately inflict pain, but neither do they seek to avoid inflicting it. They are not cruel with intent; they are careless about pain when it is outside their immediate personal sphere. This apathetic attitude in the moral sphere may be linked with certain significant elements in the theory of causation. Pain is felt keenly by the person who has it, and the response of his kinsfolk and neighbours is usually prompt. But it is apt to be treated as a symptom not merely of a bodily ailment but of some possible action by superhuman agency—black magic or witchcraft. Human pain is, then, often not just a matter of a moral judgement on a nervous sensation arising from a physical cause; it involves an elaborate process of inquiry and identification of some superhuman cause. There is a tendency all the time to transfer the interest in the pain as such to the invisible agency responsible for it. This agency is sought in the complications of intrigue, competition, quarrelling, and slander in the social life of the community. It is not the pain, but the fear of witchcraft, that is the worry. It is not the infliction of pain, but the credited practice of bewitching, that is the object of strong moral reprobation. Pain in human beings outside the social circle, or in animals, tends to be a matter of minimal interest. The physical aspect is subordinate to the social aspect, and it is for this that the moral attitudes are reserved.

A moral system is related to the structure of the society it serves by validating the major types of social status. This can be illustrated by considering the moral values attached to human personality in certain social situations. Take first the case of the slave.

Our history of slavery in Europe and North America is still recent. Emancipation is still less than a century old. Yet our capacity for moral indignation has been so effectively developed in this regard that few social states of man are now more repugnant to us than that of the slave. Legal ownership of a human individual as a chattel is associated, to our minds, with the most utter and degrading control of his personality. In some more remote parts of the world, as in some Muslim areas, slavery is still permitted or exists in a covert way as a relic of a much more widespread institution. But it is interesting to note that in these communities the legal control of a slave and rights to his services are usually accompanied by a very distinct respect for his personality. The master has his duties as well as the slave. The latter in time often attains the position of a valued retainer in the household. Not infrequently emancipation has meant hardship for the slave, whose master is now free to cast him off. What are thought by Western humanists to be the evils of slavery often lie not in the actuality, but in the possibility, of exploitation.

That legal control by purchase can go hand in hand with respect for a personality is seen also in the apparently shocking custom of buying children. In Malaya these are not slaves, but acquisitions to the family. A Malay woman wanting another child occasionally buys one from Chinese parents. (Malay parents will not sell a child, it is said.) The child is usually a girl baby, and is initiated into Islam as soon as the purchase is complete. The price of such a child in 1940 was about $20 to $30, according to health and prettiness, but is now higher.[1] Desire for a child is the ruling factor among Malays, and such a bought child is treated in the same way as an ordinary member of the family. This is facilitated by the custom of the Malay peasant of borrowing and lending children to relatives fairly freely. Respect for its personality is shown by the fact that it is ordinarily referred to by the putative parents as their own child, or adopted child. To be called a " bought child " would be derogatory, so it is not told that it has been bought lest its feelings be hurt.

Moral standards connected with the preservation or taking of human life also show the close relation between the form of the society and the nature of the judgements passed upon social action.

Observation seems to indicate that in all human societies there is a basic moral view that it is good as a general rule to attempt to preserve human life. Strenuous efforts are normally made to save persons of the community and even outsiders whose life is endangered by accident or sickness. Devotion in this may even lead individuals to sacrifice their own lives in the attempt. An interesting variant of this is a practice which came under my own notice in Tikopia. From affection for a relative threatened by sickness a person may dedicate himself to death by imploring the gods and ancestors who control the fate of men to take him in the stead of the sick man. It is believed that if they accept his dedication the spirits will strike him down. The methods adopted to cure the

---

[1] It has been recently reported that in France there is a " black market " in young children, who are stolen from their parents in order that they may be sold at high prices to people wishing to adopt them.—*Evening Standard*, August 19, 1948.

sick in the more primitive societies may savour to us of brutality, with the disturbance of the patient, their magic charming, and their noise. But they are well-meant, and often do seem to act as a counter-irritant. One cannot doubt the tenderness and anxiety of the closer relatives as they bend over the sick-bed. The loss of a member of the community is greeted with at least as much observable sorrow as with us. For those who have been accepted as members of the community, the morality of family, of wider kinship, of the local group, all demand the mobilization of action to attempt to save the threatened life.

Divergence from the Western moral norms is seen much more widely in infanticide. In the West this is a crime and sin. But in parts of the East and the South Seas it is regarded morally as no more than a painful necessity, as right to pre-serve the relation of family size to food resources. In China its incidence has often been commented upon. In Tikopia it is practised " proportioned to the food," as the people say. It is done by the midwife, who turns down the face of the newly born infant to smother, at a word from the father. It is done unwillingly, these people claim, with the limited family resources in mind; only after at least one child of each sex has been born is the act carried out. The infant is buried without ceremony, since it has barely lived, and has not be-come a fully fledged member of society. The Tikopia have in essence some of the views expressed by Jeremy Bentham. He did not defend infanticide. But he said that it should not be treated in the same way as the murder of an adult, since there is no " alarm " or danger to third persons involved. It is not to be justified, since it is an introduction to crime. Yet it is not " unnatural "—the epithet commonly applied to it— since the very natural motive of self-preservation occasions it. Nor is it a proof of insensibility on the part of the mother. Bentham was arguing about infanticide committed by a woman who had borne a child out of wedlock. He said, " She is devoted to infamy because she has dreaded shame too much." Bentham is in agreement with the Tikopia as regards the infant's lack of recognition as a full social being. " The offence is what is improperly called the death of an infant,

who has ceased to be, before knowing what existence is." [1]
The general position of people such as the Chinese or the
Tikopia in regard to infanticide is that human life, especially
newly born human life, has as such no absolute value. It has
some small relative sentimental value, but the preservation of
it is to be judged in relation to a social and economic situation.
Where other checks on expansion of the population are not
effective they regard this as preferable to engendering conditions
of food shortage which would be the cause of human misery.

Now turn to judgements of homicide. As members of a
Christian community Westerners are used to the formulation
" Thou shalt not kill! " In modern European society we
do not take this literally; we regard the taking of human life
as morally justified in certain circumstances. The text of
the Revised Version of the Bible, " Thou shalt do no murder,"
expresses the position more closely. That is, it is the " un-
lawful killing of a human being with malice aforethought "
that is condemned. We therefore ask what types of killing
are lawful. Two such types are clearly that killing which
represents the exaction of the death penalty for crime; and
the killing performed by soldiers upon the enemy in war.
The first is an affair of members of the same society; the
second is the outcome of hostile relations between the members
of two societies. But in either case the ultimate decision on
the lawfulness of the killing does not lie with the person who
performs the act. It rests with the State, the society in its
political form. The nature of the moral judgement therefore
depends on the social circumstances. There are some who
question the right of society to be the arbiter in such instances,
who maintain that it is wrong in all circumstances for one
human being deliberately to take the life of another. Such
people will not accept the morality of either capital punishment or war.[2] Another view which is not so much a denial

---

[1] Jeremy Bentham, *Theory of Legislation* (ed. by C. K. Ogden, 1931),
pp. 264–65, 479, 494.

[2] It will be noted that this may be different from the view which has
prevailed in Portugal and most Scandinavian countries, that capital punishment should be abolished, not necessarily because it is wrong for the State
to impose such a penalty but because it is inefficient or otherwise inexpedient.
But this abolition may also, of course, be associated with moral views.

of the right of the State to validate the taking of human life as a claim for that right to be extended, and for individuals to have a more personal decision in the exercise of it, is seen in the arguments about euthanasia. Certain extreme physical conditions, such as decrepitude, incurable disease with acute pain, render it a moral act, it is argued, for life to be taken from the person concerned, using proper safeguards against abuse. The difficulties in its application are obvious—to decide which conditions are appropriate and which are not for such action, and to overcome the emotional reluctance to take the final decision at a given point. Unless the individual's consent is obtained, it also has the disadvantage of opening the way for the general view that members of the community may be justifiably removed from it by death not because they are a danger to the community but because they are a burden on it. Homicide in more primitive societies shows analogous variation in moral judgements. Moral approval or disapproval of killing depends on whether the person slain was a member of the killer's own community or of another community. In the latter case the anger of the killer's group may be directed against him on moral grounds, not because of the taking of life as such but because his act has endangered the safety of the community by inviting revenge. Hence compensation to the group of the murdered man is a normal procedure. Similarly within the community, while direct moral condemnation is applied, compensation to kinsmen and ritual atonement tend to be included among the reactions. Even the issue of euthanasia arises in semblance, with the same divergence of moral views. Cases are not unknown in primitive society where a man with an incurable loathsome disease has prayed his kinsfolk for death. Their refusal, on emotional grounds, has led him to appeal to the gods and ancestors to kill him by spiritual means.

But the absence of a specifically moral condemnation of the taking of human life by others, in certain circumstances, is brought out by attitudes to suicide, or to attempted suicide. In many primitive societies disposal of one's own life is regarded as not purely a private affair. But it is semi-private. An attempt at suicide will be prevented if possible by any member of the community—people do not stand by and watch calmly while someone tries to kill himself. But their interference is not accompanied by any particular moral condemnation of the attempt. The act is disapproved on grounds of stupidity, or incorrect judgement. The person is weighing up his situation inadequately, it is held, and treating as insoluble what is only temporarily embarrassing. Or it is disapproved of on grounds of sentiment. As in the case of Pa Rangifuri cited in Chapter II, it is the wrench to the family and kin sentiment that is stigmatized, not the suicidal act as such. A converse attitude may occur, as in Japan, where suicide may be even facilitated by friends, and classed as praiseworthy, as the *seppuku* ritual practised under the feudal system, and, later, by men of the gentry whose honour had been compromised without remedy. The contrast with the modern European attitude is most marked. Attempted self-destruction in Europe is a legal as well as a moral offence. This may be linked with the religious view, that the individual is regarded as endowed with some elements of divine purpose, of which he is in some sense an agent, and is therefore not free to dispose of his moral envelope as he wishes. Yet eighteenth-century Europe recognized the moral if not the legal right of a gentleman to sacrifice his life, if need be, in a duel. This "affair of honour" might be tantamount to suicide for the weaker man.

We can now set out more precisely some of the general characteristics of primitive moral judgements from the angle of social actions and relations. That there are many empirical differences in the evaluation of the same or similar types of action in different societies is a commonplace. But this has an important and less-well-recognized corollary. The lack of complete isolation, even for the most primitive society, means that members of one society are continually being offered moral comparisons. Most of these they tend to reject. Their own individuality and integration as a community are strengthened by the crude contrast of moral values. But contact and the presentation of new ideas have some effect. Individuals and ultimately communities may modify their moral standards in response to a complex set of motives. In parts of North-Western Australia, for example, groups of aborigines who have previously practised a so-called four-section system of social alignment have come in recent years to be confronted with knowledge of a more complicated arrangement—the eight sub-section system. Like players at draughts who have become convinced of the superiority of chess, some of these communities are struggling to adopt the new system. They are told by the other aborigines, and believe, that it is morally right to make the finer differentiations which the new system lays down in allocating marriage partners. Sometimes a compromise is worked out when parties from communities practising different systems marry. In spheres other than kinship and marriage—for instance, trading relationships—contact of people from different communities may lead to some softening of the edges of moral judgement on certain types of conduct—e.g., eating habits. In some ways, then, there is a definite tendency for the sphere of moral judgements to widen as the sphere of social relations extends and interests become common. A contrary tendency is the formation of more specific, even individual, judgements as interests narrow down. In group action, differentiation of evaluations of conduct helps in group demarcation, and may serve as a focus and symbol of integrated action.

It appears also from our brief survey that there are differences in the quality of evaluation of the same or similar conduct in various circumstances. The physical act of killing another person is viewed morally in very different terms, according to the range of social action involved and the degree of responsibility imputed. The extent to which social relations are affected, as within a group, or between two groups in a community, or throughout the community, is an important criterion in giving weight to moral judgement. In many cases of killing, for instance, it is immaterial from the moral point of view whether the act was accidental or premeditated. Moral condemnation and material compensation or seeking of revenge follow equally in either event. But the circumstances of the action, even the motivation, may be taken into account. In ancient Maori warfare, for example, which was conducted with ferocity, and where the killing of an enemy was normally approved, killing in treacherous circumstances did appear to evoke some moral disapproval. It was described by a special term, *kohuru*.

The survey also brings up the general question of the relation of moral rules to religious sanctions. How far is the good a function of the sacred? In the universalist religions such as Islam, Judaism, Christianity, Buddhism, there is a specific integration between them. The sacred books and other sources of religious training proclaim and help to enforce the moral law. In primitive religions the relation is apt to be more diffused. In some cases the High God or other supreme culture hero is alleged to have given particular moral pronouncements. More often, he is regarded as having simply ordered that men should continue to practise the ceremonies he instituted, or preserve a structure he set up. The myths of a people thus give only a tacit moral backing for their modern cultural forms. This general positive sanction, this aura of approval which is thus cast over the institutions, is reinforced by the role of ancestors in cultural transmission. In relatively stable social conditions " to have done as our fathers did " is a good thing in itself.

Religious sanctions often operate strongly in a negative sense, giving grounds for disapproval of conduct, and supplying an interpretation of misfortune, illness, and death in terms of the anger of ancestors at breaches of the moral law. In Tallensi ideology filial piety is an important moral principle. For a man to remain for years in foreign parts and neglect to make sacrifices at the ancestral shrines is dangerous, especially if he is the eldest of a group of brothers, and therefore primarily responsible for carrying on the family cults. If his wife or children die, if he gets a continual run of bad luck, this is attributed by diviners to his having " rejected his fathers." He will probably return home to rebuild the parental homestead, to avoid worse, perhaps his own death.[1] To the Tikopia, the ultimate sanction against incest between very close kin, say half-brother and half-sister, is the moral indigna-

[1] M. Fortes, *The Web of Kinship among the Tallensi*, Oxford, 1949, pp. 173-74.

tion of their dead parents. The parents may take no action during their lifetime, for shame at the scandal. But after their death, the Tikopia aver, their ghostly anger is expressed in the killing of any offspring of the incestuous union. In a variety of ways, in primitive beliefs, agencies from the spirit-world intervene to punish the derelictions of men. This punishment is conceived as being in some circumstances automatic, as when the breach of a taboo necessitates compensatory suffering, the spirit agency concerned being a morally neutral instrument of chastisement. But the motivating force behind the spirit action is often conceived to be anger on a moral basis. Failing to sacrifice, sleeping with a clan-sister, insulting a chief, killing a fellow kinsman—actions of such a kind may be difficult to deal with effectively in human terms. But moral judgement on them is projected into the spirit sphere, whence it is brought back in the form of diagnosis of ills and misfortune, and adjustment made on this basis.

Yet the application of moral judgement in the religious field is by no means uniform. Spirit attitudes may be described as the basis for the moral law, yet spirit behaviour as described in myth may itself break precisely those rules which are held in regard in the contemporary society. It is common in mythology to find gods lying, thieving, committing adultery and incest, killing, to serve their ends. Even in the narratives of the Old Testament some of the actions of the Almighty and incidents approved by Him savour of sharp practice or of moral short-sightedness, by modern standards. Uzzah was struck dead for trying to be helpful and steady the Ark over rough ground. Jacob was continued in the Divine favour after cheating Esau and his father over the blessing in a quite barefaced way, and even his behaviour when dividing the flocks with Laban was in questionable taste. The mythical sanction for morality is selective. Sometimes, as Radcliffe-Brown has pointed out, it appears to work by contrast rather than by direct precept or example. Sometimes it ignores early peccadilloes in favour of more recent achievements.

We have discussed so far mainly the bases of moral evaluation of conduct. Mention must also be made of the effects of moral judgement, the organization of moral sanctions. In many spheres moral sanctions operate in a diffused way. The individual who is the object of them is made to feel their force by the words and gestures of his fellows rather than by any physical constraint put upon him. The diffuse moral sanction of contempt, applied through public opinion, is often a powerful means of securing conformity. Among the Tikopia, as among the Eskimo and other peoples, the public chanting of songs expressing moral disapproval or scorn is one way of bringing a negative moral sanction to bear. In Tikopia also positive moral sanctions are conveyed in a similar way, by laudatory songs, which are expected to be acknowledged by a gift from recipient to composer.

In the more primitive societies, breach of a moral rule is reckoned to provoke suffering. But this is conceived as almost entirely physical. The results may be delayed, and only attributed by oracles or divination. In the meantime, the moral delinquent may actually be suffering keenly from emotional disturbance. But the primitive concept of punishment does not include the idea of unhappiness as a factor to be counted in the payment for sin. It is the visible token, the physical effect, that is treated as the true and proper sanction. It is in line with this that primitive ideas of the afterworld place so little emphasis on punishment for the guilty soul. There is not much interest in the fate of the human spirit after death, from the moral point of view. In this concentration on observable effects these primitive societies have in some ways a more effective means of control of social action. They do use the concept of mental or emotional suffering, however, as a punishment for moral offence, by linking it with family sentiment. If there is to be any fairly close observable relation between moral breach and physical punishment, the system must be elastic; there must be a wide choice of factors. If a child falls ill, the only moral offence that can be sought and reasonably identified may be in the behaviour of a parent. If a person commits an observed breach of the moral law, the only observable illness or misfortune in his vicinity for some time afterwards may be that of a child or other kinsman. Hence the morality of parental and other kin ties is invoked as a sanction against offence.

No ordinary father will deliberately commit a wrong act if he is going to suffer for it in seeing the sickness or death of his child.

This leads us to consider further the relation of moral rules to the social structure. It is clear that in any society the structure of kinship is strongly supported by morality. The reciprocal obligations between parents and children, or between brothers and sisters, are justified basically by reference to moral principles. The transmutation of biological relations into social relations is intelligible for the ordinary member of society only in terms of appeal to customary notions of what is right. In the many primitive societies where kinship provides the basis for the economic and political structure, extrafamilial extensions of kinship also have an important moral weight. In some Australian aboriginal groups it is the custom for a man to seek a wife from the family of his mother's cross-cousin. Specifically, he looks for a daughter of his mother's mother's brother's daughter. This latter woman and her husband, his distant aunt and uncle, are his potential mother-in-law and father-in-law. In the rules of such a society, it is right and proper that he should cultivate these people, perform services for them, and help to provide them with game. These services are done in the hope of a substantial return in the shape of a wife. But there is also a distinct moral obligation on a man to perform them. The moral system is oriented in support of the structure of kinship and marriage arrangements.

In the more complex societies—for instance, where there is a more developed class structure—it may be less easy to see the direct bearing of the moral ideas. It is true that in a Polynesian or African society with a system of chieftainship, for example, there is a morality of obedience of people to chief which transcends the rendering of economic or political obligations. This is reinforced by two factors. One is that the chief is normally not simply a leader in a political sense; he is also the leader of a prominent kinship group in the community, and as such can draw upon the moral fabric of the kinship structure to support his authority. The other factor is that the chief himself is bound by a morality of responsibility. In the Maori phrase, he is the " stake to which the canoe is tied "; or again, his people are " the hairs of his legs." They depend upon him. He moves, and they follow; if he is weak, they succumb. The distributive system in a primitive community is such that a chief reaps only a relatively small advantage from his superior command of wealth. In the absence of many durable types of accumulation, his capital stocks are best handled by feeding them out—often literally—to his dependants, as a basis for long-term service obligations. But there is probably always a kernel of discontent at the appropriations of a chief. And especially when contact with the Western economic system provides new outlets for using resources, concepts of social justice tend to be stimulated to demand some readjustment of the chief's privileges. Hence class morality is apt not to be a direct reflection of current structural alignments. The existing moral rules may conceal and minimize tension, not express unanimity.

The fulfilment of the moral obligations laid down by structural requirements is conditioned by individual interests. But more than this, moral judgements play a large part in giving the impetus to divergence from what appear in general as the norms of conduct. As interpreted by individuals in application to their own particular situations, ideas of right and wrong provide an important justification to social action. A simple example from Tikopia will illustrate this. A chief in that community has a structural obligation to instruct his heir, normally his eldest son, in the ritual procedures, and especially in the sacred ancestral names, of the *kava* cults which are the basis of Tikopia religion.[1] It was said of one chief when I was there that he had not been properly instructed in these fundamental matters. The reason was that as an eldest son he had not remained by his father's side, as he ought, but had gone to live in another district. The old chief, angry at this desertion, as he considered it, did not make known the esoteric matters to him, but to a younger son. In the course of time the father died. The eldest son was elected as chief. In accordance with the moral obligation on

[1] See my *Work of the Gods in Tikopia*, 2 vols., London, 1940 (London School of Economics Monographs on Social Anthropology, Nos. 1 and 2).

such occasions, a kinsman who has the sacred knowledge in his possession should make it known secretly to the new chief. That is the right thing to do, in the interests of the clan and the chief who has to carry out the rites for the good of all. In this case the younger brother did make known the secrets of the cult, but, it was said, not completely. He was angry that his brother had been selected as head of the clan, while he remained a commoner. So some of the information died with him. Here the major structural obligation is clear —to transmit the esoteric data, in proper conditions. But each of the three parties varied their behaviour from those conditions. The eldest son should have been by his father's side to receive the old man's confidences easily. But, for reasons which seemed to him good—family friction, ease of working land, nearness to wife's kinsfolk, maybe—he moved to live elsewhere. He had a moral justification for moving. But the old man had a moral justification for feeling aggrieved; why should his heir put his own convenience above his father's? So he turned to the younger son. This man, too, had a moral justification for holding back some of the sacred data. He had gone to the trouble of learning it, but had not been elected to the title of chief. Why should he bother too much about his elder brother, who had shirked his responsibility at a critical time, when his father was approaching old age? Here these men were not simply each meeting his own selfish interests; they had each a moral basis for so acting. One can understand the social action only by reference to these moral evaluations.

From analysis of such material we can see the relation of a moral system to social organization. Every structural arrange- ment has its moral attributes of obligation. But these have to be interpreted by persons in the light of their own position at the time. This has also its moral concomitants, or its inferences for moral judgement on action. It is not simply economic interest or status–desires that dictate the action. The moral evaluation supplies a force of justification that may override structural requirements. The various moral evalua- tions possible within the system do not in themselves suggest any automatic hierarchy of interests or action. Yet the limitations inherent in the nature of human resources demand some arrangement of time and energy in proper sequence. Hence decision is required. The role of moral judgement is to give such decision a validity which ensures that it shall be effective in action. Morality is socially born, but individually nourished. It is in the capacity to generate and adapt moral force that man derives one of the most potent springs to social action.

A moral system, then, includes the idea of an elaborate interlocking set of judgements by individuals on their own conduct and that of others, continually being formed, reformed, and exploding into action. In this complexity of moral evaluations and in clashes of moral interpretation lie the seeds of social change.

It will be useful to put this analysis of morality briefly again in its general anthropological perspective. The anthropologist is not discussing the existence of ethical notions on the philosophical plane. But what he does show, in line with the studies of Durkheim, Westermarck, Hobhouse, Ginsberg, and others, is the existence of standards of right and wrong, and sensitive judgements in their terms, in all human societies studied. These standards vary greatly in differentiation and in social range. They are in obvious relation to the structure of the societies where they are found. But behind this variation is a real measure of uniformity. Moral judgements spring immediately from individual emotion fused with a component of reasoning. But they are based ultimately on social inoculation, especially in childhood. Morality has important social functions, and exists in virtue of them. Right and wrong, good and evil, justice, duty, conscience, are operational concepts, gripped into social action. Morality, then, is that system of rules and standards which gives significance to the activity of individuals in relation to one another in society. It gives meaning and value to conduct. It justifies conduct, even in opposition to major structural principles. Associated with the perception of inconsistencies in action, it may even set the seal on opposition as one of its social functions. Morality is a social cement between individual means and social ends.

P

There must be, then, a system of morality in every human society. It is relative in the sense that social ends vary, and so must the emotional tone that is given to them. But as some common factors are discernible in the basic requirements of all societies, so certain moral absolutes exist. It must be assumed that for a society to continue to exist there must be some regulation of conduct among its members. This must have reference to some fundamental principles. No human society which depends for its existence on a minimum of family arrangements could exist without some regulation and restraint in sexual affairs. Licence in one direction, as in premarital intercourse, is compensated for in another, as in restrictions on adultery, or on sex relations between members of the same kin group. There is everywhere, as Malinowski so clearly demonstrated, sufficient stability of human sex relations to allow the minimum of care for infants. Every society must also in some way or another place a curb on violence. This demands some general principles about the relative value of non-violence and overt harmony in social action. It is from such a standpoint, whatever be his pre-conception about religious or other sanctions for basic morality, that the anthropologist approaches his subject. He does not abjure moral universals. He seeks them in the very nature of his social material.

Morality, then, is not merely subjective. It is objective in the sense of being founded on a social existence which is external to the individual, and to any specific social system. This does not mean that one has to appeal for its validity to some exterior agency, absolute and independent of the social world. It is preferable to look for a more general theory which will subsume the thesis of the exterior agency itself, together with that of morality, in terms of a humanistic analysis.

See Appendix for some recent works in this field.

CHAPTER VII

RELIGION IN SOCIAL REALITY

RELIGION is one of the great driving forces in human activity, both individually and socially. Not only does it give occasion for elaborate institutional assemblies, it also gives sanctions for a wide range of conduct. It provides a referent for the explanation of many events in human life which seem obscure and demand a meaning. It can even be appealed to for basic principles of interpretation of history and the existence of the world itself. It constitutes a system parallel to and in many ways opposed to the logical-empirical systems of science. Yet at many points it is gripped by human interest into situations which man attempts to handle by scientific techniques—for example, into those of illness, where medicine and the consolations of religion may meet. Historically, religion has been a source of obscurantism, of persecution, of cruelty, and of war. Yet with it have been associated some of the finest flowers of art. It has promoted philosophy through humility, self-examination, and the desire to push back the bounds of knowledge. It has led many men to do much for their fellows by the charity and love it may enjoin.

It is, then, one of the most important, yet one of the most debatable subjects for anthropological discussion. Anthropologists have not shirked the task. The names of Tylor, Robertson-Smith, and Frazer; of Durkheim, Marett, Hubert, and Mauss; of Preuss, Söderblom, and Wilhelm Schmidt; of Goldenweiser, Radin, Lowie, Edwin Smith, Malinowski, and Radcliffe-Brown recall the vast body of comparative and analytical studies already done, and their continuation by others today. The data accumulated on the character and functions of beliefs in gods and demons, ideas of the soul and the life after death, principles of mana and taboo, myth, miracle and magic, ancestor cults and nature cults, propitiatory and sacramental rites, have enabled large regions of human religious experience to be mapped out on a comparative basis. The anthropologist has shown that to be understood scientifically religion must be defined in a broad way. At its centre is belief in some kind of superhuman power. But the idea of such a power may be in much less coherent anthropomorphized form than that ordinarily conveyed by the concept of spirit or Deity. The emotional content of such belief is at least as important as the intellectual content. Belief alone does not constitute a religion; the rites and mundane practices associated with belief are an essential constituent of the whole. The antinomy between faith and works, a matter for argument by Buddhists or by Christians, may have meaning for a doctrine of salvation, but none for a definition of religion. Religion is a medium through which the individual can obtain some of his keenest experiences and handle some of his most fundamental personal problems. But it must be considered also in its collective bearings. Individually interpreted and supported, it is socially shared and transmitted, and in this lie some of its most important characteristics. The anthropologist has been able to show how, when regarded as it must be in such a broad way, religion is universal in human societies. This is an empirical generalization, an aggregate of a multitude of specific observations.

But the anthropologist has gone farther. He has argued that religion is a necessary corollary of man's social existence. This theme was developed, for instance, by Malinowski.[1] In substance, form and function, he said, religion has a unity in all human societies, and grows out of the necessities of human life. On the sacramental side, at crises of life, it gives a purpose and direction to the course of the individual's existence, and emphasizes the value of personality. On the side of practical interests, especially in the domain of magic, that "embodiment of the sublime folly of hope," it enhances man's capacity to act by giving him confidence in his own power and a basis

[1] In two important works, *Magic, Science and Religion*, Glencoe, Ill., 1948; and *The Foundations of Faith and Morals* (Riddell Memorial Lectures, University of Durham), Oxford University Press, London, 1936.

for organization in meeting the trials and difficulties he encounters in coping with Nature. This view Malinowski put forward as a believer in the value of human culture and human personality, but not in any specific religious tenets. He argued that as a rationalist unable to accept what purport to be the eternal truths of religion, he must at least recognize them as "indispensable pragmatic figments without which civilization cannot exist."

With this position I am very much in sympathy. But I think it needs further examination, on several general grounds.

Such views do not arise inevitably from consideration of the anthropological evidence. Susan Stebbing has remarked that every scientist turned philosopher tends to find support in his special studies for the metaphysical theory which *on other grounds* he tends to find attractive. This was said primarily about physicists. But with it in mind it is no surprise to find that there is a diversity of opinion among anthropologists as to where the basic functions or reality of religion lie. There may be no great support for the view commonly held by theologians and some others who study "comparative religion," that its crowning development, which gives a final meaning and solution to the problems of existence, was the revelation of Christianity. But there is not general agreement that all religious beliefs are in the last resort an illusion or fiction.[1]

The competence of the anthropologist to pronounce on the content as well as on the form of religion would be sharply denied by schools of thought to whom science is like electricity, safe only when properly insulated. The arguments here are varied, and may be summarized by propositions such as follows. Science has as its field the natural world of physical fact, and works by the method of reason; there are phenomena

[1] It may be noted that Malinowski, brought up as a Roman Catholic when a child, and dogged by personal and family illness in grim shape for much of his life, had an obscure belief in fate and an almost obsessional interest in the fear of death. It is, I think, no coincidence that he found in the twin beliefs in Providence and in Immortality the cardinal affirmations of all religion, and that he stressed the vital functions to humanity of a faith in which he himself, perhaps, subconsciously would have liked to share.

beyond the physical world, not susceptible to the control of reason. Science studies those things which exist and live; it cannot affirm or deny anything meaningful about the source of being or living. Science deals with the data of ordinary sense experience, what may be called external knowledge; it cannot give any proof that an individual does not have a different form of experience, an inner knowledge which cannot be apprehended or measured by ordinary means. Hence it cannot disprove a person's statement that he knows mystical states with a direct experience of God. Again, science must deal with the predictable and determinate; the more science advances the clearer it becomes that there is a point beyond which prediction and determination are impossible. Recent work in atomic physics, for instance, by showing the uncertainty relations in respect of the measurement of the position and velocity of electrons, has revealed an ultimate indeterminacy in the nature of the universe which is incapable of treatment by science.

One need not accept such views. But it is significant that there is a strong body of opinion which welcomes the researches of anthropologists in so far as they demonstrate the universality and illustrate and elucidate the workings of religion, but deprecates any anthropological attempt to pronounce on the nature of religious reality.

Anthropological consideration of the basic nature of religion has an added interest at the present time because of what is thought to be a crisis of faith in the Western world. To many this appeals primarily as a crisis of Christianity. There have probably been few periods during almost the last two thousand years when Christianity has not been undergoing some kind of critical change. But rarely perhaps since the Roman persecution of the early centuries and the Muslim invasion of the Middle Ages has it faced such a direct challenge as now. Arnold Toynbee would place the origin of the present discontents of Western Christendom well back—in the sixteenth and seventeenth centuries, which saw a subordination of religion to politics. Others would lay the blame at the door of Galileo and Newton. The seeds might well lie still farther back, in an economic rather than a political refusal to accept the authority of the Church. But Toynbee regards the sceptical attitude of mind of the last few centuries as the supreme danger to the spiritual health, and even the material existence, of our Western civilization—the spiritual vacuum hollowed out in our Western hearts by the progressive decay of religious belief. To some extent Christianity in the last century and a half has compensated for religious lethargy at home by proselytism upon the heathen abroad. Other keen competitors are now in the field. Buddhism and Hinduism are both seeking converts, while Islam is especially active in African and Asiatic fields. But Christianity has a more dangerous enemy. If in the nineteenth century the major challenge was from the scepticism of evolutionary materialism, in the twentieth century it comes from the faith of revolutionary materialism. This offers not only a theory of society and man's destiny which is more simply formulated, if no less fundamentally obscure, than that of Christianity. It has also that burning conviction of the rightness of its aims which is one of the choicest possessions of religion itself. Here Islam and the other religions face the same problem as Christianity. Men must have a moral basis for action. This can be provided in various ways, in which historically in both the Orient and the Occident philosophy and religion have taken their share. To be effective, a moral system must be expressible in symbols which in one way or another can be related to current experience. Religion is often appealed to as the only source of the morality which can measure up to the magnitude of the problems created by modern technological advance. Yet in the Western, as in the Oriental world, the traditional religions have by their compromises allowed some of the most important symbols of distributive justice to pass to their Communist opponents. One result of this has been that when Communism has taken power as a political system, a change is apt to take place in the religious patterns. This is not simply a change in authority and a yielding to pressure, as is usually alleged in the West; it indicates a voluntary change in the symbols of moral expression through a real re-alignment of views.

In the face of all such issues the anthropologist must continually consider his problems afresh. They provide him with new data for comparison, they invite him to test again the personal assumptions he must make in his study. He is concerned mainly with the interpretation of material from primitive societies. But in the field of religion, above all, it is hard to draw the line of primitivity. So all ideas about the general nature of religion, from whatever source, are of interest to him, either as examples of religious behaviour or as theoretical stimulus. For a detailed consideration of the nature of religion the anthropologist would need to rely heavily on the work of historians, sociologists, and psychologists, as Max Weber, Tawney, Troeltsch, Wach, Talcott Parsons, William James, Leuba, Allport. Here a much more limited examination of some of the problems is all that is possible.

In the first place, a sketch may be given of typical elementary social situations which give a basis for religious action.

Man as an individual is subject to biological and psychological drives to action. This action is goal-oriented, value-governed. To attain the full range of his goals, man must live in society, and so derive the advantages of co-operative action. Social living means on the one hand processes of learning and processes of adaptation, and on the other hand processes of sharing of knowledge and definition of the unknown. The sharing and learning processes provide behaviour for imitation and ideas for communication; they generate values, orientations for behaviour, and assign qualities to relationships. In relations with the external, natural environment, social living provides possible solutions to problems of ignorance, uncertainty, anxiety, and even fear. Some of these solutions are empirical, even technical. Others go beyond the ordinary empirical sphere and may take on a symbolic character. Such are the solutions offered by productive and protective magic, which in systems of ritual and belief symbolically safeguard the yield from agriculture or fishing, allay storms at sea, and bring the canoe-traveller home, give health to the sick and successful issue to women in childbed. But social living in itself has its drawbacks, and even dangers. Social relations involve not only co-operation but also friction—criticism, slander, quarrelling, rivalry, and the risk of personal violence.

Solutions are provided here, too.   In the empirical field the
social controls of etiquette and of law, for instance, resolve many
difficult situations.   But these cannot cope fully with the subtle
workings of the human psyche.   Solutions of a socialized
kind are therefore provided in which the individual can operate
a symbolic system more to his liking.   Concepts of evil
principles, of sorcery and witchcraft, of demons, provide
more acceptable explanation of social failures than does the
notion of human inadequacy.   Reinforced by ideas of sacrifice and scapegoat, of the devil and of hell, they provide
outlets for aggressive impulses which need not react physically
on other members of the society.   A solution of another kind
is provided by prayer.   This offers an outlet for aggression
and a release from emotional tension.

It does this in a variety of ways : by statement of desire in
overt form, by projection of mental images as objective
reality, by an elaborate process of identification of the self
with other members of the society, and even by response to the
æsthetic qualities of the word-patterning and imagery used.
But the social world does not bear on its face the obvious
stamp of completion and fulfilment of human desire.   Its
empirical techniques are clearly inadequate, its symbolic forms
do not easily meet the search for the full resolution of the
problems of existence.   The process of projection is therefore
carried farther, to concepts of divine entity.   This combines
the extreme qualities, actual and desired, of the human personality, and in knowledge, power, and love provides the full
plan and the full meaning to human life.   Rites such as those
of worship provide movements of association with the grand
design for living, while those of communion make a more
intimate inclusory gesture.

This skeletal indication of some of the main fields or type
situations for religious action has helped to specify some of
the important complexes ordinarily recognized.   Magic,
witchcraft, prayer, worship, communion, and sacrifice are
not found in all religious systems, but they are of wide currency.

No really satisfactory theoretical classification of religious
behaviour has yet been made.   The categories generally

used are those of descriptive association, complexes of a factual kind, like those just mentioned. A distinction is usually drawn between ritual, the mode of action and belief, the mode of conception, in religion. But neither of these categories is easy to define, and they are closely linked. However, they do give starting points of different emphasis from which to begin the examination of religion.

Ritual may be defined as a kind of patterned activity oriented towards control of human affairs, primarily symbolic in character with a non-empirical referent, and as a rule socially sanctioned. When we are speaking of religious ritual in particular, the non-empirical referent is ordinarily a god or other spiritual being or superhuman force such as *mana*. There are many kinds of religious rituals. Some distinction may be drawn between them by intention, expressed in the language which is a normal part of any ritual. Some kinds of ritual may be termed *hortatory*, since they attempt to control by a process of admonition. Many magical rituals are of this type. Such is the simple performance of a Tikopia who takes out a new net one night when he is going after flying-fish. When his canoe gets to the mouth of the channel, beyond the reef, and the fleet is about to begin fishing, he dips his new net, which is long-handled and rather like a lacrosse net, into the sea. At the same time he calls out: "Here! rise properly, flying-fish, To the canoe of man."

The address is partly to the flying-fish, urging them to rise and soar above the surface that they may be caught. It is also intended to stir up any spirit guardian of the net or the canoe to use his powers. Many magical rituals use much more elaborate spells and an array of ritual substances or "medicines" to aid the process. But the integral association of words with other actions in the ritual complex is an important feature. There is a felt need to verbalize in order to be sure of the reality of the performance. The word in itself is not necessarily magical in virtue, but it is an essential validating element. Other kinds of ritual proceed not by the language of command, but by that of entreaty. The spirits are asked to grant the performer's wishes. This is the type of expression often used in rituals of *propitiatory* intention, in order to gain the favour of the spirits, or of *piacular* intention, in order to expiate an offence. The difference between the language of command and the language of entreaty was taken by J. G. Frazer to be the essence of the distinction between spell and prayer. Further, he took it also as the distinction between magic and religion. One difficulty here is that of cross-relationship. It is not uncommon for hortatory ritual to be performed in reference to gods or ancestors, invoking them in the language of admonition and command. Moreover, language of entreaty is not infrequently mingled with that of admonition. It is for this reason, the difficulty of drawing any very clear line between spell behaviour and prayer behaviour, that many modern anthropologists include magic under the general head of religious behaviour. They differentiate it where necessary by the absence of any very clear spirit referent and the relation of such ritual actions to an immediate clear-cut end.

It is convenient, however, to draw a distinction between rituals which are *sacramental* and those which are not. Sacramental rites have as their essential feature the notion of some change in the persons performing or attending the ritual, or for whom it is being performed. In the traditional Catholic view, the sacraments comprise baptism, confirmation, the eucharist, penance, matrimony, the taking of orders, and extreme unction. In most primitive societies, and in many Western Churches, matrimony is not a sacrament, neither is the counterpart of the taking of orders. By sacrament in the strict sense is meant a ritual which by its outward forms serves as a visible sign of an inward or spiritual state—a state of grace. In primitive religions the inward state cannot be defined in the same theological terms. But, as Marett showed, there are in primitive societies many rituals analogous to those just cited.[1] In fact, the rites of the Christian Church are but species of larger religious genera, not an absolute standard by which all others are to be measured. Baptism has its analogies in the reception of an infant into its family and community by rites in which lustration by water is not infrequently an element. Confirmation has its analogies in the

[1] R. R. Marett, *Sacraments of Simple Folk*, Oxford, 1933.

elaborate initiation rites which are so characteristic of Australian aborigines, East African, and Melanesian peoples. Penance finds its parallel in the piacular rites of folk such as the Manus who seek by public confession the expiation of sin.[1] Extreme unction has less close analogies; the emphasis here in primitive societies is rather on promoting the appropriate state of the person after his death than on giving him the final spiritual easing out of life. But funeral rituals are many and elaborate. The rituals known to the anthropologist as *rites de passage* are the most important of the sacramental rituals in primitive societies. They are characterized, however, by a permanent transition of state of the persons primarily concerned, as at initiation, whereas other sacramental rites such as communion involve only a temporary change.

The *non-sacramental* rituals represent the exercise of control not over the inward state of the principal parties but over the action of some external object or person. That is the object of the various forms of productive, protective, and destructive magic, and the main aim also in the general field of worship. In rituals of divination the aim is retrospective or proleptic knowledge in order that control may be exercised over external events. In spiritualist performances—for example, those of the common type when a person is sick—both divinatory and protective aims are important. But a sacramental element is often also present, since as part of the process of recovery through such ritual a change in the patient's inner condition is often thought to be necessary.

If sacramental rites have as an important component a technique of identification, non-sacramental rites commonly use a technique of projection. In all types of ritual, however, the anthropologist is concerned primarily with the kinds of social relations that are produced or maintained, rather than with the inner state as such of the participants. Rituals reflect and express structural arrangements of the society, and of component though divergent elements in it. They provide occasion for group assembly, and reaffirm social values. They

[1] R. F. Fortune, *Manus Religion, Memoirs*, American Philosophical Society, No. III, Philadelphia, 1935.

stimulate economic productivity and condition the system of disbursement of resources. They allow individuals to handle social apparatus to advantage. It is from this point of view that the study of mystical experience, for instance, must be undertaken. The mystic does not necessarily perform any ritual. But his inner experiences do not remain locked up in his own mind; they affect his personality, his outer relations, his status in his society, and the way in which he behaves to others.

Most series of ritual actions presuppose some concomitant of religious belief. This involves the acceptance, by a mixture of cognitive and emotional attitudes, of a set of propositions regarding the sacred and the supernatural. Religious belief helps to provide organizing principles for human experience. In its content, its form, and its expression it is related to the attempts of people to give coherence to their universe of relations, physical as well as social. This it may do by several processes. It relies on the non-empirical formulations of experience—that is, on those which are not capable of verification by the methods of empirical science. This involves to a large extent what may be called a shifting of the index-pointer of reality. It is not just a flight from reality. It is a series of assertions that reality extends to the ideas of God and the soul, to principles of good and evil; or that the ultimate reality is spiritual in nature. The second process is the assertion of the truth of the beliefs, not in any conditional sense, but as final and absolute. The primary figures of the belief are indeed often identified as being the quintessence or the source of the very notion of truth itself. The third process is the attribution of moral rightness to the religious belief. Not only is the substance believed to be correct, accurate in knowledge, but also it is regarded as good that the attitude of belief should exist. The essential matter of belief is also commonly regarded as supplying the source of moral goodness. Compare this with the attitude of a physicist who is investigating the nature of the atom. He relies almost wholly upon formulations that are verifiable by scientific techniques, or that he tries to make verifiable. He may assert that his formulations are true, but he does not do so in any final sense. He knows that they are open to review at any time. He may think that it is a good idea that people should study the constitution of the atom, but he thinks it no virtue to believe in atomic constituents for their own sake. Nor does he impute to these particles the source of any virtue he may see in the whole process of study. In other words, religious belief invokes notions of absolute truth and morality to give authority to formulations which cannot be verified by ordinary means. An important question is, why should this be so? I shall answer this question towards the end of this analysis.

The conceptual content and emotional quality of religious belief vary according to its function—that is, according to its relation to other elements in the total system. In a social system, variation is given according to the sets of concepts held by other people. In particular, in the more highly differentiated societies, the existence of a church means a specific organization for the maintenance of belief in definite forms, often crystallized in dogma and creed. In such cases the implicit authority of the individual's belief may be transferred in part explicitly to the organization. In a personal system of action, the individual uses his belief as a means of adjustment of his relations with others and the external world. In order to do this effectively, he must be able to translate the beliefs as transmitted to him into terms of his own experience. Moreover, he must be able to give them sufficient quality of abstraction and generality to serve him for social interpretation.

The notion of a system implies an interconnected series of elements, and hence a tendency to resist a change in their connections. A system of religious belief, in view of the character of authority, already mentioned, which it accrues to itself, is peculiarly prone to defend itself against attack. On the other hand, it offers a tendency to intellectual elaboration, since in this is a covert freedom from control. Neither a primitive society nor a Church in Western civilization can apply sanctions to thought and feeling beyond a certain point. Imaginative activity is difficult to confine. Exploration of the logical possibilities implicit in the basic propositions of the belief is apt to proceed, even in the primitive field where often it is supposed there is only a faithful adherence to dogma. In Tikopia, for example, with its panoply of gods and other spirit beings, there has been clearly imaginative development of the pantheon along the lines of the system familiar to the people in their ordinary life—the kinship system. Gods and ancestral spirits are furnished with wives, endowed with offspring, with bond-friends, and depicted as composing songs and having adventures with mortals. This is apparently due in large measure to spirit-mediums, who in a state of dissociation have freedom to elaborate the system with their fantasy creations. Yet it is not pure fantasy. It is related to social requirements, to the status-seeking of individuals, and the other emotional satisfactions, as well as to the need for decision on matters of social import. Between elements of the social system and of the personal system there is continual adjustment.

On the other hand, a belief system may proclaim the " sacrifice of the intellect." Joy may be asserted in intellectual aversion, a deliberate choosing of emotionalism. Only in a special context, perhaps, have ever been asserted the epigrams attributed to Tertullian : " *Credo quia absurdum* " : " I believe it because it is ridiculous," or " It is certain, because it is impossible." But, as Max Weber has pointed out, there is no " unbroken " religion working as a vital force which is not compelled at some point to demand such a sacrifice. It is part of the character of religious belief to transmute this into an acquisition and a banner.

Our problem here is not to attempt to denigrate and destroy the non-empirical. In the æsthetic field, in social relations, and even in the creative constructs of scientific theory it has great value. But what we must do in a study of religion is to provide hypotheses which will account for its use and the forms its use takes in different circumstances.

The anthropological method of study, here as elsewhere, is that of empirical science, comparative inductive study. To help the explanation I take an example of a religious rite in which I participated years ago among the Tikopia of the Solomon Islands. Twice a year these heathen Polynesians perform a cycle of ceremonies lasting several weeks, in which offerings are made to their gods and ancestors. Valued objects of their culture, such as canoes, temples, and foodstuffs, are re-sacralized, and dedicated once more to their task of catering to the needs of the people. Among these rites is one connected with the yam harvest. It is a kind of firstfruits ceremony. It is known to the people as the Hot Food (*Kai Vera*). It is performed by the people of one clan, led by their chief, who is highest in the island hierarchy. In native eyes he is responsible for the religious control of the yam and its fertility, for the benefit of the whole Tikopia community. Tubers of the yam are picked out, and carefully counted, one for each man who will be present at the ceremony. They are then scraped, by women who wear new bark-cloth skirts for the occasion, to mark its sacredness. An oven of red-hot stones is prepared in the usual Polynesian style, and the yams are set therein to cook. While they are being removed from the oven in due course, the participants assemble in the clan temple, sitting in a curved line around three sides of the building. On the fourth side—the most sacred side—sits the chief of the clan, alone, facing inwards, like all the other men. Every man except the chief is provided with a large green leaf like a banana leaf, a couple of feet long and nearly a foot broad, which he holds cupped in his hands. As is the native custom, everyone is sitting cross-legged on the coconut-leaf mats on the floor of the building. Speech is only in whispers, for the rite that is to be performed is very sacred. As we sit there, an air of tense expectancy has seized everyone, and I am told that the rite is one that is carried out in great haste.

At last the sound of hurrying bare feet is heard on the path outside. In through the low thatch doorway bursts a man, bearing in his arms a basket full of the steaming hot yam tubers. Passing swiftly along in front of the line of men, he gives a yam to each. He does not hand it politely, but hurls it to the recipient, who must catch it in the leaf. Immediately each man receives his tuber he bends over it and makes a bite at it. His first effort is a mumble, for the yam is piping hot. But in a short time one of the company has succeeded in nipping off a piece of the vegetable and swallowing it, while his comrades are still struggling in keen competition with the heat. As soon as the man has gulped down his bit of yam he gives a little whistle. This is the signal for everyone to stop their efforts. As soon as the whistle, or little chirrup, is heard, everyone puts down his yam and there is a general relaxation of tension. The whistler is identified. People chaff him and one another at their ludicrous attempts to bite off and swallow the burning morsels. After more jokes and conversation, when the yams have cooled, an ordinary meal takes place.

The contrast between the strained expectancy and hushed voices of a few minutes before and the relaxed ease and good fellowship and rather boisterous laughter of the present is very marked. How is it that such a simple collective performance involving nibbling at some hot yams should be apparently an affair of such sacredness? What is the content of what must be a symbolic rite?

For the Tikopia the interpretation of the proceedings is this : the yams are under the protection of a god, the Supreme Deity controlling the fortunes of the island people. This ritual is believed to demonstrate to him that the people have cultivated his vegetable and are celebrating a ritual which he instituted as a culture-hero in times long past. They eat the yams at a ceremonial meal, symbolized by snatching at the hot morsels. The first man to swallow his morsel is deemed to have the special favour of the god for the coming season. Moreover, the god himself is thought to be present to watch the performance. He descends to inhabit for a brief space the body of his representative the chief. It is his eyes which look out from the chief's countenance and observe the conduct of his people on the occasion.

It is clear that to understand its meaning properly we must consider a range of ideas which are not comprehensible from consideration of the performance alone. In fact, this series of acts is intelligible only as part of an elaborate sequence in which other elements of offering and invocation of spirit beings are of vital importance.

Let us examine these elements one by one. The god is conceived as a being of superhuman attributes, though he was once a man and lived upon earth. Respect, awe, and even

Q

fear are dominant emotions in regard to him. He has many names, but a title which is often used for him is *Te Atua Fakamataku*, the God Causing Fear. Every Tikopia when I was there—even Christians—believed in his power, and in his ability to injure or succour the people of the land. Like other gods, he is manifest in the thunder. But the noise of his staff as he trails it rumbling through the heavens is more powerful than that of the others. These beliefs, with their strong emotional content, do not stand isolated in vague concepts. They are bound into a system which has as one of its vehicles of expression and concrete representation a set of tales or myths. These stories manifest the glory and the achievement of the god. They tell how as a human culture-hero he did mighty works in the island, using a tree as his staff, clearing whole acres of brushwood and planting whole cultivations at one stroke. Finally, struck down by a treacherous adversary, he was about to slaughter his foe. But he yielded to the entreaties of a female deity, and allowed himself to die and go to the after-world of spirits unsullied by any act of mortal revenge. Arrived there, he went to each of the gods in turn and compelled them to concede to him their power, that *mana* which is the force lying behind supernormal achievements. Such stories of origins are brought up to date by tales of contemporary events, miracles in which the ordinary course of nature is bent to the will of the god when he intervenes in the affairs of men.

Yet such a being, supreme ruler over the affairs of the Tikopia people, is believed not only to control the cultivation of the yam, but to be at times incarnate in that lowly vegetable. All the major foodstuffs of the Tikopia—taro, coconut, yam, breadfruit, sago—are each under the control of a deity whose head or body is represented by the foodstuff in question. When therefore the men nibble at their burning yams, it is the body of the god which they hold in their hands. At the sacramental moment it is the flesh of the god which is swallowed. Here, then, is a primitive communion feast, analogous to many other feasts in which the celebrants partake of the flesh of the deity, and so secure greater unity with him. This Tikopia ceremony is not a travesty of the Eucharist. It would

appear to be a rite of considerable antiquity in Tikopia, long
before the first European contacts took place. Moreover, it
has much in common with various primitive rituals analysed
by Frazer, Durkheim, and other anthropologists.

The Tikopia rite conforms closely, in fact, to Durkheim's
example of supreme religious activity, the totemic ritual of
Australian aborigines. There is the same close association of
a symbolic kind, between a social group, a clan, and a natural
species. There is the same assembly of clan members, to
partake of the symbolic object. There is the same aura of
the sacred round the proceedings. There is the same effer-
vescent social environment—tension, drama, competition,
release—that " super-excitation " which Durkheim regarded
as a prime generating condition of religious emotion. In
Durkheim's view the Australian totemic festival is religion
in its elementary form. The religious force is ultimately
given by the collective, anonymous force of the clan. The
animal or plant which is the clan totem serves as the clan
emblem. There is a transference of sentiment from the one
to the other. This is the more complete and marked, since
the emblem is something simple, definite, and easily represented, while the clan is complex and difficult for its members
to conceive of. So the emblem or symbol is treated as if it
were the reality. The clan is represented in the mind only
by the totem, and the totemic emblem is like the visible form
of the god. So Durkheim's argument runs. Now we can
agree that respect for a totem and for religious forces in general
is not just a translation of the way in which physical things
affect the senses directly. Like the bread and wine to the
Christian, the yams to the Tikopia mean far more than their
taste conveys. Moreover, in this respect the role of the collec-
tivity, the group determination of sentiment, is very important.

But alternative structures of belief are possible, even
in Durkheim's optimum conditions of totemic festival.
To the Tikopia the yam is the visible form of their god.
To some degree, it is an emblem of the Kafika clan. But its
sacredness is very limited and detachable. It is not only for
a brief space in the communion rite that it is treated with

great respect; for much of the agricultural cycle it is regarded
as taboo to common hands.   But after harvest and the festival there are many occasions when the yam is treated as an
ordinary vegetable.   Its sacredness, too, is not contagious;
it is not communicated to things in any permanent relation.
It is less of an emblem for the god and the clan than a vehicle
for commemorating the god by the clan.   And as compared
with Australian totemism, the relations of man and yam in
Tikopia are not on the same level and of equal value as
Durkheim would argue.   The Tikopia make a much clearer
separation of man from Nature than the Australian aborigines
do.   Their god was never a yam, as aboriginal culture-heroes
were once kangaroos and emus.   The identification of god
and totem is of a different kind, with a much more elaborate
degree of personification by the Tikopia.   The collective
solidarity of the Tikopia is much less overt in the religious
sphere.

In Tikopia the god is consciously present at the rite, not
only in an inactive form.   He is there active, endowed with
human attributes of sight, and with the power of understanding.   Peering through the eyes of his priest-chief, he
looks to see that men do not make sport of his rites.   He is
subject to all the human emotions.   If he detects an infringe-
ment of the rules of seating or other behaviour, he is believed
to strike the offender or his family with disease or death.   On
the occasion when I was present the god uttered no word.
He came and went in a flash.   But one of the characteristic
features of Tikopia religion, like that of so many other primitive peoples, is that the gods are believed to appear to men in
human form.   It is not that the body and limbs of the human
being are regarded necessarily as those of a god.   But in
Polynesia, at least, the god is regarded as using the human
medium as a vehicle for his pronouncements to his people.
Such spiritualism is widespread in primitive societies.   Though
we dignify it, it is known also in our own Western society.
In essence it is part of a general pattern by which god manifests himself to man in some concrete, easily apprehensible
form which carries more conviction than a vague and voiceless
entity.   Man likes as far as possible to be sensible of immediate,

not remote, control. This is basically Durkheim's argument but put in a more general, non-totemic setting.

Just as the speech of a god through his human medium carries force and conviction of reality, so the speech of man to his god is a matter of great significance. The verbal element is vital in the contact of man with deity. In theory one can communicate by mental effort, or by feeling alone. In practice thought and feeling both tend to express themselves in words uttered or silently formed. I have already mentioned the distinction usually drawn between the words of a spell, regarded as being almost automatic in their operation, an assertion of man's power over that which he addresses, and the words of prayer which rely for their effect upon an appeal, a beseeching of the deity. Useful in theory, such a distinction is often not easy to make in practice. Prayer comes often near to attempted compulsion, as is seen by the theory that reiterated prayer must bring an answer sooner or later. The spell, on the other hand, however unalterable and self-sufficient its wording may purport to be, is often conceived to rely for its power in the last resort upon spiritual beings. In invocation to such beings, though the form of words may be an appeal, the use of their names may have almost a magical quality. In Tikopia each god or ancestral spirit of importance has several names, which are regarded as the private property of the various social groups having the right to appeal to these spirit beings. The conception is that the deities are seated in the heavens when the appeals are made. Each hears his name, rises in his seat, and peers over the edge of the heavens to see why he has been called. Use of an incorrect name brings no response, while use of his name without reason or for sportive purposes brings down his anger.

In all this the concept is one of control of the affairs of man by unseen spirit beings whose powers far surpass his. But they are believed to share with him most of the ordinary human attributes of sensation and emotion. The gods of the Tikopia are pleased with offerings and with thanks; they are ashamed if they are accused by men of having acted unjustly; they are angry if men try to cheat them, withhold from them the first fruits of the earth, or insult them. In Tikopia ideas, foods of land and sea, winds and storms, thunder and lightning, sun and rain, sickness and health, all depend on the controlling power of these spirit beings.

Tacit in the relationship of the Tikopia to his gods is the idea of reciprocity—a theme discussed in Chapter II. When the yam is about to be harvested the Tikopia are anxious that the crop should be adequate, at least for the purposes of this communion feast. They argue like this: if there are not enough yams for the celebration the god will suspect that his people are hiding away from him the produce which his bounty has afforded them, that they are unwilling to give to him the acknowledgement which is his due. He therefore will become angry and visit them with misfortune. Should therefore the yam crop be too poor to supply an adequate meal, they supplement it, with some misgiving, from other vegetable foods in order that the ritual may be performed and the god satisfied. However, while the Tikopia are firm believers in the power of their gods and in the rights of these gods, they are also realists. Their method of making offering to the gods is not one of wasteful sacrifice. They have a theory of what one may call essences—that is, that every material living thing has an immaterial separable counterpart, which in the case of man may be called his soul. This essence, being of the same order of reality as the spirit powers themselves, is what spirits subsist on. Therefore, when offerings of food are set out to them, they do not need the solid material, and only small token morsels are actually thrown away to attract their attention. The food is set out in quantity before them, their attention is attracted by word and sign, and when time has passed for them to have abstracted the essence, the substance is withdrawn and converted to ordinary human use. It is, in fact, a most economical principle which allows justice to be done to the gods without too much loss to men (Plate XI).

The theme of reciprocity in religion has many analogies. It appears, for instance, in a less material form in our own religious thinking and behaviour. It is sublimated as the offering of a pure and contrite heart or of praise and thanksgiving for benefits received. Milton has described this subli-

mation of the reciprocity motive in part of the dialogue
between Satan and the Son of God. The Saviour has rejected
the glory with which the Enemy of Man has tempted him.
Satan speaks :

> Think not so slight of glory; therein least,
> Resembling thy great Father; he seeks glory,
> And . . . requires
> Glory from men, from all men good or bad,
> Wise or unwise, no difference, no exemption;
> Above all Sacrifice, or hallow'd gift
> Glory he requires, and glory he receives. . . .

The Son of God replies :

> And reason; since his word all things produc'd
> . . . of whom what could he less expect
> Than glory and benediction, that is thanks,
> The slightest, easiest, readiest recompense
> From them who could return him nothing else . . .
>
> .   .   .   .   .
>
> Yet so much bounty is in God, such grace,
> That who advance his glory, not their own,
> Them he himself to glory will advance.[1]

The reciprocity which the Tikopia and most other primitive
peoples stress so much in their religion is of a material kind.
So also are the ordeals which a person may have to endure
before he is regarded as being a fit recipient of the bounty of
the god. In Tikopia the ceremony we have just discussed
embodies a very simple kind of ordeal. It would be ludicrous if it were not for the solemn way in which the members
of the assembled group treat it. But there are many other
kinds of ordeal in primitive society, particularly in connection
with initiation rites, which impose severe bodily pain upon
those who are attaining a more developed state. To the
primitive the concept of the ordeal of the heart in thrusting
aside the desires and lusts of the flesh in favour of better things
rarely enters the religious scheme in any direct way. But
although it is not overt, although an ethical system of values
does not usually stem immediately from religious roots, there
is in every primitive religion some ethical or moral standard.

---

[1] John Milton, *Paradise Regained*, Book III, Nonesuch ed., p. 377.

In Tikopia the religious beliefs and rites are regarded by the people as good. In conversation with a stranger who has seen them they will defend them by asking: "Friend, are these things wrong? They do not involve the slaying of men. They are only to make good weather, to increase food, and to feed the people and give them health."

The system of religious beliefs of the Tikopia is highly consonant with the rest of their social structure. The people are organized into clans and lineages, authority essentially being in the hands of the men of senior descent. Each kinship group has its own spirit guardians, consisting of gods and of ancestors of the senior man of a group, arranged in hierarchical order. When this man dies, his spirit, after being purified and taken in charge by his gods and ancestors, goes to join them and take its place in the hierarchy according to the same kind of rules and precedents as operate in the world. The future life of the spirit is in fact organized along much the same principles as on earth. There are even divisions of the heavens corresponding to the social divisions occurring among the Tikopia themselves. The concepts of these people about the future life are thus in a sense a reaffirmation of the kind of structure and of the social values which they know among themselves. Religion is thus largely a supporter of the social order, and much of its strength springs from its correspondence with the collective organization. On the other hand, there is room in it for personal advantage and manipulation of the system. Compensation, even in a society where the social structure is fairly clear cut, as it is in Tikopia, is by no means out of the question. It is true that in a primitive religion there is usually no thesis that the poor and the meek in this world shall be the inheritors of the next. Such a thesis to a primitive people like the Tikopia would seem a patent absurdity. He who has power and authority in this world is most likely to retain and exercise it in the world above. In this way the religion has a personal meaning for those of rank. But also it provides avenues for people of talent and imagination. In particular, those men who have special psychological characteristics are apt to find in spirit mediumship a way of passing beyond the bounds of the ordi-

narily recognized social alignment of hereditary kind. Such
men as mediums, diviners, priests, or prophets speak with
authority, it may be in a voice not their own, which is the
voice of God. Often they wield an influence not at all commensurate with the lowly status they occupy in the economic
or kinship sphere. Sometimes they are the founders of new
cults based upon their apocalyptic vision or upon their perception that society needs a new message. And in all the
ordinary business of life men and women like the Tikopia
feel that their personal prosperity, and indeed survival, depend
on maintaining, or on having maintained for them, right
relations with the gods and other spirit beings. Their crops,
their catches of fish, the safety of their houses from hurricanes,
their water supplies, their own freedom from accident, and
the maintenance of their children's health, all lie within the
hand of an unseen power. Here, then, is a vivid personal
interest of an emotional as well as of an intellectual kind which
is one of the mainsprings of the perpetuation of religious
belief. But it also tends to facilitate change.

It is now time to recapitulate a little. Starting from a
simple but rather dramatic performance in a thatched temple
on a remote Solomon island, I have tried briefly to sketch in
the outlines of some of the main elements in religious belief
in one primitive culture. But much the same elements appear
over a wide range of primitive cultures. Spiritual beings,
spirit mediumship; incarnation, communion; reciprocity
between god and worshipper; names and other speech of
power; myth, miracle; ordeal; symbolism; ethical values;
control over social and economic affairs; collective elements
and personal compensation—each has a variety of implications, could be studied in its comparative variations and at
one point or another is of great importance in the field of
religion. It will be clear that the religious beliefs of such a
people are not simply a set of intellectual ideas to be changed
when a more logical set of ideas is presented. They are
deeply infused with, indeed based upon, emotional attitudes
of great strength and practical relevance. This is borne out
by the way in which, when such a people is converted to
Christianity, this process of conversion rarely if ever appears

to transmute the whole fabric of ideas about the unseen world. There is recognition of the existence of a god superior to and more powerful than the old god; he may be even called the One God. And there is recognition of Jesus as the Son of God who came to save the world from sin. But usually there is no acceptance of the idea that the old gods and spirits do not exist. The missionaries say they are false, and the people accept this as meaning that they are evil and deceitful or simply outworn and inefficient. But they still believe that they exist and can interfere in the affairs of men if allowed. In fact a common concept is that the old gods, angered at their rejection, try to interfere, to punish their former ad- herents with illness and misfortune, and are only restrained by the powers of the gods of the new religion. Such at least has been the case in a part of Tikopia. The people accepted Christianity, but regarded this as in no way denying the existence of their own gods, but merely superseding and subduing them. I have myself seen ceremonies to cure a Christian chief from the evil attentions of one of his old gods. It was generally believed that the god had lodged within his belly in the form of an eel and was threatening him with death. I have also had séances at night with a native Christian spirit medium, who used to come to me in a state of spirit possession and speak with the voices of the gods from the other world. It may be thought that this kind of happening is restricted to a savage people only recently converted to the Gospel. But from many other parts of the world—Africa, and the Orient—it is quite clear that Christianity is not neces- sarily exclusive of belief in the old spiritual order. In China, as is well known, the missionaries have had to draw some rather fine distinctions between commemoration of ancestors by tokens of remembrance at annual ceremonies and worship of those ancestors by offerings which supplicate their assistance.

Consideration of this material from Tikopia against the vast background of information assembled by anthropologists allows us to elaborate our earlier statements about the social functions of religion.

In the first place, it is evident that a system of religious belief and ritual may be a strong positive element in social organization. The assertions by Durkheim, Radcliffe-Brown, and others that the essential function of religion is in the regulation, maintenance, and transmission of sentiments on which the constitution of a society depends, express an important general principle. Religious rites unite the members of the society in common assembly, under an ægis which cannot be easily disputed, and so reaffirm their solidarity and enforce social interaction. Religious beliefs can supply not merely a theory for this social interaction, but also wider principles of order in the whole social universe. They can give an organizing medium for ideas of social structure. They also give a frame of reference for attitudes towards nature. The position of man *vis-à-vis* other living things and the manner in which he proceeds to exploit natural phenomena are to be defined in their most general terms, in regard to some religious principles. Religion, then, promotes the establishment and maintenance of social patterns outside its own immediate field. But it has also the important function of the expression of social existence in symbolic patterns. It does not only guide men in their social actions; it serves them as a way in which the principles of social action can be rendered in metaphorical terms. This anagogic function of religion follows different forms in different systems. Primitive religions do not use parable. But myths and other traditional tales and the corpus of descriptions of spirit activity represent the lines of approved human activity. When the Tikopia god glares out from the eyes of the chief at the yam ceremony to see that his worshippers conduct themselves appropriately, this epitomizes the principles of good behaviour between participants in a group assembly. When god is pleased with man, that means that man is pleased with himself.

Another important function of religion may be the provision of authority, for belief and action. Unity of action in ritual assembly and on other occasions is not merely suggested by the religious patterns. It is enjoined. A particular type of order in the social universe is not merely offered as a solution to the problems of divergent aims. It is presented as the only true solution, and the only one which is morally accept-

able.   Absolute criteria are given in social relations of super-
ordination and subordination—father and child, priest and
parishioner, teacher and pupil.   Not infrequently there is
some merging or blurring of status in these relations.   Ana-
gogically, priest and father are identified by the Catholic
Church, as teacher and father by Confucianism.   The authority
function of religion removes the dilemma of choice from
many social situations which would otherwise be embarrassing.
For this it substitutes the notion of rightness.   There is always
a right course of action if it can be discovered.   If there be
difficulty in discovering which course is right, then authority
again supplies the answer.   The principles of moral theology
are supplemented by casuistry, the application of the moral
law to particular cases by weighing up conflicting rights and
obligations.   The source of this authority lies at some point
in the assertion of revelation.   This revelation may be believed
to have occurred uniquely, at a certain historic moment, and
to be transmissible only by a chain of authorized persons.
It may be believed to occur afresh in the personal experience
of every individual involved in the religious system.   But
one of the methods of reinforcing adherence to the authority
is to endow its modern representatives with more than ordinary human powers.   Father Divine, the negro American religious leader, has apparently taken to himself all the attributes
of godhead, just as Shembe, the Zulu prophet of Ohlange,
took upon himself the re-symbolization of the Christ.   The
Catholic dogma of the infallibility of the Pope when he is
speaking *ex cathedra* is the exercise of the same mechanism in
a more limited way—a double-locking of the authority principle by putting its immediate human interpreter beyond
challenge.   An extension of the mechanism into the physical
sphere is the claim of invulnerability sometimes put forward
by charismatic religious leaders, in conflict with the established
power.   Reinforcement to their authority, itself often a
product of secession, is given by the thesis that the body of
the leader—and sometimes that of his followers, when properly
treated—is impervious to bullet or steel.   Such was the claim
made by a Malay leader, known as To' Janggut—the Bearded
One—in a rising in Kelantan in 1917.   Sumatra has seen

several such invulnerability cults. In recent years, during the fighting in Indonesia and Malaya, similar claims have been made. Participants in the Sioux Ghost Dance of 1890 were instructed to wear " ghost shirts " which were believed to be bullet-proof. But bodily invulnerability is a more dangerous claim than invulnerability of opinion—it is easier to put it to the test, as To' Janggut and others, like Sitting Bull and his warriors, found to their cost.

Religion has one of its most important functions in the provision of meaning for social action. It gives not merely pattern and order, but allows them to be interpreted in terms of ultimate ends. For a Muslim or a Christian, his religion centres upon God, and all his actions should bear some identifiable relation to his ultimate end of fulfilment of the will of God. In such a scheme there should be no item of conduct which is loose, without attachment to the rest in terms of meaning. All living is part of the Grand Design. From this point of view it is logical to define superstition as irrational fear of the unknown, and religion as rational worship of the known. It is in the provision of meaning to human existence, the unwillingness to face the unknown without some assurance of sensible final ends, that the greatest appeal of religion seems always to have lain to many intelligent people. Yet there may be differences of view about the nature of ultimate ends, about the relation of man to the extra-human source of meaning.

If tolerance is given to such differences, and they should be admitted, then in this aspect religion becomes one of the arts —an arranging of human experience in cognizable patterns. Many primitive societies adopt such an attitude towards the religious beliefs of others. They hold to their own, but regard them as pragmatic and contextualized. That which is adapted to their own circumstances they do not hold to be necessarily good for others. Religions which are believed to have a universalistic quality do not allow such catholicity, except on their own terms. Meaning is more highly canalized, and submitted in the last resort to some central authority.

The attribution of final meaning to action, given with authority, offers a certitude which can be a powerful stabilizing mechanism to individuals in their personal and social relations. Loss of fortune, loss of a loved one, is met by the voice of authority speaking of the vanity of earthly attachments, and of the recompense in the life beyond for the sufferings faithfully endured in the world below. At some point in every religious system, however primitive or advanced, the two themes of submission and foregoing of benefit emerge, and are matched by the theme of compensation, overt or in concealed form. The assurance in the promise of compensation, in however a diluted or etherealized manner, is an important element in the assignment of meaning to action. Compensation is conceived normally as coming in a future state. But much of it actually is given in the present state. The consolations of religion are their own reward psychologically, irrespective of any dividend that may be declared in the hereafter.

A system of religious belief also allows for the expression of concepts of imagination and æsthetic creation. One type of imaginative extension is found in the search for expressions of the infinite. In the monotheistic religious systems the idea of God explores this. God is a projection of a number of themes. In the power theme there is the concept of God as omnipotent, representing the assertion of human power desires in infinite form. This theme is shown also in the Creator aspect. Power over the universe is given specific objectification as the Demiurge, the Craftsman of infinite ability. This theme helps also to satisfy ætiological interests —in the last resort, it is alleged, no explanation can be found for the primal constitution of matter other than the process of creation, whether conceived as a series of historical acts or a continuous operation. But the human desire to know, that curiosity which seems basic in all men, finds its projection in the concept of the omniscience of God. Here, too, there is promise of compensation: for ignorant man in the hereafter, " then shall we know as we are known." The theme of love, opposite to that of self-assertion, finds its projection in the concept of God as the source of all love. The human wish for care and protection, for understanding in circumstances which get no response from companions in the society, is met by the concept of divine compassion. Even the offender against the moral law can be met by grace, the saving virtue for the soul, which can lay claim to the unmerited favour of God. The projections of morality and authority, both necessary for social life, are both envisaged in terms of a divine, infinite, unchallengeable source, which encapsulates humanity.

Such a system of projections, involving concepts basic for social action, tends to be given structural elaboration. Some systems, as those of Islam, avoid any partition of the divine essence. God must remain unique and indivisible, and one of the prime heresies is that of "giving God a partner." But in popular Muslim theology a hierarchy of human sanctions takes on symbolic form. Archangels and angels act as divine messengers, reintroducing as it were the will of God to man. In other systems, as that of Catholic Christianity, the structuring of aspects follows a simple genealogical principle, that of the family. God the Father, God the Son, and the Virgin Mother represent in various ways the themes of power, knowledge, love, morality, authority in the highest degree conceivable. Indeed, the human imagination goes even farther, and allots to them these attributes in quality and to a height not conceivable by man. In the polytheistic systems, especially those of the more primitive peoples, there is not the same emphasis on the perfection of various qualities. Gods often are supposed to be very limited in their range of knowledge, and can be deceived by their worshippers. Their powers are restricted, their affections canalized. But the people have scope for their imagination and creative fantasy in elaboration of the kinship and other relationships of the pantheon, and of the myths which validate the existence of the gods and the social institutions they are conceived to regulate.

But all these concepts do not exist simply as abstractions. They have work to do. They are expected to operate in terms of communication between gods and men, and as sanctions for human behaviour. Faced by decisions to be made, conduct to be justified, the individual uses his system of ideas regarding the divine character and its implications, and the associated rules of conduct to resolve his situation. But it is not always easy to implement this conceptual relation

between the God and his worshipper. If God is both omnipotent and the final source of the moral law, certain problems
arise. How much freedom is the individual allowed in the
taking of decisions? This is met by subsidiary concepts which
postulate some voluntary limitation on the part of the Almighty, some handing over of initiative to man. Some
preservation of free will is necessary for a theory of moral
control. Otherwise, if all human action were the direct outcome of the original creative impulse of the divine, there
could be no offence but through ignorance, and no punishment for sin. Again, how is the existence of evil to be
accounted for, unless through the will of God? And why
does God permit pain and suffering? The answer to these
problems of theodicy tends to be in terms of the instrumental
value of evil. The exercise of choice in moral courses is
regarded as having in itself an educative value. The experience of suffering helps to mould the character. The
conception is one of a deeper, more intricate personality so
formed. In essence, evil exists because it makes good
brighter. Such is the type of solution put forward by the
monotheistic religions, in which it is an important intellectual
problem. In the religions of the more primitive kind these
problems tend to be avoided. There is a division of forces in
the spirit world, into those of good and evil. But this is in
terms of immediate activity rather than long-range potential.
The forces are classified into those which are in favour of a
human individual or group at a given time, and those which
are against him. Even ancestors may be evilly disposed, and
so spoken of, if the proper offerings and deference are not
given them. This means that the problem of evil is pushed
into an external sphere. The gods are given limited powers.
They are not omniscient, and hardly omnipotent even when
roused. Moreover, they are not necessarily regarded as the
specific source of the moral law—this is more diffused in its
origins. Hence since the complete load of morality and
omnipotence is not put on the shoulders of the gods, the
problem of having to vindicate their tolerance of evil and
suffering does not arise. The primitive externalization of evil
allows of the development of other concepts. There are

extra-human forces, such as *mana*, which may come from gods and spirits but which men may capture and use for their own ends. There are ghosts and witches which can operate as contending forces with ancestors and other tutelary spirits, leaving the outcome uncertain. There are ideas of the jealousy and malignancy of neighbours and rivals which can be objectified to supply the principle of evil in black magic. In their ordinary life, both primitive and civilized man avoid pain and frustration when they can. In their religion, the primitive accepts these evils as a reality and deals with their origin by projection of them as personalized entities. The modern Christian accepts them as a reality and attempts to explain them as a moral asset or at least a moral signpost, put down by an omnipotent judge. The Buddhist, on the other hand, denies their reality, and makes recognition of their illusion part of his intellectual and emotional training. But whether conceived as entities, as attributes, or as illusion, in each case the recognition of the categories of good and evil, and their association with religious ideas, help to provide stimuli to social action and standards for the judgement of action.

The possibilities of intellectual and emotional satisfaction to be derived from religious belief are increased by the resort of that belief to non-rationality. The reliance upon revelation as the source of truth; the assurance that the hand of God can be discerned in history by insight which no historian can prove or disprove, or is even concerned with; the credit given to a reason which subsumes as well as subdues the passions; the acknowledgement of the claims of peculiar personal experiences which are not commonly shared and are declared incapable of being so shared—all this gives scope for elaborate projective development. But here also lies a danger for an established religious system. The prophet, the mystic, the spirit-medium are valuable interpreters and validators of religious belief. But they can easily escape from control. One of the important roles of a Church is to keep a firm hand over its non-rationality, and channel it into courses which do not allow too much individual initiative.[1]

[1] *Some Modern Substitutes for Christianity*, London, 1942. A series of lectures delivered by Bede Frost at the request of the Bishop of Chichester

R

Within the control of an organized religious body, however, an individual is selective in his belief. He takes or emphasizes elements which appear to be conformable with his past experience and most suitable to his present experience. The influence of his whole society, and of the church or other specifically organized group to which he belongs if religion is socially differentiated, is a powerful conditioning factor. But it is not automatic in presenting elements of belief for credence and action. It is this selective process which results in heresy, apostasy, schism, and conversion. To account for these processes is feasible only if the function of religion as a force of personal adjustment is recognized.

Religion gives a framework for social relations through the application which individuals make of it to their personal circumstances. I have already given an example in Chapter II how the obligations of religion in regard to duties to acclaim the gods, and to perform the last rites for the dead, were interpreted in moral sanctions, and were resolved in terms of mourning before feasting. Religion serves to validate many of the choices made by individuals in pursuit of ends which they regard as good. The fabric of social organization in a primitive society is composed of many such religious strands. Social relations are affected in a more specific way too. Every religious system has its human carriers, arranged in a status structure. The keepers of record have a status through knowledge; the directors of assemblage have a status through administrative functions and control of resources; the interpreters of events have a status through the manipulatory skill with which they apply rules to particular cases. In many societies such status attainment gained through the religious organization—the ecclesiastical hierarchy—is an important feature of the total social system. Important also is the way in which different groups in the society use variant aspects of

in 1942. This booklet is an attack on various types of religious systems with Christian relationships, on the primary ground that they claim an exclusive possession of truth on the basis of "alleged" private revelation or individual judgement. Cf. also my "Anthropological View of Mysticism," *Rationalist Annual*, London, 1950, pp. 47–61, and *Religious Belief and Personal Adjustment*, Henry Myers Lecture, London, 1948.

religious belief—such as myths of origin, or relations and functions of gods—as evidence for their own status assertions. Sectarian claims give useful mechanisms for social definition and emphasis of personality.

Religion is, then, much more than an emotional expression of individual awe, fear, or dependence. It is more than a reflection or symbolic expression of social structure. It is not a unified blanket stretched over a society. It is a complex set of concepts and patterns of behaviour of people in inter-action, dynamic in conditioning other kinds of behaviour, and plastic in being capable of modification to meet individual and group circumstances. Its peculiar quality of the sacred gives it not only authority as a social regulator but enables it to throw out fresh bulwarks of dogma, myth, and miracle when attacked, and to have them speedily absorbed.

What is the basis for this powerful social force? A general view is that there are real entities or powers to which religious concepts correspond. What is the nature of these? Have they an existence apart from the human beings who believe in them? If there are such entities outside the human sphere, an Ultimate Reality of a conscious order, the anthropologist cannot explore their nature scientifically. But there are alternative hypotheses. One is that these entities really exist only through the human conceptions of them. They are social constructs, corresponding in some way to reactions in social organization. God, then, exists as a human idea, pre-sumably fulfilling some conceptual and emotional needs of man, but without separate existence as an exterior entity. Such is the humanistic view—and one to which all the evidence if rationally considered would seem inevitably to lead.

There is still on such a view a field of recognition of the non-empirical. In æsthetics, for example, just as in the creative formulations of science, there are actions and results which are not capable of rational explanation. But there is no conception that they belong to any extra-human or superhuman sphere.

On this view the claims of the protagonists of religion to a special kind of knowledge of reality, to a revelation, a mys-tical experience, a traditional authority, take their place among the justificatory acts which seek to preserve the peculiar quality of that in which they have an interest. As the analysis of this chapter has shown, the assumption of a unique source of authority is precisely the kind of sanction which religion needs in order to carry on.

This argument can be further set out as follows. The processes of social living create continual problems, for which solutions are always being sought. Among the qualities that human beings like their solutions to have is a true and not merely apparent correctness. They also like some identifiable relation to other solutions in coherent, intelligible form. Solutions to most kinds of problems can be handled in technical or in symbolic terms—using these expressions in a wide sense. The areas of the two may overlap, as in much primitive medicine. Or the symbolic may enter in an unexpected field, as in the Cargo cults of New Guinea discussed in Chapter III. But together they represent the attempts of man to organize his life. This can only be done on a social basis. In the symbolic as in the technical solutions to problems every individual is using social material, is relying wittingly and unwittingly on his fellows. In the continual re-devising of solutions to meet individual problems, the relation of technical to symbolic elements changes, and this change is reflected in the fresh handling of their problems by other individuals. Historically, the technical elements have tended to advance in many fields, and the symbolic to retreat—as alchemy has given way to chemistry, magic to medicine. But technical development creates as well as solves problems. In itself it demands new forms of symbolism for the expression of its relationships. It also raises in still clearer and more urgent forms the problems of meaning, including the right use or the devices it supplies. It stimulates further symbolic usages, in the economic and political fields, as well as in philosophy and the natural sciences. Religion involves one complex system of such symbolic usages.

Religion embodies a conceptualization and projection of the most fundamental human needs and human problems. The solutions it provides are partly technical, as the act of prayer provides tension-release through verbal and other physical action. But its major elements are symbolic, with a human referent. Ideas of spirits of the dead and the rites embodying these ideas are projections of sentiments of the living. Ideas of the soul and the after-life project desires for continuity of personality. Ideas of God project wishes for more adequate and more complete control of human affairs. God's knowledge is the obverse of man's ignorance; God's wisdom is the obverse of man's stupidity and error; God's love is the obverse of man's yearning for approval, affection, and comfort from his fellows. Theo-symbolism, the representation of man's interests by personification in terms of gods, is among the most developed of symbolic concepts. Part of its most powerful appeal is its transference and inversion. Man wants care and attention, and a conviction that he is not alone in the scheme of things—therefore he assures himself that God cares. Man has created the idea of God— therefore he safeguards his own position by assuring himself that he is the creation of God. This process of elaborate build-up of concepts is primarily an emotional one, and an unconscious one. But it has complex rational aspects of analysis and theological argument, and presentation of logical relationships between different parts of the total scheme. From the most primitive to the most sophisticated religions, changes in natural phenomena are interpreted in terms which are quite rational, provided the initial assumptions of divine or spiritual interest and will are accepted. But when reason fails, then the supra-rational is called to aid. Revelation, miracle, or other super-normal process is claimed. We are familiar with beliefs in primitive religious systems that people can be killed by magic. In some such systems, as in parts of New Guinea and the Solomon Islands, there is belief that magicians can not only kill people but can revive them again afterwards, though they lead a somewhat dazed existence for only a short time, till they sink and perish finally. Europeans regard this as a supreme example of native irrationality. Yet the Christian dogma of the resurrection of the body is even more startling to everyday experience. The Melanesian magician claims only to reinsert the life. The Christian belief claims to reconstruct the physical form as well.

A religious system is defended by a range of formidable weapons, from the thunderings of *ex cathedra* authority to the subtleties of philosophic argument.   Appeals to the necessity of a faith as a mainspring of action; to the existence of unique personal insight into reality as an unchallengeable source of knowledge; to irrationality as an essential component of human psychology and the foundation of man's deepest attitudes; to the antiquity and universality of belief in an external source of moral worth—all such arguments indicate the strength of resistance to disturbance of the symbolic system of religion.   Yet, as Susan Stebbing has said, the claim to truth is not self-validating.   Exploration of religion by the ordinary process of rational analysis can lead to other views. A comprehensive hypothesis here is that religion is a form of human art.   The understanding of religion is most fully obtained not by embracing its symbolic system, but by scrutinizing it.   It is then seen as a symbolic product of human desires in a social *milieu*.   A religious system represents one way of obtaining a framework for handling fundamental problems of social organization—for reducing uncertainty and anxiety, for increasing coherence in human relationships, for assigning meaning to human endeavour, for providing justification for moral obligation.   On this rest its power and its capacity for continued adaptation and re-creation.   It is not possible for human society to exist without some forms of symbolic solutions which rest on non-empirical foundations. But it is the role of the anthropologist above all to make clear their human character and functions.

For recent works in this field see Appendix.

APPENDIX

p. viii. *Introduction to Third Edition.* These recent works on political organization are: J. A. Barnes, *Politics in a Changing Society*, Oxford, 1954; L. A. Fallers, *Bantu Bureaucracy*, Cambridge, 1956; J. Middleton and D. Tait, *Tribes Without Rulers*, London, 1958; Audrey I. Richards (ed.), *East African Chiefs*, London, 1960; I. Schapera, *Government and Politics in Tribal Societies*, London, 1956.

p. 4. This book has received a great deal of critical attention from Japanese scholars, who devoted a special number of the *Japanese Journal of Ethnology (Minzokugaku-Kenkyu)* to it. They were interested in an American view of their society, and impressed by its methodology. But there was considerable disagreement with its interpretation. Some scholars held that the book presented an "ideal type" of Japanese character related especially to the patterns of the pre-war ultra-Nationalist military group. Others, including the leading expert on Japanese culture, Watsuji Tatsurō, argued that the author would have been on safer ground if she had considered her study as that of the residue of feudal custom in contemporary Japanese society. (A general appraisal of Japanese views is given by J. W. Bennett and M. Nagai, *American Anthropologist*, vol. 55, 1953, pp. 404-11. I am indebted to Miss Chie Nakane of the Institute of Oriental Cultures, University of Tokyo, for references and commentary on this subject.)

p. 21. In *Social Change in Tikopia*, London, 1959, pp. 84–90, I have given further data on funeral transfers, and shown the degree of variation which took place as a result of decisions made in consequence of food shortage after a hurricane.

p. 29. 3rd ed., A. M. Carr-Saunders and others, Oxford, 1958. The title now speaks of "Social Conditions," not "Social Structure," since it was recognized that sociologists have come to use this term in a special sense. See also David C. Marsh, *The Changing Social Structure of England and Wales: 1871–1951*, London, 1958.

p. 33. I have examined this subject in my article "Function," *Yearbook of Anthropology*, 1955, New York, pp. 237–58.

p. 46. Arthur E. Morgan was chief engineer of many water control projects in America, and became first Chairman of the Tennessee Valley Authority. He is the author of various other books, including *Search for Purpose* and a biography of Edward Bellamy.

p. 52. *Social Change in Tikopia*, London, 1959, gives details of the limited way in which money was known to and used by the Tikopia in 1951.

p. 55. An interesting comparative paper of much broader scope, but dealing with analogous political processes, is by J. H. Beattie, "Checks on the Abuse of Political Power," *Sociologus*, n.f., vol. 9, 1959, pp. 99–115.

p. 88.   In recent years anthropologists have devoted considerable attention to the concept of peasant society, and in particular have emphasized the way in which peasantry form a class segment of a larger population, with urban centres from which much of their culture is derived. See Robert Redfield, *Peasant Society and Culture*, Chicago, 1956; Eric Wolf, " Types of Latin–American Peasantry," *American Anthropologist*, vol. 57, 1955, pp. 452–71; L. A. Fallers, " Are African Cultivators to be called ' Peasants '?," *Current Anthropology*, vol. 2, 1961, pp. 108–10.

p. 113.   Interesting data on various forms of messianic movements and their interpretation are given by B. G. N. Sundkler, *Bantu Prophets in South Africa*, London, 1948; P. Worsley, *The Trumpet Shall Sound: A Study of ' Cargo ' Cults in Melanesia*, London, 1957; V. Lanternari, *Movimenti Religiosi di Liberta e di Salvezza dei Populi Oppressi*, Milan, 1960.

p. 141.   Further data may be found in my " Work and Community in a Primitive Society," *H.R.H. The Duke of Edinburgh's Study Conference on the Human Problems of Industrial Communities within the Commonwealth and Empire, 9–27 July, 1956*, London, 1957, vol. II, pp. 103–14.

p. 150.   Elizabeth Munroe has described how the Shaikh of Kuwait agreed to the establishment of an Investment Board with its seat in London. " The idea was that he should invest a proportion of his annual revenue from oil in holdings sufficiently secure to ensure him a revenue in years when the price of oil might be low, and sufficiently liquid to be cashable at short notice if need be. The idea of making interest-bearing investments, other than in real property of goods completely within personal control, has long been repellent to Muslims mainly owing to the injunction in the Koran not to lend money upon usury; this religious scruple strengthened their inclination to mutual distrust where money is concerned. Installation of the Investment Board was, therefore, a plunge for a religious man, though to Western eyes it does not appear so very far removed from practices that had long prevailed in the bazaar, such as giving money to a merchant to buy a cargo of goods upon his undertaking to buy it back again for a larger sum at a later date." " The Shaikhdom of Kuwait," *International Affairs*, XXX, July, 1954, p. 281.

p. 164.   Plate VIIIb. The " Madonna and Child " figure was carved by a Maori craftsman in the early part of the nineteenth century for the first Roman Catholic Mission Church at Maketu, New Zealand. It was refused by the priest, and is now in the Auckland Museum.

p. 214.   Recent works of anthropological interest in the study of morals include: A. Macbeath, *Experiments in Living*, London, 1952; R. B. Brandt, *Hopi Ethics*, Chicago, 1954; J. Ladd, *The Structure of a Moral Code*, Harvard, 1957; M. Edel and A. Edel, *Anthropology and Ethics*, Springfield, Ill., 1959.

p. 250.   Recent works on religion (some referred to on p. ix) are: W. W. Goode, *Religion among the Primitives*, Glencoe, Ill., 1951; D. Forde, *African Worlds: Studies in the Cosmological Ideas and Social Values of African Peoples*, London, 1954; M. N. Srinivas, *Religion and Society among the Coorgs of South India*, Oxford, 1952; S. F. Nadel, *Nupe Religion*, London, 1954; E. E. Evans-Pritchard, *Nuer Religion*, Oxford, 1956; A. Métraux, *Voodoo in Haiti*, London, 1959; J. Middleton, *Lugbara Religion*, London, 1960; C. Geertz, *The Religion of Java*, Glencoe, Ill., 1960.

Significant studies of ritual include: Audrey I. Richards, *Chisungu: A Girl's Initiation Ceremony among the Bemba of Northern Rhodesia*, London, 1956; and Monica Wilson, *Rituals of Kinship among the Nyakyusa*, London, 1957. (See also note to p. 113 in this Appendix.)

INDEX

29387253R00161

Made in the USA
San Bernardino, CA
22 January 2016